Brave New Wealthy World

Winning the Struggle for World Prosperity

JOHN C. EDMUNDS

FT Prentice Hall

FINANCIAL TIMES

An Imprint of PEARSON EDUCATION
Upper Saddle River, NJ • New York • London • San Francisco • Toronto • Sydney
Tokyo • Singapore • Hong Kong • Cape Town • Madrid
Paris • Milan • Munich • Amsterdam

www.ft-ph.com

Library of Congress Cataloging-in-Publication Data

Edmunds, John C.
  Brave new wealthy world : winning the struggle for world prosperity / John C. Edmunds
    p. cm.
  Includes bibliographical references and index.
  ISBN 0-13-038160-8 (case)
  1. Wealth.   2. Investments. 3. Finance. 4. Economic development. I. Title.

  HC79.W4E348 2003
  330.1'6--dc21   2003048804

Editorial/production supervision: *Patti Guerrieri*
Executive editor: *Jim Boyd*
Editorial assistant: *Linda Ramagnano*
Manufacturing manager: *Alexis R. Heydt-Long*
Marketing manager: *Laura Belcher*
Cover design director: *Jerry Votta*
Cover design: *Nina Scuderi*
Art director: *Gail Cocker-Bogusz*
Interior design: *Meg Van Arsdale*

 © 2003 Pearson Education, Inc.
Publishing as Financial Times Prentice Hall
Upper Saddle River, New Jersey 07458

Financial Times Prentice Hall books are widely used by corporations and
government agencies for training, marketing, and resale.

**Financial Times Prentice Hall offers excellent discounts on this book when ordered in
quantity for bulk purchases or special sales. For more information, please contact: U.S.
Corporate and Government Sales, 1-800-382-3419, corpsales@pearsontechgroup.com.
For sales outside of the U.S., please contact: International Sales, 1-317-581-3793,
international@pearsontechgroup.com.**

Printed in the United States of America

1st Printing

ISBN 0-13-038160-8

Pearson Education LTD.
Pearson Education Australia PTY, Limited
Pearson Education Singapore, Pte. Ltd.
Pearson Education North Asia Ltd.
Pearson Education Canada, Ltd.
Pearson Educación de Mexico, S.A. de C.V.
Pearson Education—Japan
Pearson Education Malaysia, Pte. Ltd.

FT Prentice Hall
FINANCIAL TIMES

In an increasingly competitive world, it is quality
of thinking that gives an edge—an idea that opens new
doors, a technique that solves a problem, or an insight
that simply helps make sense of it all.

We work with leading authors in the various arenas
of business and finance to bring cutting-edge thinking
and best learning practice to a global market.

It is our goal to create world-class print publications
and electronic products that give readers
knowledge and understanding which can then be
applied, whether studying or at work.

To find out more about our business
products, you can visit us at www.ft-ph.com

Pearson
Education

FINANCIAL TIMES PRENTICE HALL BOOKS

For more information, please go to www.ft-ph.com

Business and Technology

Sarv Devaraj and Rajiv Kohli
  The IT Payoff: Measuring the Business Value of Information Technology Investments

Nicholas D. Evans
  Business Agility: Strategies for Gaining Competitive Advantage through Mobile Business Solutions

Nicholas D. Evans
  Business Innovation and Disruptive Technology: Harnessing the Power of Breakthrough Technology...for Competitive Advantage

Nicholas D. Evans
  Consumer Gadgets: 50 Ways to Have Fun and Simplify Your Life with Today's Technology...and Tomorrow's

Faisal Hoque
  The Alignment Effect: How to Get Real Business Value Out of Technology

Thomas Kern, Mary Cecelia Lacity, and Leslie P. Willcocks
  Netsourcing: Renting Business Applications and Services Over a Network

Ecommerce

Dale Neef
  E-procurement: From Strategy to Implementation

Economics

David Dranove
  What's Your Life Worth? Health Care Rationing...Who Lives? Who Dies? Who Decides?

John C. Edmunds
  Brave New Wealthy World: Winning the Struggle for World Prosperity

David R. Henderson
  The Joy of Freedom: An Economist's Odyssey

Jonathan Wight
  Saving Adam Smith: A Tale of Wealth, Transformation, and Virtue

Entrepreneurship

Oren Fuerst and Uri Geiger
  From Concept to Wall Street: A Complete Guide to Entrepreneurship and Venture Capital

David Gladstone and Laura Gladstone
  Venture Capital Handbook: An Entrepreneur's Guide to Raising Venture Capital, Revised and Updated

Erica Orloff and Kathy Levinson, Ph.D.
  The 60-Second Commute: A Guide to Your 24/7 Home Office Life

Jeff Saperstein and Daniel Rouach
  Creating Regional Wealth in the Innovation Economy: Models, Perspectives, and Best Practices

Finance

Aswath Damodaran
The Dark Side of Valuation: Valuing Old Tech, New Tech, and New Economy Companies

Kenneth R. Ferris and Barbara S. Pécherot Petitt
Valuation: Avoiding the Winner's Curse

International Business

Peter Marber
Money Changes Everything: How Global Prosperity Is Reshaping Our Needs, Values, and Lifestyles

Fernando Robles, Françoise Simon, and Jerry Haar
Winning Strategies for the New Latin Markets

Investments

Zvi Bodie and Michael J. Clowes
Worry-Free Investing: A Safe Approach to Achieving Your Lifetime Goals

Harry Domash
Fire Your Stock Analyst! Analyzing Stocks on Your Own

Philip Jenks and Stephen Eckett, Editors
The Global-Investor Book of Investing Rules: Invaluable Advice from 150 Master Investors

Charles P. Jones
Mutual Funds: Your Money, Your Choice. Take Control Now and Build Wealth Wisely

D. Quinn Mills
Buy, Lie, and Sell High: How Investors Lost Out on Enron and the Internet Bubble

D. Quinn Mills
Wheel, Deal, and Steal: Deceptive Accounting, Deceitful CEOs, and Ineffective Reforms

John Nofsinger and Kenneth Kim
Infectious Greed: Restoring Confidence in America's Companies

John R. Nofsinger
Investment Blunders (of the Rich and Famous)…And What You Can Learn from Them

John R. Nofsinger
Investment Madness: How Psychology Affects Your Investing…And What to Do About It

Leadership

Jim Despain and Jane Bodman Converse
And Dignity for All: Unlocking Greatness through Values-Based Leadership

Marshall Goldsmith, Vijay Govindarajan, Beverly Kaye, and Albert A. Vicere
The Many Facets of Leadership

Marshall Goldsmith, Cathy Greenberg, Alastair Robertson, and Maya Hu-Chan
Global Leadership: The Next Generation

Frederick C. Militello, Jr., and Michael D. Schwalberg
  Leverage Competencies: What Financial Executives Need to Lead
Eric G. Stephan and Wayne R. Pace
  Powerful Leadership: How to Unleash the Potential in Others and Simplify Your Own Life

Management

Rob Austin and Lee Devin
  Artful Making: What Managers Need to Know About How Artists Work
Dr. Judith M. Bardwick
  Seeking the Calm in the Storm: Managing Chaos in Your Business Life
J. Stewart Black and Hal B. Gregersen
  Leading Strategic Change: Breaking Through the Brain Barrier
William C. Byham, Audrey B. Smith, and Matthew J. Paese
  Grow Your Own Leaders: How to Identify, Develop, and Retain Leadership Talent
David M. Carter and Darren Rovell
  On the Ball: What You Can Learn About Business from Sports Leaders
Subir Chowdhury
  Organization 21C: Someday All Organizations Will Lead this Way
Subir Chowdhury
  The Talent Era: Achieving a High Return on Talent
James W. Cortada
  Making the Information Society: Experience, Consequences, and Possibilities
Ross Dawson
  Living Networks: Leading Your Company, Customers, and Partners in the Hyper-connected Economy
Charles J. Fombrun and Cees B.M. Van Riel
  Fame and Fortune: How Successful Companies Build Winning Reputations
Robert B. Handfield, Ph.d, and Ernest L. Nichols
  Supply Chain Redesign: Transforming Supply Chains into Integrated Value Systems
Harvey A. Hornstein
  The Haves and the Have Nots: The Abuse of Power and Privilege in the Workplace... and How to Control It
Kevin Kennedy and Mary Moore
  Going the Distance: Why Some Companies Dominate and Others Fail
Robin Miller
  The Online Rules of Successful Companies: The Fool-Proof Guide to Building Profits
Fergus O'Connell
  The Competitive Advantage of Common Sense: Using the Power You Already Have
Richard W. Paul and Linda Elder
  Critical Thinking: Tools for Taking Charge of Your Professional and Personal Life
Matthew Serbin Pittinsky, Editor
  The Wired Tower: Perspectives on the Impact of the Internet on Higher Education
W. Alan Randolph and Barry Z. Posner
  Checkered Flag Projects: 10 Rules for Creating and Managing Projects that Win, Second Edition

Stephen P. Robbins
The Truth About Managing People…And Nothing but the Truth
Ronald Snee and Roger Hoerl
Leading Six Sigma: A Step-by-Step Guide Based on Experience with GE and Other Six Sigma Companies
Susan E. Squires, Cynthia J. Smith, Lorna McDougall, and William R. Yeack
Inside Arthur Andersen: Shifting Values, Unexpected Consequences
Jerry Weissman
Presenting to Win: The Art of Telling Your Story

Marketing
Michael Basch
CustomerCulture: How FedEx and Other Great Companies Put the Customer First Every Day
Deirdre Breakenridge
Cyberbranding: Brand Building in the Digital Economy
Jonathan Cagan and Craig M. Vogel
Creating Breakthrough Products: Innovation from Product Planning to Program Approval
James W. Cortada
21st Century Business: Managing and Working in the New Digital Economy
Al Lieberman, with Patricia Esgate
The Entertainment Marketing Revolution: Bringing the Moguls, the Media, and the Magic to the World
Tom Osenton
Customer Share Marketing: How the World's Great Marketers Unlock Profits from Customer Loyalty
Bernd H. Schmitt, David L. Rogers, and Karen Vrotsos
There's No Business That's Not Show Business: Marketing in Today's Experience Culture
Yoram J. Wind and Vijay Mahajan, with Robert Gunther
Convergence Marketing: Strategies for Reaching the New Hybrid Consumer

Public Relations
Gerald R. Baron
Now Is Too Late: Survival in an Era of Instant News
Deirdre Breakenridge and Thomas J. DeLoughry
The New PR Toolkit: Strategies for Successful Media Relations

Strategy
Thomas L. Barton, William G. Shenkir, and Paul L. Walker
Making Enterprise Risk Management Pay Off: How Leading Companies Implement Risk Management
Henry A. Davis and William W. Sihler
Financial Turnarounds: Preserving Enterprise Value

To E. Ricardo Quiñones,
for sage advice, candor, and lucidity

Contents

Preface

This book gives an optimistic yet disturbing view of the outlook for economic well-being in the world. It argues that a new economic mechanism is at work, and that this mechanism is making people everywhere better off. It also argues that improvements in living standards will reach the people who are now the poorest, even if they are living in remote areas. The new economic mechanism is securitization. It works synergistically with other mechanisms driving economic progress, and under the proper circumstances, it can accelerate economic progress.

The established view of economic growth is that it happens slowly, and that it happens in the goods-producing sectors of a country's economy. Growth can also occur in the services-producing sectors of a country's economy, but productivity gains are harder to achieve in those sectors, so the established view gives less emphasis to the services sectors. In the established view, growth happens as the result of the gradual accretion of knowledge and skills in a country's population and as the result of investment in productive capacity. As populations become more educated and workers deploy newer capital equipment that incorporates technological advances, output per capita rises.

Now some writers are attributing greater importance to securitization and national financial systems. They point out that national financial systems can be powerful facilitators of economic growth, and can catalyze periods of supernormal growth, but they are also mindful of the volatility that national financial systems can experience and the damage that financial meltdowns can cause to economic growth.

This book asserts that national financial systems and securitization can be, and already are, much more proactive facilitators of economic growth than they have been in the past. The book goes so far as to suggest that a country's financial system can become, under favorable circumstances, a prime driver of economic growth. Investment in education and in productivity improvements can now have a new teammate helping them create economic growth. The new teammate is a well-designed national financial system. A really good national financial system brings many advantages and stimulates innovation. These advantages go beyond those that first come to mind, and the impetus they give to economic growth can be very large. A few countries have had very good national financial systems for several decades, and have gained advantages from these well-structured systems. Other countries have managed to achieve high growth rates despite having second-rate national financial systems. Recently, there has been pressure to remedy the defects in these underperforming national systems. This pressure is intensifying and will have very powerful effects even if it succeeds only partially. Some of these very powerful effects are discussed in this book.

True-life stories, in addition to data and numerical illustrations, convey some of the ideas. The stories are from my overseas work and depict moments when I learned how important it can be for a country to have a well-designed national financial system. There are also stories about moments when I noticed something that did not fit the preconceived views I previously held about population, labor supply, or the distribution of income. The ideas in this book are allusive and not a rigorous statement of a thesis. The ideas do not aim to supplant or overturn any existing consensus view. They aim to add some interesting enhancements to the view that the main determinants of a country's standard of living are the level of education of its population and the technological sophistication of its productive apparatus.

The topics and treatment put finance in the leading role and explain economic growth, wealth, and prosperity as if finance were the main determinant. This exposition aggrandizes finance and infuses it with Herculean capabilities for creating wealth. The narrative and stories underscore how important finance has become. The experiences I had in the countries where I worked gave me this "finance-centric" viewpoint. The discussion dwells on stock and bond markets, cross-border capital flows, banks, and mutual funds, and attributes to them the power to create wealth and also the power to transfer it and destroy it. The discussion indicates how, and under what circumstances, a country's financial system can facilitate or hinder real economic growth. The stories and the examples show that there are times when a country's financial wealth can rise much more quickly than its annual output of goods and services. When rises of that sort have occurred in the past, they have often been unsustainable. But under some circumstances these rises may go on for a long time and bring prosperity to many people, and then stabilize without rising too high.

This book proposes that some countries can benefit from a policy that initiates and fosters long, sustained rises in the market prices of the businesses, real estate, and capital equipment located within their borders. This policy of fostering asset booms is risky, and there are only a few instances when countries have implemented it successfully. There are countries that would refuse to consider it, and many experts would feel that this policy diverts emphasis away from building new capacity and raising productivity. Nevertheless, some countries have put this policy into effect and have done well with it, and many countries could benefit from trying it. This policy is an appealing way to jump-start a stagnant economy, especially if its asset prices are depressed. The policy is more feasible than it used to be, and there is now a larger experience base to guide policymakers who opt to try it.

The foot soldiers in this book are the middle-class savers everywhere in the world. These savers try to find securities that will yield positive returns and not suffer from violent price fluctuations. It is easy to sympathize with their efforts to find and buy these securities. They make these efforts in good faith and do not wish to bring harm to anybody. Yet in the aggregate their efforts can have powerful destabilizing effects. This book gives optimistic scenarios for the future effects of their efforts.

Another theme in this book concerns world population growth. Abundant evidence indicates that world population growth is slowing and that world financial wealth is growing; these trends can lead to labor shortages in several regions. The shortages might occur first in skill categories that are hard to automate. In parts of North America there have already been shortages of workers who deliver personal services to wealthy people. Among the many job categories that fit that description are housemaids, gardeners, chauffeurs, nannies, personal trainers, nurses, tutors, and kitchen laborers. If the number of wealthy people continues to grow, and if people who are now in the upper-middle class increase their spending on personal services, the shortages could reappear in North America and become widespread by the end of the decade. That is one of the possible outcomes regarding labor supply that this book discusses. A possible consequence is that real wages might rise in parts of the world. If those increases occur, the rise in real wages could ultimately reach the poorest people in the most remote parts of the world.

The ideas in this book span a range of academic disciplines, and hopefully are not at variance with any of those disciplines. The stories are not neat illustrations of textbook principles or laws. They are experiences that I had, and are more suggestive than definitive. Nevertheless, they led me to the synthesis that this book describes. My explanations use the reasoning and methods of finance. That is the academic discipline I have been in for much of my career, and is also the field in which I have business experience. Readers whose expertise is in other fields may prefer their own explanations and may reach different conclusions.

Eleven chapters seek to develop an argument that has many features and give a view of how growth can happen and how the poor are going to escape poverty. Data support the argument, but I cite only a few figures here and there to indicate orders of magnitude and trends. The intention is to suggest that the world may already be on a path to prosperity, not to convince the reader beyond all doubt.

Each chapter emphasizes a few features of the argument. By the end all the features should be in plain view. In some chapters I may seem excessively critical of financial practices that most people do not consider very damaging. Other parts of the argument depend heavily on projections. But the full argument is quite gripping, and as it gradually dawned on me, it shook me out of my complacency. My education had given me an attitude of casual certainty and confidence. I knew all the doctrines and the controversies. Then this set of ideas began to take shape in my mind. If this book is successful, it will pique the reader with illustrations and stories that one by one are interesting and together are provocative, disturbing, and hopefully convincing.

The argument begins with securitization, and Chapter 1 describes what securitization is and gives an example of how it works. The chapter also argues that some countries have already harnessed the new force and others are trying to harness it, and that every country must reassess its growth policy in view of the new wealth-creating power that securitization exerts.

Chapter 2 describes experiences I had over a three-year period in Costa Rica that led me to the argument in this book. The country's economy was going through a really bad period when I arrived, and as I tried to calibrate my frame of reference, one relationship seemed glaringly anomalous. I tried to work around the anomaly, but it did not go away. I continued running into it, and finally an explanation began to form in my mind. That explanation developed over time into the argument in this book. As the argument developed, it continued drawing my attention back to Costa Rica's national financial system and why it was so vulnerable to upheavals and long periods of paralysis.

Chapter 3 is about three economic booms I witnessed and how each ended. The booms had some similarity, but their endings were extremely dissimilar, and one of the three ended in a complete collapse. My explanation for the dissimilarity is that the national financial systems of the three countries were quite different from each other. In particular, the rules, conventions, and practices of their national stock markets were very different. Each country's stock market had a different role in the economy and different rules for distributing gains and shouldering losses. The institutional underpinnings of each country's national financial system determined how gentle or brusque the end of each country's boom would be.

Chapter 4 puts forth the idea that financial assets can catalyze economic growth. Financial assets (bonds and stocks) have become more than mere counters of past accomplishments. Financial assets can transmit pressure to increase real output and can reward progress more quickly and effectively than previous reward schemes did. Financial assets gradually became a central feature of the U.S. economy after the reforms from 1933 onward strengthened the institutional foundations of the U.S. financial system. The huge pile of U.S. financial assets rests on institutional foundations that are resilient and have shown they can continuously reform and reinforce themselves. In many countries the national financial systems are still defective. Many countries have high savings rates but waste a large part of their savings because their national financial systems do not allocate capital efficiently or allow it to be stolen. The Asian Tigers had national financial systems that seemed to work well but suffered from defects. The Russian default showed that its rough-and-tumble national financial system did not have enough checks and balances and was vulnerable to fraud and embezzlement. The U.S. pursued the strategy of raising the market values of stocks and bonds, especially from 1980 to 2000, and did extremely well with that strategy. The U.S. became the sole economic superpower because that strategy worked well.

Chapter 5 begins with stories about three grossly defective national financial systems that I witnessed. The three systems all consisted mostly of commercial banks that misallocated capital. They loaned too much to real estate developers who took years to finish buildings. These national financial systems did not lend to young people with ideas for new businesses. The result was the overbuilding of unproductive luxury office buildings and apartment towers and economic stagnation. The national financial systems I observed did little to promote social mobility. Highly educated young people in those countries were unable to find work and were unable to get capital. After the stories, the chapter indicates a few of the design flaws that undermine national financial systems and describes how the U.S. financial system reduces its vulnerability by fostering new-style financial institutions like mutual funds that do not suffer from such severe design defects.

Chapter 6 poses and then answers a rhetorical question: Is it workable for every saver in the world to put all his or her savings in the United States? Because so many countries have defective financial systems, savers outside the United States might simply bypass their countries' financial systems and put their money in the United States. If this would give them high yields, many of them would do it. The chapter gives an explanation for the robust performance of U.S. stocks and bonds from 1990 to 2001, then argues that there is an upper limit to how much the assets in the United States can be worth. Even if the United States takes extreme actions to make its financial assets worth more, there will still be an upper limit, and that limit will be too low. For all the savers in the world to achieve their objectives, financial assets issued outside the United States will have to perform better. The securitization process must spread to other countries more completely than it has done already. The emerging countries have the greatest untapped potential to issue stocks and bonds. Their success as issuers to date has been very limited, and the yields their securities have delivered to portfolio investors have been too erratic. They will be under increasing pressure to improve their national financial systems so that they can do better at issuing securities.

Chapter 7 gives some micro-level examples showing why third-world countries have not been more successful as issuers of securities. It describes three projects and discusses the financing of each. The Nicaraguan flour mill, the Nicaraguan jeans factory, and the Philippine electric generators were all badly structured deals. None of the parties in these deals had the correct incentives, and in each deal the protections against fraud and embezzlement were glaringly inadequate. The chapter discusses the design flaws in these deals and suggests a better way of designing the financing of the Philippine generator project. There is a calculation of the cost of defective design, and the chapter concludes with a summary of how much a well-designed national financial system can contribute to growth.

Chapter 8 argues that the worldwide value of financial assets will grow much faster than world population. It tackles the population controversy and sides with the experts who say that world population will peak sooner than 2050 and will never reach 9 billion. It computes that dollar values for financial assets per capita will rise quickly, especially after 2020.

Chapter 9 puts forward the idea that the world is on track to experience a labor shortage in parts of North America. The chapter begins with three stories illustrating labor shortages in Mexico, starting with the striking example of the waitress shortage at The Cowgirls Restaurant in Mexico City. It describes the demographic transition that drastically dropped the total fertility rate in Mexico. The chapter gives projections that the Unites States might soon demand more unskilled Mexican laborers than Mexico will be able to supply. The demand would spill over to Central America and absorb all the unskilled laborers that Central America and Panama can supply. The demand would spill over and ultimately become strong enough to support full employment worldwide. The argument is speculative and optimistic, and there are many possible roadblocks on the path to full employment. Depending on how productivity grows and how much substitution occurs, there could ultimately be higher real wages in many parts of the world and labor shortages in some regions outside North America, particularly after 2030. The chapter discusses the key inputs to and possible errors in these forecasts.

Chapter 10 discusses how the growth of financial assets may lead to higher incomes for the billions of people around the world who are now poor. The chapter begins with a story of extremes of wealth and poverty that I witnessed in Haiti in the 1970s. The business of exporting human blood was profitable enough to account for the high incomes of the few people who benefited from it. That experience depicts income disparity at its worst. The chapter argues that the world's distribution of income has become more egalitarian since the worst days in the 1970s, and that it will continue this trend. The income disparity is now moderating for hard-nosed, pragmatic reasons. People in the middle-income and poor countries now have a more pivotal role in the world economy than they had before. Their new role is to become buyers of stocks and bonds. The younger cohorts in the rich countries will not have enough buying power to buy the securities that today's savers are buying. Prices of stocks and bonds will fall unless people in the middle-income and poor countries become buyers and buy enough to bolster the total demand for securities, particularly from 2008 onward. The middle-income and poor countries also have a new role in the world economy: to become issuers of securities that yield high returns. Calculations illustrate that a new symbiotic relationship can develop between the rich countries and the poor countries. Savers in the rich countries need to buy newly issued, high-yielding bonds issued in the middle-income and poor countries. Those portfolio investments will allow the rich-country savers to accumulate enough profit to pay for their retirement and not burden the younger cohorts in the rich countries. Calculations also show that if enough people in the middle-income and poor countries buy stocks and bonds, a decline in prices of stocks and bonds may not happen from 2008 onward as savers in the rich countries sell their holdings to pay for their retirement. The symbiotic relationship can work well enough to prevent the retirement crisis looming in the rich countries. The calculations put a new face on the pressure to raise incomes and reform national financial systems in the middle income and poor countries. The pressure coming from the rich countries and is no longer altruistic; it is selfish.

Finally, Chapter 11 begins with an affirmation that society is gradually winning the struggle to bring an adequate standard of living to everybody in the world. It describes the frightening challenges the world faced in the 1970s and the resistance to change that third-world oligarchs displayed. It argues that many indicators are improving and that pressure through financial systems is gaining strength. It ends by arguing that savers can achieve superior results if they diversify their portfolios internationally, and if the yields on stocks and bonds in the emerging countries improve.

1   A New Force and the Race to Harness It

The world is becoming wealthier. This fact does not make everyone happy. Many dismiss the new wealth as an unstable edifice that easily can come crashing down. Others worry that the new wealth will continue to accumulate in the hands of the few and never reach the vast masses of the world's poor. This book argues that the new wealth is becoming stable, resilient, and self-propagating, and is able to withstand hits that would have brought it crashing down in the past. This book also argues that the new wealth will reach everyone on earth and will raise the standard of living of the billions of people who are now desperately poor.

Forces are at work making wealth grow rapidly and making it more resilient. A big reason for optimism is that national financial systems are improving in many countries, which means they do a better job of allocating resources and protecting the savings entrusted to them. Another reason for optimism is that a mechanism called "securitization" is at work. This mechanism creates value, and some of that value reaches the poor.

The new wealth is a huge, rapidly growing amount of bonds, common stocks, insurance policies, certificates of deposit, and other financial assets. The worldwide total of these assets has grown rapidly since the beginning of the 1980s. The total grows because middle-class people around the globe are buying more of these assets every month. People are willing to buy financial assets because of the improved safeguards now existing in many countries.

The idea of middle-class people saving every month is not disturbing, nor is the improvement in the protections their savings now enjoy. What is disturbing is that the worldwide total of financial assets has grown so quickly and has acquired so much power. The large number of people buying bonds and common stocks every month is one reason why worldwide wealth, in the form of financial assets, has grown so rapidly. Another reason is securitization—a process at the core of a controversy spanning issues ranging from sovereignty to the distribution of income. This process has the power to deliver windfall profits and to make everyone's economic life more volatile. Securitization, in its modern form, is a new force; some countries have harnessed it, but others have not. To explain what securitization is, and why it is such a powerful and controversial force, a definition and an example follow.

Securitization

The securitization process transforms the ownership of large, cumbersome assets into smaller bits tailored and packaged so that individual investors find them attractive and buy them. It is like a manufacturing process that starts with a bulky slab of raw material and transforms it into bite-sized finished products of a suitable size for consumers, and it packages them so they are convenient to use. The securitization process converts the ownership of illiquid, unwieldy assets into stocks and bonds that are worth more money. The stocks and bonds are easy to trade and fit the needs of investors. This process is one of the main ways by which financial markets create value. Securitization starts by buying a big, valuable property, changing its legal form of ownership, and then putting professional managers in charge. The managers direct the property's income stream to bondholders and stockholders, so they get income from the property without having to become personally involved in managing it themselves.

The assets that securitization uses as raw material can be any valuable property too large for most buyers to afford, and which most buyers would not want to manage—for example, a parcel of downtown real estate, a large cattle ranch, or a winery with its vineyards. Any big asset like these is difficult to sell because only very rich buyers can afford it, and only a few buyers would be interested, because whoever buys it would have to manage it. Securitizing an asset that is big and requires management makes its ownership accessible to millions of investors who are not rich and who cannot manage the asset.

Consider another example: A large municipal airport is valuable, but most investors would not be interested in buying one because it would cost too much and they would have to manage it. Securitizing the airport raises the number of potential buyers immensely. Millions of investors who otherwise would not have any interest in buying the whole airport would consider buying a few bonds or some stock in the company that owns the airport. These investors might buy an ownership interest in the airport if several conditions are met. The investors would have to feel confident that the airport is in the hands of a competent management team, and they would have to see a legal structure that gives them a strong claim on the airport's income. They would also need to be able to buy securities in small denominations so that they would not put much money at risk. Another condition is that there would have to be a liquid market for the securities, so that later they would easily be able to sell the securities without paying big fees to brokers.

Continuing with the example of the airport, suppose that it belongs to a city, and the city government wants to sell it. First the city tries to sell the airport to a rich buyer. Suppose that there are only a few rich buyers who know anything about airports, and they do not bid very much for the airport. After that, the city government looks for a way to get more money from selling the airport and consults an investment banker, who recommends securitizing it.

Securitizing an asset like the airport begins by changing its legal form of ownership so that it belongs to a corporation. The corporation then does the necessary paperwork to get permission to issue bonds and stock on the local stock exchange. After the paperwork has been completed, the corporation that owns the airport hires auditors and lawyers to issue reports. These inform investors that regulators, auditors, and lawyers have checked out the corporation and certified that the bonds and stock it will issue are valid. At that point the investment banker can start trying to sell the bonds and stock issued by the corporation. If the bonds and stock appeal to investors, and offer features competitive with other bonds and stock in the market, investors buy them. The total price collectively paid by the investors is usually much more than an individual rich buyer would have paid for the airport. The process of securitizing the airport involves five sets of people: the city officials, lawyers, auditors, investment bankers, and the investors who buy the securities. The steps of the securitization are:

1. City officials convey the airport to a corporation that the lawyers create.

2. Lawyers certify that the airport really exists and that the city officials are acting legally when they convey it to the corporation.

3. After the corporation becomes the legal owner of the airport, the corporation files papers with the local stock exchange and the auditors certify the corporation's financial statements.

4. The corporation issues securities.

5. The investment bankers sell the newly issued securities to the investors, who pay cash.

Each investor then owns a part interest in the airport, and together the investors own the whole airport. The city government, which was the previous owner of the airport, gets most of the cash that the investors pay for the securities. The lawyers, auditors, and investment bankers get fees. The parties to the transaction each end up with something they prefer over what they had before the deal. The investors get stocks and bonds that give them claims on the airport's future income. The city gets cash to spend, and it gets more cash than it would have acquired if it had sold the airport to one rich buyer.

To summarize this example, the city officials decided to securitize the airport because they could not get an adequate offer from any of the rich individuals they contacted. Securitizing the airport brought in more money because it dramatically increased the number of potential buyers, and because it transformed the ownership into smaller, convenient, bits. These small bits of ownership were designed to fit well into personal portfolios. Thousands of middle-class buyers bought the bonds and stock, because the bonds and stocks fit their needs. Their aggregate buying power added up to more than the low price a single rich buyer would have paid.

Why does this work? The main reason is that millions and millions of people in the world buy small amounts of bonds and stocks every month. They are always looking for affordable investments that suit their needs. Some of these investors are looking for very safe securities, and others are willing to take greater risk. The investment banker sees that the airport's income stream can fluctuate but will almost always be above a certain level. This allows the investment banker to partition the airport's cash flows. Every year, the airport has some amount of cash flow, and that amount varies. There is an amount that always comes in—even in a bad year, such as following the September 11th terrorist attacks—and that is the safe part of the airport's cash flows. In addition to that safe part, extra amounts come in during good years, and those are the risky part of the airport's cash flows. The investment banker sets an amount of bonds and an amount of common stock to sell. The bonds get the first claim on the airport's cash flow, and they are the safe securities. The common stock gets the part of the airport's cash flows that is risky. In some years the stockholders do not get a dividend, but the bondholders always are paid their interest. The common stock is not as safe as the bonds, and its claim on the airport is subordinate to the bondholder's claim, so common stock is called a "junior security."

An important result of this hierarchy is that the airport's fluctuating income stream serves as collateral for bonds that are quite safe. Older investors who cannot take much risk are willing to buy the bonds, and younger investors who can tolerate some risk are willing to buy shares of the common stock.

Another reason this works is because it separates ownership from management. If a buyer must purchase the entire airport, only rich buyers who know how to manage airports will consider the opportunity. After it is securitized, millions of investors, including investors who live a long way from the airport and have never seen it, will consider buying a few bonds or shares. They would consider taking the risk because they would not have to invest much money, and they would not have to manage the airport.

There is another reason why securitization works. It provides diversity and choice to the market. To see how the diversity and choice would benefit investors, assume that hundreds of thousands of assets like airports, apartment buildings, and factories have all been securitized. Consider that tens of millions of small investors have portfolios of stocks, bonds, and mutual funds. When there are many securities to choose from, the millions of small investors can easily adjust their portfolios so that their holdings are always in line with their preferences. As people age, their tolerance for risk changes, so they sell riskier securities and buy safer ones as they become older. Also, many investors alter their holdings in response to what they see happening in the economy. World events make many investors alter the geographical mix of securities in their portfolios. When enough different securities are in the market, these individual investors can achieve whatever mix of holdings and degree of risk they want. If there were no assets like the municipal airport being securitized, then securities markets would not offer a wide enough range of different securities. Investors would not be able to fine-tune their portfolios easily, and they would have a harder time finding really safe securities to buy.

Does Securitization Create Value?

Many people have difficulty accepting that an asset can be worth more after it is securitized; they do not acknowledge that changing the ownership structure of an asset changes its value. There are also many people who state that although securitization creates value in the United States and other rich countries, the process would not work in all other countries. Let us consider each of these concerns.

The concept of ownership is multilayered and laden with intellectual and cultural baggage. In the case of securitization, ownership simply means claims on future cash flows. These claims are first priority or lesser priorities. Some buyers will pay premium prices to buy first-priority claims, and other buyers will buy lower-priority claims. The investment banker makes a profit by creating priorities of claims on an asset's cash flows and selling each cash flow for a price that depends on its priority.

The second concern is central to the argument in this book. Indeed, there are countries where securitization does not create value. For this process to work, the country must have a securities market with the proper safeguards. It also must have a legal system that promptly and successfully enforces financial claims—especially junior claims. Countries lacking these institutions are at a serious disadvantage because they are not able to create value in this way. Many people in poor countries do not appear to rank this as a very serious disadvantage. Instead, they emphasize that the technology of the poor countries' manufacturing sectors is outdated, and they view technological backwardness as the main reason they are poor. Securitization, however, has now become a powerful wealth-creating process. Consequently, good financial and legal infrastructure, along with education and technology, has become an essential prerequisite for economic progress.

National Financial Systems

Every country has a national financial system of some sort. This always includes a treasury and a central bank. Most countries issue a national currency, but now a growing number of countries have abandoned the policy of issuing a currency. All countries have commercial banks and an assortment of other financial institutions. The other financial institutions are savings banks, insurance companies, mutual funds, and a stock exchange. At that level of broad description, most national financial systems appear to be quite similar.

However, the similarities among national financial systems are deceptive. In substance and effectiveness they are not similar. Some work much better than others, and some work really badly. Others work so badly that people will go to great lengths to avoid putting money into them.

A national financial system is supposed to perform many functions. Most obviously, it should gather the country's savings and allocate them to the most productive uses. Another of its roles is to signal what are the most promising new paths of expansion for the economy. It is also supposed to provide a market where owners can sell their holdings promptly and receive fair compensation for what they are selling.

There are several ways of telling whether a country's financial system is working well. If the system works well, it can gather the country's savings without having to rely on coercion. Many national financial systems have been unable to do that, because the citizens do not trust the system's integrity. Another sign that a national financial system is working well is if the system is sometimes able to attract inflows from abroad. Foreigners will go to the trouble of moving their savings from their home country into the successful national financial system if they calculate that the advantage of investing there exceeds the inconvenience and cost of moving the money.

Several statistical indicators signal whether a national financial system is good. Some of these indicators are more obvious than others. The most obvious is the size of the national financial system as compared to the country's annual output. If the national financial system functions well, the total amount of bonds, stocks, bank deposits, insurance policies, and other financial assets should be much larger than the country's annual output. This indicator is not entirely reliable, but it does show if the country's financial institutions have a large role in the economy. They acquire and hold that large role only if people are willing to do business with them.

Another indicator is the size of the country's bond market. Many countries rely too heavily on commercial banks. It is better if each borrower's debt obligations are publicly traded and quoted on a daily basis. The terms of each bond and the market's assessment of each borrower are continuously on display. When the bond market is large relative to the amount of bank loans outstanding, transparency in credit allocation is greater.

A really good indicator is the size of the country's stock market. More specifically, there are three size dimensions that matter. One is the country's aggregate stock market capitalization—that is, the total value of all the shares listed on the country's stock exchange. This figure should be as

large as the country's annual output or larger. A second dimension is trading volume. In some countries the daily trading volume on the local stock
exchange is small, which indicates that most common stocks are illiquid; a
buyer may have a hard time selling the stock at a price that is near the price
of the previous trade in that stock. A third dimension is the number of
common stocks traded heavily every day. In many countries, hundreds of
common stocks are listed, but only a few are really liquid in the sense that
they trade every day.

The stock market indicators are a particularly sensitive gauge of how
well a national financial system works. The reason is that stock shares are
junior claims, and in a badly functioning financial system, junior claims are
not worth very much. The shares trading daily on stock exchanges are
shares that pass frequently from one investor to another. Those shares participate in the company's income stream and in its upside potential, but do
not usually have much influence in determining who controls the companies. Company control usually rests in the hands of wealthy individuals
who have large blocks of shares. These large blocks are "control blocks"
and are usually not for sale. When there is a lively market for a company's
shares on the local stock exchange, and the control is not in dispute, it is a
healthy sign. It means that minority shareholders enjoy good protection.
People who buy minority shares are risk-takers. If controlling shareholders
are able to deprive minority shareholders of their rightful returns, minority
shareholders refuse to participate. High daily trading volume is a sign that
risk-taking is rewarded.

National Financial Systems as Engines of Growth

A country's productive sector is its engine of growth. However, a country's financial system can make a big difference in its growth, and two
points about the financial system's role are particularly important. One is
that the productive sector cannot grow unless it receives capital to buy
new equipment that incorporates the latest technological advances. That
capital must be raised and allocated by the country's financial system.
Many countries allow their capital to be channeled to unproductive investments, which deprives their productive sectors. Others select key industries in which to concentrate their national efforts. They lavishly allocate
capital to those industries and deprive other industries that could be as
promising. A national financial system must give the right amounts of

capital to the right activities at the right time. This task is hard to accomplish by any known method, but doing it effectively is now a key determinant of economic success. Consequently, a well-functioning national financial system can be an engine of growth, just as powerful as a large, successful, world-class export industry.

The second point is that securitization itself creates value. A country with a well-functioning national financial system can grow rapidly by fostering securitization. The growth occurs because securitization raises the wealth of the people in the country who own properties and businesses. When the preconditions for securitization are in place, investment bankers make enticing offers to business owners because investment bankers are confident they will be able to sell the securities they plan to issue. Those offers raise the market prices of all assets that are suitable raw material for securitization. Wealth is not income, and wealth is not output. But when asset prices rise, owners may spend more money and may also refurbish their properties. Their increased spending will raise the income and employment levels in the country. These two points show what a pivotal role a country's financial system can have in spurring growth.

The magnitude of the gains that securitization can bring is large. The earlier example of the municipal airport indicates that securitization increases the number of potential buyers, and this can increase the market value if enough buyers want to own the securities. The amount of the increase varies and can be very large depending on how much it broadens the market for the asset. The finance sector, in that sense, can be an engine of growth. It can repackage the country's businesses, buildings, equipment, and other assets and transform the ownership into securities that will be worth much more than the market prices that those businesses, buildings, and equipment commanded before the repackaging.

Asset Booms Contrasted with Bubbles

When asset prices rise, people become nervous because they worry that asset prices might crash. This is true everywhere, because every country has witnessed an asset boom of one sort or another. There have been frenzies to buy land, buildings, common stocks, and sometimes all three at the same time. Booms usually rise too high and then collapse. So, people are wary of sudden increases in asset prices.

There can be sustained, gradual increases, however, and these do not have to end in collapse. It is possible for an asset boom to happen in a sober and reasonable fashion. The new, higher prices of assets can be a result of new conditions that are going to prevail into the future, not the result of excessive optimism. The recent European monetary unification provides examples. The market prices of Italian and Spanish government bonds rose from 1994 to 1998 as the date of the monetary convergence approached. The rise was neither sudden nor excessive. It was erratic, but persistent. The timing of the rally was rational. In 1994 there was some doubt that the euro would come into existence by 1999. As the months passed, the 1999 start date looked more realistic, and traders bid up the prices of the bonds. By May 1998, market participants were certain that the euro would enter into effect on schedule. After that, the rally ceased, and the bond prices stayed up in their new higher range.

The bond rally was rational because the euro is a more stable currency than the lira or the peseta. The euro replaced the national currencies permanently, so the new, higher price range of the bonds was reasonable in view of the change in the monetary regime. The bond rally was accompanied by a stock market rally, and real estate prices also rose. Consumer goods prices experienced no big jump, and there was no subsequent collapse in asset prices. There were no big losers who threw themselves out of skyscrapers. The asset boom was gradual, and asset prices rose to new levels and then fluctuated around those new levels.

The United States' prosperity of 1994–2000 was another asset boom of a more mixed character. It was similar to the European bond boom, but in some respects more frenetic. Prices of real estate, investment-grade bonds, and common stocks all rose. Some categories of common stocks rose too high. In that sense, the United States experienced a rational, sustainable asset boom and a partial bubble at the same time. The bubble affected a few parts of the stock market but did not extend to other asset categories and did not extend to the entire stock market. The bubble collapsed but did not cripple the financial system or cause massive damage to the economy.

The Japanese experience of 1985–1989 was a bubble that extended to every asset category, from common stocks to land to golf club memberships. When it came down, it brought chagrin and stagnation that has lasted longer than a decade.

A bubble usually requires a restriction of the supply of the asset that speculators are so anxious to acquire. In Japan the supply of common stock and the supply of land were both severely constrained, so when buyers outnumbered sellers, prices rose sharply. When supply is not so constrained, prices rise more slowly, and investors have more time for sober reflection. Also, if prices rise slowly, there may be enough time for supply to increase.

An economic policy that seeks to raise asset prices appears risky. A gradual asset boom can easily turn into a frenzy, and that is the risk. To a country with high unemployment and depressed asset prices, the risk may be tolerable. The country might choose to run the risk of having to deal with the excesses of a boom in the event that its policies would start one and then be unable to control it. There has been enough experience with asset booms so that government policymakers can prevent them from overheating. That is another reason for running the risk.

A Fully Securitized Country Contrasted with a Completely Unsecuritized Country

Asset values now matter more than they used to. Assets are no longer inert or stationary, because securitization turns them into liquid wealth that can move easily to where opportunities are best. The difference between rich countries and poor countries still is measured in terms of income, but it is more revealing to measure the difference in asset values. That difference is larger and is widening more quickly. Relatively unsecuritized countries are falling behind more quickly than the income statistics indicate.

It is revealing to contrast two hypothetical countries. The fully securitized country has a sophisticated financial system that delivers returns to people who put in money, and protects small investors against fraud and inequitable practices. The unsecuritized country has an opaque legal system, hazy land-ownership records, weak financial market regulation, malleable auditors, and a tiny, rigged stock market.

The fully securitized country has higher income per capita than the unsecuritized country. That difference is striking, but what is more striking is the difference in financial wealth between the two countries. If the securitized country is a typical first-world country, its income per capita might be eight times higher than the unsecuritized country's. But the difference in wealth per capita may be much greater; the securitized country's wealth per capita may be as much as 30 times greater! Moreover, the securitized country's wealth is in negotiable form, so it is more dynamic and more able to move in search of higher yields. The unsecuritized country's wealth is more sedentary and inert, so its reach and influence do not extend as far. For measuring the economic well-being of the two populations, income per capita is more appropriate. For measuring economic power in cross-border dealings, wealth per capita, and the mobility of that wealth, are more revealing indicators.

Implementing a Finance-Driven Growth Strategy

A country can embark on the new path to prosperity without fanfare and without soul-searching. It does not have to acknowledge that it is prioritizing financial wealth creation. All it must do is take a few steps that are easy to justify and simple to put into effect. These steps will set in motion a growth process. A constituency in favor of taking further steps along the new path will form.

Here are four steps that a country can take. All four are improvements in fairness, transparency, or efficiency. Vested interests may oppose them but will have a hard time making their objections sound legitimate.

1. Foster a local corporate bond and commercial paper market. Local well-known companies should be able to sell bonds and commercial paper directly to investors instead of borrowing from banks. Raising money this way bypasses commercial banks, so it saves fees and administrative expenses.

2. Pick a few flagrant violators of insider-trading laws, try them, convict them, and put them in prison for long sentences. Assign a high-profile legal team to find all securities-law violators and punish them. Fund that watchdog activity adequately and permanently. Most countries already have laws against insider trading in common stocks but do not enforce them. Middle-class savers in most countries shun local common stocks because they feel that well-connected insiders will get too much of the profits.

3. Create a truly independent oversight watchdog for every pension fund. The absolutely essential role of a pension fund is to protect the savings of the workers who contribute to it. The oversight watchdog who is responsible for the pension fund should serve the workers and be accountable to them. There are many pension fund managers in the world who have conflicting mandates. A reform that establishes appropriate protective arrangements should enjoy widespread support.

4. Foster affordable title insurance for deeds to land. In many countries it is hard to get clear title to a parcel of land, and title insur-

ance is too expensive. These facts impede land transactions and prevent land from being used as collateral. A smoothly functioning mortgage market is a stimulus to social mobility, and it liberates capital to pay for improvements to land and buildings.

The list is not exhaustive, but it does show the types of rule changes that governments can implement. These rule changes should be enough to set new financial activity in motion, but there may be so much skepticism, fear, and inertia that the government will have to give stimuli. For example, insurance companies may be unwilling to issue title insurance policies unless they receive sufficient assurance that the government will cover their losses. To jump-start the local stock market, the government may have to do more than throw a few wrongdoers in prison. The watchdog agency must have real teeth and must show over and over that it catches violators and successfully brings them to justice.

The effects of these rule changes and stimuli will be large and will very quickly yield visible results and direct improvements to the well-being of ordinary people. For example, if affordable, reliable title insurance exists, the value of the country's houses and apartments will rise quickly. People who want to buy houses will be able to get mortgage financing on better terms. That will increase the demand for housing and may spark a building boom. Also, investors who do not intend to live in the houses will bid for them. The increase in the market value of the country's houses and apartments could be a large figure compared to the country's annual output.

Competition to Harness the Power of Securitization

Countries can continue to rely on a growth strategy centered on improving productivity in manufacturing. The strategy will work for them, and their standard of living will gradually improve. However, the strategy of harnessing securitization will deliver faster growth and will expand the pool of money that moves across borders in search of opportunities. If several new countries successfully harness that new force, the prospects worsen for countries following the traditional growth strategy. Countries that raise the value of their assets will have enough buying power to buy businesses in other countries that do not try to raise the value of assets. Countries that have successfully increased their wealth will be able to increase it more by buying businesses in countries that have not modernized their national financial systems.

The competition among countries is now on a different plane. Historically, markets for goods were the decisive arena. The country with superior goods became richer because its exports would pay for more imports from the poorer countries. Competition for production superiority is still important, but is no longer the sole determinant of a country's prosperity. Some countries with especially good national financial systems have been able to make financial services one of their exports. They have also been able to get part of the profit of manufacturing businesses located in other countries. They earn fees for raising money that those businesses use, and they earn fees for performing other services that those companies need, such as providing insurance.

Origins of the Pressure to Harness the New Force

People have always saved, except in times of severe crisis. National financial systems in all countries offer products for savers, such as savings accounts. These products used to be simple and imperfect, and in many countries they still are. In the countries that prioritize financial innovation, the products have become more sophisticated. The new products meet the needs of individual savers, including young savers and those approaching retirement. The new products have well-designed legal protections, and many are tax-advantaged.

Savers have come to trust the new savings products and have put ever-increasing amounts of their savings into them. This behavior has created steady, rising demand for new issues of bonds and stocks. Securitization would not have become such a powerful wealth-creating force without this steady demand.

During the 1990s savers bid up the prices of the bonds and common stocks that existed. Their buying drove up prices because the amount of new supply did not keep pace with the demand. This created opportunities for new issuers to place bonds and stocks in the market. It also widened the wealth gap between the countries with better national financial systems and the countries with worse ones.

Countries with inadequate national financial systems are feeling pressure to reform those systems for several reasons. First, savers in the rich countries will not achieve their objectives if they keep paying higher and higher prices for bonds and stocks issued in the rich countries. They would pay too much for those securities and consequently would not earn high enough yields over the time period they would own them. Savers in rich countries have so much buying power that some of the buying power will need to spill over. They will need to buy securities issued in the countries that are now poor. So far, they have not bought many of these securities, which are called "emerging markets bonds and stocks." These emerging markets bonds and stocks will have to yield returns commensurate with the scarcity of capital in those countries and the intrinsic risks of business activities there. The risks that stem from inadequate safeguards against fraud and abuse of minority shareholder rights must be eliminated.

Second, savers in the poor countries will need to become buyers of bonds and stocks. So far, some savers in a few middle-income and poor countries have done so, but the number of buyers in those countries must rise sharply in the coming decades. The role of savers in poor countries will be to augment the buying power of the younger cohorts in the rich countries. Soon there will not be enough savers in the rich countries, because in those countries Generation X is smaller than the Boomer generation. When the Boomers will be selling the bonds and stocks they currently are buying, there will be a chronic excess of selling unless savers in countries that are now middle-income or poor add their buying power to Generation X's buying power. Chapter 10 provides a calculation of the necessary number of new savers and the average amount each will need to save. If the number of savers in the middle-income and poor countries grows quickly enough, their buying will forestall a retirement crisis in the rich countries. That is why there will be such intense pressure to modernize the national financial systems of the middle-income and poor countries. Those systems have to reform completely enough to gain and keep the trust of the savers in those countries.

Favorable Conditions
for the Securitization-Driven Growth Strategy

Countries currently in the middle-income or poor categories have a tempting opportunity to adopt a policy that will stimulate growth. They can give this policy a try without having to discontinue or de-emphasize their existing policy for promoting growth. They can easily and inexpensively take clear and decisive steps to make their national financial systems more fair and transparent.

This new policy of enforcing fairness and transparency is controversial. Any poor or middle-income country that makes its national financial system more fair and transparent is not only helping its own middle-class savers, but it is, in effect, fostering securitization and is also opening its doors to inflows of foreign portfolio investment. Securitization and foreign portfolio investment have profound effects on a country. Both undermine the dominance of the oligarchs who have previously exercised control over credit allocation in the country. Both increase the size and profitability of the national financial system. Both shower quick fortunes on talented young people. Both raise wealth more quickly than they raise income, and both also make the country's economy less stable. Both increase the country's exposure to the caprices and vagaries of international financial markets.

When a country takes the first steps to improve fairness and transparency in its national financial system, the occasion may not seem momentous. On the contrary, the occasion might seem minor and unremarkable, as the country implements long-overdue remedies to unfair practices that have been causing harm for years. Yet those first steps will quickly raise the prices of bonds and stocks in the country and awaken hopes that have lain dormant. The price rises will begin to spill over into the real estate market, and business owners will begin to ask higher prices for businesses they are selling. The people who benefit will express their desire for more steps along the new path.

External inducements and threats will add to the internal pressure to take more steps along the new path. The major external inducement is that foreign portfolio investment will flow in. As foreigners see the country taking steps to reform its financial system, they will make small purchases of bonds and stocks there. As the foreigners make profits on those small purchases, they will begin making larger purchases. The major threat is that other countries will reform their national financial systems faster and more successfully. If that happens, those countries will attract more foreign portfolio investment, and will raise their wealth sooner. Then business owners in the successful countries will be able to buy businesses in the countries that lag behind. The purchases will give the buyers immediate capital gains. The wealth gap will widen, and the countries that reform more slowly will fall behind in the new competitive struggle.

Chapter 2 recounts the events that made me see the new force and showed me its power to transform inert assets into more volatile, fast-moving agents.

2 An Idea Germinates

Personal experiences I had during a three-year period convinced me that there is potential for a sustained rise in the market values of many assets in the world. I saw houses, farms, businesses, and industrial machinery for sale at distressingly low prices. Many of those prices have recently begun a sustained rise, which can continue for many years before reaching an upper limit. The personal experiences that gave me that view are the subject of this chapter.

The desire to bring an adequate standard of living to all the people of the world took me on an odyssey of overseas jobs that brought me face-to-face with poverty and intransigent barriers to prosperity. Battling these obstacles was a task that engaged my energies and challenged my expertise. I never gave up hope, and despite frequent setbacks, I remained cheerful and optimistic.

During the first few years I worked overseas, I did not question a central tenet of my education: that low productivity is the prime cause of poverty. Everywhere I turned were production systems crying out for improvement, and the poorest people were using the most primitive production methods; this is why the explanation provided by my training seemed adequate, and until I worked in Costa Rica, increased productivity appeared to be the solution.

A new idea formed in my mind the last few months of my three years working in Costa Rica. The new idea supplemented the conventional explanation for the country's economic recession. My job in Costa Rica was particularly frustrating because the nation had been quite prosperous before falling into a deep recession from which it could not recover. I had really good friends there who were brilliant and imaginative, and we spent long hours together casting around for mechanisms that would pull the economy out of its rut. We sifted through stacks of books and publications, and we asked anybody and everybody for ideas, but we kept going around in circles.

My investigations kept bringing me back to a paradox. The first few times I encountered it, I rationalized it and put it out of my mind, because it definitely didn't fit with my view at the time. However, the paradox continued popping up; a friend noticed it, and he and I spent a few minutes trying to concoct an explanation. Teasingly, during seven years I had spent working in three countries, that one nagging inconsistency kept coming up over and over. All my neat little models of equilibrium looked just the way they were supposed to, except for one thing that didn't fit the picture.

> ### The assets weren't worth enough money!

That was the incongruous fact that I noticed when I started working in Costa Rica in 1982. The prices people were quoting me were much too low. I had been there only a few days when people started offering to sell me big-ticket items, and it immediately hit me that the asking prices were much too low. A guy offered me his car for $500, and I thought he was kidding because the car was pretty good. I knew the guy from my days in Nicaragua, and he wasn't trying to cheat me. The car would have been worth at least $2,500 in the United States. The price he was asking was completely out of line with what it cost to rent a car—about $50 a day. New cars cost three times more than in the United States because there was a very high import duty on them. That's why renting a car was so expensive. So, the price he quoted me was wrong for that reason, too. If new cars were so expensive, and it was so expensive to rent a car, used cars should not have been so cheap. The mystery deepened when I was shown a nice house that the owner offered to rent me for $700 a month. That rent seemed reasonable enough, but then I found out a day later that the owner would sell the house for $15,000. The selling price was completely out of line with the monthly rent. He was asking less than two years' rent. Normally, a house is worth ten or fifteen years' rent, and in the other Latin

American countries where I had been, owners would quote prices as high as twenty or twenty-five years' rent for houses or farms.

The anomaly applied to every kind of productive asset. Houses and cars were not the only cheap big-ticket items. After I had been there a few weeks, I started hearing about every sort of business, and all of them were on sale. Restaurants, hotels, gas stations, farms—the whole country seemed to be on sale at bargain prices!

The first thought I had about the high prices of big-ticket items was that there must have been an acute shortage of dollars. Everybody seemed to want dollars, and everyone I met was anxious to convert dollars for me into local currency. That was what had always been the story in every developing country I had been to (ten or fifteen at that point), so I thought this was just the same story one more time. Ten minutes after meeting me, people would offer to change dollars for me. Sometimes they would offer to do it as a courtesy, to save me the trouble of going to the bank, or to give me a better rate than my hotel was offering. Sometimes they would tell me they needed dollars because they were going to the United States, or their grandmother needed an operation, and the operation was so delicate it would have to be done in New York.

But the situation in Costa Rica was different, and I could see that the usual explanation didn't hold water. There was more going on than the garden-variety shortage of dollars that every third-world country seems to experience from time to time. When there is a shortage of dollars, locally produced goods are very cheap and imports are very expensive. In that regard the situation in Costa Rica seemed fairly mild. Most prices for items of daily use were pretty close to what the same items would cost in the United States. Hotel rooms were a bit cheaper and so were clothes, but electric appliances were more expensive. Prices in the supermarket displayed the normal pattern: Food prices were a bit cheaper for items produced locally and a bit more expensive for imported items. Butter was $1 a pound, which is about what it cost in the United States at that time, and beef was cheaper; for example, tenderloin steak was $1 a pound and filet mignon was $2 a pound. Imported food was higher, such as $1.50 for a can of tuna fish, or $5 for a small jar of Nescafé instant coffee. Locally produced instant coffee cost about half as much as Nescafé and was right next to it on the shelf.

Dollars were somewhat scarce, import duties were high, and there was nothing unusual about that. I had been trained to expect that, and my training provided the first explanation that came to mind. Local labor and land were cheap, and foreign exchange was scarce, so the products made locally, with local inputs, would be cheap. Imports would be expensive, and prices of everyday items would reflect the abundance and scarcity.

The big disparity was in the prices of land, buildings, businesses, and used cars and trucks. My training did not explain that disparity, and the more I learned about these prices, the lower they seemed. Farms and beachfront houses were very cheap. Sometimes the asking price would sound reasonable, but soon it would become obvious the owner would take much less. Office buildings were available also, at prices well below what it cost to build them. The skyline was dotted with half-finished buildings, and nobody was completing them because they could buy a finished building for less than it would have cost to finish one. Entire businesses were for sale, at prices so low that the buyer could repay the cost of buying the business in two years.

The disparity between the prices of big-ticket assets and the prices of everyday goods kept coming back to me, and my friends and I talked about various ways of calibrating exactly how large it was, and about what could be causing it. Tax evasion was one explanation we tried, but that didn't explain much of the disparity. The controls on foreign exchange seemed like a promising explanation, but we did not get very far with that either.

> *It was like waking up in a land of giants*
> *and then noticing that all the giants have tiny feet.*

To me the disparity was striking and disturbing, and I struggled to arrive at an explanation that would conform to the principles of financial economics and monetary theory. I could not brush it aside and simply go on with my work, which required me to understand the economy and all its idiosyncrasies. Also the disparity clashed with other things I was seeing; Costa Rica is a very nice country, and retirees from the United States were coming there to enjoy the good life the country offers.

The final sledgehammer blow came when, two years after I arrived, I ran into a friend who knew someone who had just bought a 300-acre coffee farm for $4,000. A farm that size, with mature coffee bushes and all the buildings and installations, should have been worth a hundred times that amount. The farm was in Nicaragua, and at that time the Sandinista government had been in power for five years.

That transaction was so striking that I asked my friend to tell me all he knew about it. Several facts helped me make sense of the transaction. First, the farm was technically owned by a Panamanian corporation, and the buyer had actually bought only the shares of the corporation. This meant that neither the buyer nor the seller paid any taxes on the transaction, and the Nicaraguan government did not receive any notification about the transaction. Second, neither the buyer nor the seller lived in Nicaragua at that time. Both had been born and raised in Nicaragua, but had moved to Costa Rica at the time of the Sandinista revolution in 1979. Third, the crop had already been harvested, processed, and sold. The next crop would not be very large unless somebody bought copper sulfate and sprayed it on the coffee bushes, because they were infected with coffee rust, a disease that decreases output. Copper sulfate is not cheap to apply, and the seller did not want to spend that much money in Nicaragua at that time. Fourth, land titles in Nicaragua were in a state of flux. The Sandinista government had issued land titles to soldiers who fought against the Somoza regime. These had as much legitimacy as the preexisting titles. Furthermore, local political committees called Revolutionary Tribunals would issue land titles to deserving people. So, it was not clear if the title to the farm had much validity. Fifth, the Sandinista government appeared popular at that time, and there were no signs that it would lose an election six years later.

What the buyer really bought was not a farm but a very expensive lottery ticket. The farm was slowly falling into decrepitude, and its equipment and installations were being scavenged and put to work elsewhere. The workers lived there in poverty, growing food on some of the land and harvesting the small amount of coffee that grew despite the coffee rust. If things changed, the buyer would get a return on his investment, but for the months and years immediately after he bought the farm, there was no point in even going there to see it.

The last point my friend told me about the transaction was that the seller had been offering the farm to everybody he knew for months before he finally found a buyer. The price was not the result of some capricious fit of frustration. The seller was not drunk when he sold the farm, and the buyer did not win it in a poker game. I questioned my friend closely on that point, and he assured me that the price was what came out of a long search for a buyer. It was correct; it was not too low. That was all the farm was worth at that time.

This transaction stayed on my mind as my work in Costa Rica approached its end. It was just one more striking example of an asset that wasn't worth as much as it should have been. But it was an extreme example. It had somehow fallen to 1 percent of what it should have been!

A few months later, as I was looking at a field of coffee bushes in Costa Rica, the first glimmers of the solution came to me. Figuring out what was causing the disparity had taken me a long time; it did not dawn on me until about two months before I left the country, and I shared the explanation with a only few friends. The explanation came out in a jumble, and most of them didn't immediately follow what I was saying. Finally, they appeared to grasp it, and they encouraged me to keep working on it.

There is an axiom in finance called the Law of Markets. In its simplest form it says that identical items cannot sell for two different prices for very long. There has to be an arbitrage opportunity. Somebody will buy the item for the lower price and sell it for the higher price, and keep doing it until the price discrepancy disappears. That is the version that economists know. In finance the law applies to portfolios, and it says that if two portfolios have the same cash flows, their prices have to be equal.

The Law of Markets allows an exception if two markets are separated by insurmountable barriers. If the barriers are effective enough at preventing goods from flowing between the two markets, identical items can have very different prices in each market. Most barriers, however, are not really insurmountable, and the price difference is usually no greater than the cost of getting the item from one market to the other. This is especially true in finance, where money in one place is easy to turn into an equivalent amount of money in some other place.

I latched onto this axiom. It had to work if I just stuck to the guiding principle that the items are identical, and I kept telling myself that the barriers separating the markets are not really insurmountable. I began making diagrams on sheets of paper. The diagrams had boxes representing countries and arrows going from one to the other representing flows of goods or money.

I tried to design deals that would take advantage of the pricing discrepancy. In finance, this is what you always do. It is supposed to be feasible whenever the prices are far enough out of line. You start by creating portfolios that have the same cash flows, then you buy the portfolio that is cheaper and sell the portfolio that is more expensive. The difference is your profit. In this case it was very hard to create portfolios with the same cash flows. I was trying combinations of Costa Rican and U.S. assets and having trouble because the Costa Rican currency did not have a stable relationship to the U.S. dollar. There were arguments that the Costa Rican currency was undervalued, and yet there were persuasive arguments that it was going to weaken against the U.S. dollar and become more undervalued.

The box I kept referring back to was the one representing Costa Rica. I made a tiny opening it in to represent the official market for foreign exchange. Only a miserly trickle of foreign exchange went out through that tiny opening, nowhere enough to satisfy the demand. The government never had enough foreign exchange to supply the official market for foreign exchange with enough dollars to meet all the requests, and there was a huge backlog. Requests that had been approved had approximate dates associated with them indicating when they might be paid. This was good evidence of the unsatisfied demand for foreign exchange. You could buy a place in the queue, or you could buy somebody's claim that was going to be paid before yours. You could give, for example, $70 in cash and get a claim of $100 that was going to be paid in a year. The steep discount rates on these transactions were another indication of the shortage of foreign exchange in the official market.

Finally, my paper was covered with arrows and dollar signs. The deal I was designing kept becoming more complicated. There had to be some way to take advantage of the extremely low prices of houses, businesses, and farms in Costa Rica. Most of the boxes on the paper had only a few lines going to or coming from them, but the box representing Costa Rica had so many lines going to it and coming out of it that it looked like a tangle, and I could hardly read the label in the box.

Time and again I started with a clean sheet of paper. I designed deals involving coffee farms, coffee beans, hotel rooms, houses, raw land, and used cars. In most of the deals one of the parties, a person based in Miami, was going to put a dollar-denominated certificate of deposit in escrow in Miami. The cash flows from the certificate of deposit would be paid to the owner of the asset in Costa Rica.

This gave me a way of bypassing the most obvious constriction point, the official foreign exchange market in Costa Rica. There was never enough foreign exchange in the official market, and to convert local currency to foreign exchange was a tortuous paperwork procedure that could last months.

The other barrier was Costa Rica's national financial system. It was in gridlock for the entire period I lived there. To circumvent the Costa Rican financial system, I used offshore corporations, escrow agents, future-dated checks, and all the rest of the paraphernalia of financial engineering. One problem was that forward contracts and future-dated checks were both illegal in Costa Rica, but legal in Panama. I had to create bullet-proof forward contracts.

I'll spare you the rest of the details and cut to the chase. I finally designed a deal that would work. The deal bypassed Costa Rica's financial system completely and relied as little as possible on Costa Rica's legal system. It looked good on paper, but it would have been hard to do in real life. By that time I was back in Boston, and from there it would have been especially hard to do the convoluted deal I had envisioned.

Instead I showed the deal and variants of it to my friends. Most of them just shook their heads, looked at me skeptically for a few seconds, and changed the subject. One of them thought the deal was interesting, and asked me about it several times. I had written a draft that included a description of the deal, which was an arbitrage transaction. She took my draft and worked on it. She proved mathematically that if a company were set up to do an idealized version of the deal I had envisioned, its shares would theoretically be worth an infinite amount of money. In finance, that is a good way of proving that an opportunity exists, although it does not prove that there is a practical way to take advantage of it.

At that point we had something we could publish in an academic journal. The article came out in a prestigious European management journal.[1]

But my fascination did not end there. I continued to push that line of research whenever I could, and I kept seeing more and more instances of asset prices that were way out of line. I continued traveling to third-world countries and finding that asset prices often seemed too cheap. The pricing gap would sometimes narrow, and then would widen again. The gap refused to disappear, and theory says that it's only supposed to occur occasionally and not last long when it does. Wherever I went, I ran into example after example of underpriced assets. My experiences made me believe that the vast majority of the businesses and income-producing properties in the world are undervalued, and can rise in value for many years without becoming overvalued. And where the undervaluation was most extreme, the country's financial system was always grossly defective.

A Belief Grounded in Early Experiences

These overseas experiences, beginning while I was in my twenties, showed me how many assets can be worth much more than they are worth today.

An earlier set of experiences convinced me that countries can create wealth very quickly. When I was a young boy, I lived in Japan, and I happened to be there during the boom years. From 1953 to 1973, Japan achieved one of the highest rates of real economic growth ever recorded. I arrived there in 1955, at the impressionable age of eight, and remained until 1962. I was the perfect age to observe the miracle. I was old enough to understand it, and see in down-to-earth, workaday vignettes how the Japanese did it, but not old enough to know then how extraordinary that accomplishment was. They made it look easy, and it was only later that I learned how hard it really was.

This childhood experience gave me an inner confidence that kept me optimistic through times when countries where I was working were failing to break out of poverty. Whenever I suffered setbacks or faced moments of doubt, I would just think about the Japanese during the time I lived there—quietly, steadily building an industrial powerhouse right before my eyes. Then I would feel renewed optimism and new resolve to find the path to progress.

The Campaign to Raise Market Values Gets Underway

Some countries already are succeeding at increasing the value of existing assets, and many countries have put in place the legal and regulatory infrastructure to support higher valuations. The stage is set for a sustained rise in the market prices of assets. The rise will spread unevenly, and the countries that participate earlier will benefit vis-à-vis the countries that lag behind.

Chapter 3 describes three economic booms in different countries and how each boom ended. The revealing moments occurred when the slowdown began at the end of each boom. What happened at that point in each country was very different. The national financial systems and the conventions and practices in each country's stock market played key roles in determining whether the boom would end with a soft landing or with a crash.

3 Three Booms and How They Ended

The young woman had a forced smile on her face and she looked harried. She was trying to deal with three people at once, and about a dozen people crowded around her. She was taking names and adding them to a handwritten list that covered both sides of a sheet of paper.

It was a Friday evening in 1998 in Cambridge, Massachusetts, and the young woman was the hostess at an expensive restaurant. She wore a stylish evening dress and had an air of professional authority. She had developed a firm manner to use with customers who became overbearing. The restaurant was not particularly in fashion, but it was very good and had a good location near Massachusetts Institute of Technology. She told people without reservations that they would have to wait an hour and forty-five minutes to be seated. It was already 8:15 in the evening, past the peak times of 7:30 and 8:00.

We had come from a restaurant a few blocks away, where the crowd was even bigger and the wait even longer. That one was the trendy place with a chef who had just been written up in a gourmet magazine. We were a party of five and we did not have a reservation, so our situation was more or less hopeless. They had said it would be more than a two-hour wait. We left and came to the second restaurant.

When we arrived and tried to put in our name with the hostess, we quickly ascertained that the crush of people surrounding her was too dense to allow all five of us to approach. I was the member of our group who made the push to get our name in. It took me a couple of minutes of discreet jostling to get close enough. After I finally succeeded in telling her how many we were and getting our name on her list, I came out feeling discouraged. Looking for another place to eat seemed a good idea.

Finally, we settled on a Chinese restaurant a short distance away and walked to it. That was crowded too, but we got a table and immediately the waitress brought us some tea. For several minutes we were still too frustrated to start choosing dishes.

"Where did all those people come from to jam both restaurants? Why aren't they home eating pizza like they always are?" Rick said.

"Yeah," I said. "Those are restaurants where guys take women they are trying to impress. But the people there didn't look like they were on their first date."

"Maybe they all just got their credit limits upped, and they all decided to celebrate," offered Judy.

There was silence as we all considered her remark. In fact many of the people had probably gotten higher credit limits on their credit cards. We knew because all five of us had received increases in our own credit limits. That was not why we were trying to get into those restaurants, however. None of us was anywhere near the limit on our credit cards. We were all beyond that sort of day-to-day struggle about money, cruising along at a higher level, marveling at how much our stock portfolios had gone up in the week that just ended. Everybody at the table had made gains of at least $5,000 that week, and a couple of us had made more.

The economic boom in Cambridge and Boston was white-hot around that time. We had not seen anything like it there since 1985 and 1986. The boom continued for two more years, getting absolutely manic before slowing down in the second half of 2000. Cambridge's economy slowed down a bit, but never went into the kind of decline we had seen in 1990. Instead it simmered along, waiting for the stock market to recover its breath after its tech stock binge in the last quarter of 1999 and the first quarter of 2000. House prices kept rising, and hiring clerical staff continued to be difficult.

That boom in eastern Massachusetts was longer and stronger than the typical cyclical peak of a normal business cycle. Massachusetts has violent economic cycles, and maybe the 1994–2000 boom was just one of those. But it did not work on the same principles as the ones before it.

There have been many economic cycles in recent times, and each is slightly different. Cycles usually have a boom phase, and those times are when you can most easily see the underlying forces that make each of them tick. The night my friends and I could not get a table at one restaurant was one, and it sticks in my mind. It was an occasion when I could see, as well as feel, how the high-tech boom in Massachusetts and California worked. There had been other moments of illumination, one before that, and one about two years later. Both happened in other countries.

What follows are descriptions of those two moments when I was witnessing other booms and saw how each worked.

In early 1991 I was living in Madrid in an apartment just a couple of blocks off the main boulevard. It was a Saturday morning in March, and I was shopping at El Corte Ingles, a big department store facing the main boulevard. I was with my six-year-old daughter, and we were standing in line to purchase items. Suddenly, I noticed that the guy in front of me and the guy behind me both were buying much more than I was. The guy in front of me paid. His purchases came to the equivalent of $400. I paid. My purchases came to $80. I decided to stand there for a minute and verify that the guy behind me was really buying more than I was. He was; his purchases came to $120. One of the guys in line behind him was talkative, and started talking to me about one of the city's professional soccer teams.

"Sorry I don't know much about soccer," I said, "and I just moved here a couple of months ago, so I don't know who's leading the league. But I do want to tell you, I can't help thinking that this is really beyond belief. Statistically, the people in this line don't exist."

"You mean they need to get more clerks here?" he asked. The line was about ten people long.

"Well, yes," I answered, "but what I mean is it's statistically impossible for all these people to be buying so much stuff. They're not supposed to have that much money."

He laughed. "Yeah, we are buying lots of stuff, aren't we?"

"That's just it. The statistics say the income per capita in this country is below the European Community average. So how can all these people have enough money to buy all this stuff?" We were in the housewares section. The customers were buying fancy tools, ornate light fixtures, and expensive curtain rods. Some could barely carry their purchases. The shopping carts in that store are small and were not much use for the bulky items the customers had selected. The items they were buying were not essentials, and some of the items were completely frivolous and way overpriced.

"Must be the underground economy," he said. The next customer paid. His bill came to $200. The guy I was talking to put his purchases on the counter. He kept talking to me while the clerk rang up the total. He did not pay any attention to her.

"The underground economy must be pretty big," I said.

"Oh, it is," he said, looking at me instead of at the clerk who was adding up his purchases. "Everybody's got some little business on the side, or some stack of 1,000-peseta notes stashed away. Lots of payments are under the table here. Don't pay much attention to the statistics around here."

"That'll be $260," the clerk said to him.

He gave her a credit card and turned to me again. "The tax collectors are starting to get tough now, but it used to be a breeze to keep things from them." He signed the credit card receipt, took his purchases, said good-bye to me, and left.

Madrid was enjoying a boom in 1991, and it did not cool off until a year and a half later, after the 1992 Olympics. The boom was in some respects a typical cyclical boom, but it had several sources of impetus that gave it some distinctive features. One source was the desire to be modern, and that had been sustaining the economy since 1975, the year Franco officially died. Younger Spaniards, who suspected that he had been dead for months, celebrated their release from the cultural straitjacket and rigid conservatism the prudish dictator had imposed on them. They rejoiced with an outpouring of energy that they still displayed though 16 years had passed. They lunged forward, trying to make up for 40 years of austerity and puritanism. I found out how they felt one evening after going to the movies with some Spanish friends. The movie was about The Doors, the California rock group from the 1960s. The movie is full of lurid scenes of sex, drugs, and rock and roll. It realistically described what those days were like in California. The Spaniards were jealous because they had missed all that.

The liberation that young Spaniards felt caused them to try to embrace the future and grasp four decades of progress all at once. It filled them with determination to be European, and to leapfrog the regional conflicts and infighting that had characterized Spain for centuries. The Civil War was a catastrophe, and its shadow lingered over the country for decades. It left the economy in ruins, and recovery was agonizingly slow. Many of my friends and coworkers called the 1950s the Years of Hunger.

The Franco dictatorship lasted so long that 40-year-olds had no personal recollections of the Civil War. That made it easier for them to leave it behind when the dictatorship ended. They decided to live for the moment, and for the future. They did not settle old scores or spend their energies on reprisals. They dedicated themselves to modernizing the economy and the society. That energy gave a strong underlying tone to the economy, and that energy was still vibrant in 1991.

Another source of strength fueling Spain's boom was the European economic convergence process. Spain gained full membership in the European Economic Community in 1986, and the country's economic modernization that had begun in the late 1970s accelerated. Full convergence happened in 1992 when the borders with France and Portugal opened completely to truckloads and trainloads of goods, which gave the economy another shot in the arm. The Barcelona Olympics in 1992 were a celebration of Spain's full emergence as a modern, rich country.

The rise had happened so fast that the Spaniards themselves did not believe it. Young people would tell me in earnest sincerity that the country was poor and backward. They aspired to reach the level of France's income per capita. In many ways, not only economically but also culturally, they viewed their country as inferior to France. I, the outsider who had hardly been there long enough to know for sure, had to tell them that they were burdening themselves with an inferiority complex that no longer had any analytical basis. Their economic growth was rapidly bringing them to parity with France. I assured them that soon they would overtake France, and I urged them to think of that accomplishment as only a checkpoint on their long march to prosperity, not as their ultimate goal.

The third boom that serves as an exemplar for this discussion happened in Buenos Aires and reached its peak in the first half of 2000. During a brief trip I made to that city early in 2000, an event brought the reality of this boom to me with full clarity.

Buenos Aires should qualify all by itself as one of the wonders of the world. It is a huge city, bigger than Paris and Madrid combined, and it has spectacular architecture, broad boulevards, enormous parks, and a waterfront that stretches for dozens of kilometers. It has all the attractions of urban life and is remarkably free of the inconveniences. Although it is a very long way from New York or Europe, it is worth the trip just to see it and feel its ambience. It looks modern and bustling, and until recently it was extremely safe. The people are well dressed and highly educated, and have a glamour that matches Avenue Foch in Paris. They speak a lively dialect of Spanish that sounds like Italian. They are full of opinions and insights, and each of them seems to have a lot to do, but they are often willing to stop a moment and give directions to a foreigner.

Buenos Aires looked like an ideal place to have an Internet boom. The telephone companies had been privatized a decade earlier, and telecommunications hookups were up-to-date. Spaniards and Chileans had bought the electric companies and had installed enough electric-generation capacity so there were no more blackouts as there had been in the bad old days. There were millions of university graduates, many of them scientists and engineers.

There were other, less obvious reasons why Buenos Aires was an ideal place for an Internet boom. The city is rich, and so is Argentina most of the time. For many reasons the country is vulnerable to economic calamities like the one that broke out at the end of 2001. But in early 2000 the country looked like a particularly promising place for e-commerce. Argentina has many far-flung areas that are hard to reach and barely connected to the provincial capitals. In many of those remote places are small numbers of highly educated people who have money and very few chances to spend it. They have cell phones and many have computers, and they quickly hooked up to the Web. They receive newspapers and magazines, but cannot easily buy anything except the bare necessities. They take trips to regional centers, and from time to time they visit Buenos Aires, but the rest of the time they must make do with what they have. Mail-order catalogs should be a good business, but the postal service is unreliable.

These educated, computer-savvy people living in remote areas were an ideal target for e-commerce. The concept was that these people were going to buy the full range of consumer goods over the Web, instead of having to wait until their next trip to the city. Entrepreneurs appeared who were going to create delivery systems that would reliably put the purchases into the buyers' hands. Other entrepreneurs worked on payment mechanisms so that the customers would not have to give their credit card account numbers over the Web.

Between 1998 and the early months of 2000, 475 Internet startups received venture-capital financing.[1] That might seem like too many for a country of only 37 million people and whose gross domestic product (GDP) per capita was only about $8,000. But many of the startups targeted the entire South American continent and were intending to expand to Spain and the Hispanic market in the United States. Many of the startups had offices in Buenos Aires and the section of Miami Beach nicknamed Silicon Beach.

The moment that revealed what was going on occurred at a cocktail party. A few short conversations showed me the inner workings of the Buenos Aires Internet boom. The cocktail party was in a glassed-in restaurant atop a five-star hotel in Buenos Aires with a spectacular view of the waterfront, from the Presidential Palace and the financial district to the rail yards and grain-loading facilities upstream. The lights of the renovated restaurant district on the waterfront glittered in the foreground, and in the distance were the running lights of the ships on the river, which is very wide there. No view in Manhattan or London could be more striking. It showcased the city's modern vibrancy, the historical mainstays of the country's economy, and the melodramatic locus of its politics in one broad panorama.

The people at the cocktail party were young business people, foreign-educated, multilingual, savvy about business, and in tune with the stock market. I knew many of them, and several spoke with me in complete candor. We conversed as old friends who were catching up with each other after a long absence.

The conversations were all about Internet startups. Everybody in the room was pushing a business plan, and they were all talking about who had left his job already, and who was going to tell his boss the next week. They had all gotten pieces of each others' companies. They were too savvy to think that every company and every entrepreneur in the room was going to make it big, so they all took the prudent step of swapping bits of their stock with each other. They also pooled bits of their stock to endow a scholarship fund.

The most revealing conversation was about two people who had already left their jobs.

"Did you know Alonzo and Carmen?" one of them asked me.

"No, I think I only knew people who knew them."

"Well, Alonzo was making $100,000 a year working with Bank Boston, and Carmen was making $125,000 a year working with McKinsey—and they both quit!" he exclaimed.

"Wow!" I responded. "They must already have gotten their startup capital."

"No, they hadn't by the time they quit, and anyway they're not both working for the same startup." He waited for me to acknowledge the leap of faith the young couple had taken. Their combined income from the two high-octane jobs would have put them at the top of the food chain. When I looked impressed, he continued, "Alonzo's is a personal-finance site, and Carmen's is one aimed at women who are working and have kids and a husband."

"Carmen's sounds like a niche that is pretty big and undersupplied," I said. "I'll bet working mothers here have hardly anywhere to turn. That Web site could probably make good money with just a bulletin board giving names and phone numbers of baby-sitters!" Although Argentina is very European and cosmopolitan, it has lingering undercurrents of traditional sexist roles for women.

"Yeah, it's going to have everything from piano lessons to clothes to furniture," he continued. "They'll immediately roll out a version for Brazil too."

There were several remarkable points about the Buenos Aires Internet boom. The first was how many of the business plans appeared to have identified a market segment that really needed the service the Web site would provide, and the consumers in the segment had enough income to make the Web site profitable. A swath from Rio de Janeiro to Buenos Aires to Santiago in Chile has as many middle-class people as France. It is a rich but hard-to-reach market.

The second remarkable point was that every person with the right credentials in Buenos Aires was involved in a startup. It was not only a game for people from rich families. The key requirements for getting venture capital were an MBA from a U.S. school and some work experience with a U.S. company, preferably a bank or a consulting firm. There were local venture capitalists, but the foreign ones were setting the pace. The foreign venture capitalists looked very carefully at the team and at the business plan, but did not pay as much attention to the founders' family backgrounds and social connections. In that sense the boom was a meritocracy and not the usual offshoot of the oligarchy.

The third remarkable point was that Argentine women were involved in the boom as much as the men were. There were about 15 women at the cocktail party, all with top credentials and high-paying jobs with big, fast-track companies. Many were married. They were doing much better than women in Argentina had usually been able to do. Yet they were taking the leap to become entrepreneurs with the same fearless fervor as the men.

After the cocktail party I was too exhilarated to go back to my hotel. I should have been tired, but instead I was brimming with energy. The young entrepreneurs' optimism made me feel wonderful. I walked through the city streets to the renovated waterfront, and then along the pedestrian mall at the edge of the river. The river had always been the artery of commerce that built and sustained Buenos Aires, first taking silver from the mines of Peru and Bolivia to Spain, then taking grain and beef from the endless expanse of the pampa to London. Now it would be relegated to insignificance, soon no more important to Buenos Aires than the Hudson River is to New York. Thoughts of glittering new prosperity raced through my mind. I imagined a wave of new businesses that would be so successful, it would make Argentines forget their golden years spanning 1885 to 1929. As I walked I could see the rolls of fiber-optic cable where construction crews were laying new lines. The new lines ran parallel to the river. In my imagination I saw them transporting more commerce and bringing more prosperity than the river had done in its heyday. It was two o'clock in the morning before I finally calmed down enough to walk back to my hotel and get some sleep.

The three booms—Cambridge, Madrid, and Buenos Aires—were all different. The first two rose on solid foundations and the third one did not. All three ended. The Cambridge boom ended with a mild slowdown, hardly noticeable anywhere except in the stock market. The Madrid boom ran into a mild recession before igniting again in 1994 with the first leg of a stock market boom. And the Buenos Aires Internet boom came crashing down, ending in disappointment fully a year and a half before the bigger collapse of the country's currency and banking system. This book offers an explanation why these three booms had such different endings. To express the explanation concisely, the difference was in the financial systems of each country.

Each boom had a solid economic rationale. The new products and services were real improvements over those they sought to replace. The new companies in Cambridge were rolling out software and pharmaceuticals that really helped people live better. The new businesses in Spain pushed aside the old, stagnant, protected oligopolies that had dominated the economy during the Franco dictatorship. The Buenos Aires Internet companies were bringing the full range of consumer goods and services to a rich market that earlier had been too hard to reach.

None of the three booms was a collective delusion. These were not booms driven by speculators paying higher and higher prices for land they had never seen or frantically buying a few frivolous items that are not really unique and that nobody really needs. They were booms driven by new investment in businesses that had good ideas, good products, seasoned management, and feasible plans for reaching profitability.

The Cambridge boom went into a mild slowdown, the recession of 2001. This recession was a half-hearted readjustment, hardly worth calling a recession. It could have been worse, but the Federal Reserve aggressively cut the key interest rate 12 times, which softened the downturn. In the real economy, the recession mostly consisted of some inventory liquidation. There was no enormous amount of overbuilding except in telecommunications, and no big sector of the economy suddenly faced obsolescence. The biggest part of the decline happened in the stock market. Tech stocks and Internet stocks had become overpriced, and had to come down and find new levels where their prices looked reasonable to investors. This took some time and taught some investors to diversify their holdings. The decline in other parts of the stock market was not as severe.

The Madrid boom went into a slowdown because the economy could not sustain the intensity after the buildup to the 1992 European convergence and the Barcelona Olympics. Regional disparities and structural inefficiencies dragged down the growth rate. The unemployment rate was chronically high, and the government had never put a high priority on breaking the rigidities that allowed the rate to remain so high. Postponing the confrontation had always made sense. There were also big government-controlled companies that were instruments of the state and did not maximize profit. Instead, they channeled subsidies and provided soft jobs for thousands of people. After the government signaled its willingness to tackle these formerly fenced-off anachronisms, the Madrid stock market began a rise in 1994 that was to take it steadily higher for the next four years.

The Buenos Aires Internet boom collapsed because investors realized that they were never going to get payoffs commensurate with the risks they were taking, even if the companies succeeded. The growth of Internet hookups was fast in the big cities but disappointingly slow in the countryside. The customers were willing to visit the new Web sites, but they did not buy the merchandise and they did not respond to the advertising. The patterns were consistent with what happened in the United States and Europe, but more severe. The shakeout began and quickly took its toll on the startup companies.

Disappointing growth of e-commerce was not what really killed the Buenos Aires Internet boom, however. Everybody knew that some of the startups would not survive. There were two really fatal blows. One was that Latin American customers would not give their credit card numbers over the Web. Customers were reluctant to do that in the United States also, but U.S. customers had better protection against fraud. If a customer in the United States gives a credit card number over the Web to a U.S. Web site, and a hacker then breaks in and gets the number, the customer does not suffer serious financial losses. In Latin America the customers did not have such good protection. The legal tradition in Latin America treats individual financial obligations more seriously. Bouncing a check, for example, is a serious crime in most Latin American countries. Credit card holders in Latin America did not want to find out how bulletproof their legal protection against fraud would be. A hacker who gets credit card numbers in Latin America can do grave harm to the credit card holders. There are ways of dealing with this problem, but they did not succeed in overcoming the customers' fears of buying online.

The second fatal blow was that there was no improvement in the legal standing of minority shareholders. The legal tradition in Latin America gives minority shareholders very little protection against abuses. The majority shareholder is, in many senses, the owner of the business. Minority shareholders are like junior creditors, but they have much less leverage. Many of the Buenos Aires Internet startups were incorporated in the United States to make the shares appealing. But the habits of ignoring minority shareholders were deeply ingrained. The market for initial public offerings on the Buenos Aires Stock Exchange was moribund. There was hope that the market would revive, but the revival did not materialize. The Buenos Aires stock market was in a long slide, and the Internet boom did not reverse that decline. The only real hope for a quick payoff was a buyout from a big company, or an initial public offering on the NASDAQ. As the disappointing revenue numbers came in, the Buenos Aires companies had to scale down their plans and cut back drastically. The euphoria ended. Some companies survived, but most of the shareholders ended up with almost nothing.

A massive flaw in the foundation of the Argentine economy doomed the Buenos Aires Internet boom from the start. The flaw is that white-collar crime is not severely punished. Embezzlement, fraud, insider trading, and the manipulation of stock prices are all illegal and have been illegal for years, but the problem is that they are not punished. In the Argentine stock market a prototype variety of capitalism rules; the strong take money from the weak, and the informed take money from the ignorant. The people with the best chance of succeeding have information that in the United States would meet the definition of inside information. Alternatively, they are trading in cooperation with the group that is in control or is manipulating the stock for its own benefit. This characterization is harsh, and Argentina is struggling to correct the abuses of the past. But, whether it is still accurate or not, that flaw sealed the doom of the Buenos Aires Internet boom. The stigma of past abuses cripples the financial system of that great city and undermines every financial institution in that beautiful and potentially wealthy country. Internet companies can flower only where robust capital markets give high returns to investors according to the risks they take. The minority shareholder who owns 0.01 percent of a company's stock needs protection from the "owner" who controls 51 percent of the company's stock. U.S. regulators are tireless and zealous in defending small investors, but regulators in other countries are less aggressive and usually do not have enough staff to bring lawsuits on behalf of wronged shareholders.

The Buenos Aires Internet companies were particularly vulnerable to a feature of Argentine law. When a company operating in Argentina defaults on a loan, or fails to pay an Argentine supplier, the creditors have a very strong position versus the shareholders. This meant that whenever one of the Buenos Aires Internet startups failed to meet its revenue targets, its shareholders began to fear that they would lose everything. In the United States, by contrast, the shareholders' position versus other claimants is not as weak. Consequently, shares of a U.S. company operating entirely in the U.S. retain more value in the face of bad news. Even when the U.S. company's position looks almost hopeless, its shares will retain some value, because every once in a while a U.S. company comes back from the brink of extinction, and the shareholders score a big recovery. In Latin America local creditors—to the detriment of the shareholders—are more likely to step in and act decisively to protect their interests. In that way a 50 percent shortfall in revenue can lead to a 100 percent loss for a minority shareholder. The prospect of such severe losses was enough to spell doom.

The effect of this sad outcome on future risk-takers in Argentina will be profound. The devastating losses suffered by investors in that boom were an unintended consequence of some Argentine laws that do not look as damaging as they turned out to be. Those losses presaged the complete collapse of the country's entire financial system a year and a half later. That larger collapse had many causes, but some were the same as those that doomed the Buenos Aires Internet boom.

The savvy young entrepreneurs at the cocktail party knew that many of the startup firms were going to fail. But they did not imagine how ineffective their strategy of swapping bits of each other's stock was going to be. During the whole boom, only a few people who got rich had time to cash in. In the aftermath of the boom, big companies and wealthy oligarchs bought up most of what was valuable.

The Cambridge boom came down gently, had a soft landing, and appeared capable of gearing up again for another period of sustained growth. It could have crashed much harder, but did not. Among the reasons why it did not is one of the most important points this book makes: Risk-taking is rewarded in the United States. This is not just a statement about U.S. culture. It is a statement about how the U.S. financial system works. Investors who lost in the tech stock and dotcom frenzy remain willing to gamble again in hopes of finding the next big winners. The U.S. stock market retains credibility as a place where small investors make profits over the long term.

The Madrid boom was a classic business-cycle peak, and it ended with a slight recession. The Spanish business cycle that ended in the second half of 1992 happened in the real economy; investment went into bricks and mortar, new equipment, and process improvements. The cycle had a financial dimension, but that dimension was smaller than the cycle in the real economy, and it marched faithfully to the drumbeat of the real economy. That cycle was the last one in Spain to occur primarily in the real economy. The next cycle was predominantly financial. Spain learned the secrets of how to create paper wealth, and after that its prosperity grew more quickly than before. The growth did not show up as much in GDP statistics as it did in the total value of Spanish financial assets.

The Buenos Aires Internet boom came down with a thud. In some respects its collapse was more discouraging than the collapse that brought down the entire Argentine financial system a year and a half later. Young, university-educated Argentines are emigrating to Spain and Italy because the Argentine economy is doing so badly, and a really discouraging thought must be weighing on their minds. Even if the banks somehow get back on their feet and the economy recovers, the most a young Argentine can hope for is a job. The society will still not reward risk-takers.

These three booms and their endings are exemplary. They illustrate clearly how important the rules and practices in each country's national financial system are. All three booms look similar in their early stages, but in truth each is different in the ways that investors expect to gain wealth. In the U.S. boom, investors tried to buy stock in the companies while they were in the startup phase—to copy the success that early buyers enjoyed when they bought IBM, Xerox, and Polaroid shares in the 1950s. They were intending to make capital gains and then reinvest the gains in the U.S. stock market. In Spain investors were trying to buy real estate and Swiss and German government bonds. They were not thinking of the stock market during 1991 and 1992. In Buenos Aires investors tried to buy stock in the companies while they were in the startup phase, but they did not intend to keep those shares or any other Argentine common stocks. They were going to cash out their gains and reinvest in safe assets like U.S. Treasury bonds and condominiums in Miami.

The difference in wealth creation among the three booms is larger than most people would imagine. The U.S. boom created an order of magnitude more wealth than the Spanish boom did, and two orders of magnitude more than the Argentine boom did. And after the three booms ended, the wealth that remained from each was also very different. The U.S. boom left more wealth than the other two did, even adjusting for the relative size of the three economies.

Why did the U.S. boom create so much more wealth and leave so much more wealth after it ended? The answer is that the U.S. considers the stock market to be very important and gives it a higher status than other countries give their own stock markets. Without exaggeration one can say that the central institution of the U.S. economy is now the stock market. The bond market is also a major institution in the U.S. economy. Americans pay close attention to the stock and bond markets, and the U.S. legal system gives strong protection to small investors who buy stocks and bonds. Companies in the U.S. seek to create value in the stock market. Every action that U.S. companies take is aimed at raising their stock price. Any action that lowers a U.S. company's stock price is a mistake, no matter how prudent that action may have looked. The total value of a U.S. company's stock and bonds is usually much larger than its annual sales and many times larger than its annual profits. A change in its stock price can be a much larger amount of money than an increase in its annual sales or profits.

Savvy people in the United States used to measure their economic success the way people do in many other countries—in terms of annual income and in terms of property they own. A big salary, a fancy house, a new car, a second home, and a country-club membership were the marks of success. Now Americans measure their economic success by looking at their portfolios. Stocks and bonds are the new indicators of economic success. In the United States, a really rich person has a huge portfolio of stocks, corporate bonds, municipal bonds, and other financial assets. Americans have become conversant with many kinds of financial assets, like Treasury bills, savings accounts, commercial paper, and mortgage-backed securities. Americans who want to get rich now try to build up a big portfolio of financial assets. Wealth has now become financial.

Chapter 4 looks at how stocks and bonds came to be so important in such a short span of time.

4 Financial Assets: Catalysts of World Prosperity

A resplendent portfolio of financial assets is now the definitive emblem of economic success in the United States. Stocks, bonds, and mutual funds are not just baubles that rich people show off to impress the masses, however. These financial assets have become the prime mover of economic activity, the impetus that drives the wheels of progress and makes great cities hum and bustle. Their preeminence is relatively new, both as the gauge of success and as the motive force of economic activity. In bygone days, other possessions connoted economic success and symbolized status, and other prime movers drove the American machinery of production. For individuals, an earlier indicator of having "arrived" was to have attained some magic threshold of income, and before that, the mark of economic status was to own land. For nations the measures of economic prowess were aggregate statistics, such as cargo loadings, tons of steel produced, gross shipping tonnage, or kilograms of gold in reserve, and the prime movers were kilowatts of electricity consumed per worker, or capital investment as a percentage of current output. Now these old gauges no longer track the pulse of the economy, so they have lost their claim on the public's attention. For both individuals and countries, the

41

paramount metric today is financial assets, and their dominance as the index of power and the wellspring of prosperity keeps increasing.

Financial assets pile up more quickly than the physical assets and the output that collateralize them. Many may think this fact is transitory and ephemeral, and that the pile of financial assets rests on shaky foundations. They may think the buildup shows that a speculative mentality has taken over. But, in a few countries, the institutional underpinnings of the pile of financial assets have become strong and are capable of supporting the enormous pile of financial assets. Nevertheless, many skeptics argue that financial assets have risen above their normal station and will fall back into their traditional role as minor appurtenances to tangible wealth.

The skeptics' feelings are understandable but wrong. In countries where the stock and bond markets work well, the groundwork took a long time to build; but once the markets stood on a solid regulatory and fiduciary framework, they grew rapidly. They now play a catalytic role and will continue to play that role in the future. The stock and bond markets now move the wheels of production. They are not a mere reflection of economic reality; they are the largest part of economic reality.

How did financial assets so quickly and completely reach the newly dominant position they now hold? How did the apparently fragile edifice of paper assets develop such solid underpinnings, and how did it buttress itself with support beams that are stronger than steel? The story is a true-life saga in which elemental vices like corruption and fraud gradually come under control. It is a story of false starts and failures finally ending in success. The forces that triumphed at last are more virtuous than those that lost. It is a happy story because in some places on earth, well-functioning stock and bond markets largely replaced other, less-efficient ways of allocating capital. People have become very wealthy through those stock and bond markets. Prosperity radiates from those markets and reaches hundreds of millions of people. The story is not happy for everyone on earth, because some people are not lucky enough to live in countries where there are well-functioning stock and bond markets, and some people are not lucky enough to own the correct financial assets, the ones that deliver positive returns. Prosperity will reach them, but for now, there are billions of people it has not yet reached.

Financial assets come into existence when a saver invests money and gets a document representing debt or ownership. Historically, most of these documents were not negotiable; the owner of the document could not easily sell it, so the document was illiquid. Now a much higher percentage of those documents are negotiable, and dealers gather in large, liquid markets where anybody with a document to sell can get cash for it.

This transformation from documents that were impossible to trade to documents that are easy to trade is a giant step forward for the world's economy. It catalyzes and enables the huge upward surge in world prosperity now in progress. This transformation has not happened everywhere. In some countries financial contracts are valuable only because of the personal bonds between the provider of capital and the user; in those countries the legal system is not what enforces financial contracts. In those countries investors rely on social pressure for protection and assess the personal qualities of the people they do business with. Debtors pay their obligations to protect their reputations, not because the legal system compels them to pay.

The transformation to the modern modality of investing and lending will be complete when every borrower will submit his or her application to the market instead of submitting it to specific lenders one-by-one, and the loan document will become a security that trades in the market. The transformation will be complete when all income-producing assets in the world economy, including businesses, farms, office buildings, and mines, belong to corporations that list their shares on stock exchanges, and when every debt contract is written in a legal manner that allows it to be traded on stock exchanges. The transformation is the full changeover to securitization. The transformation brings many advantages, and Chapter 1 mentioned some of them. Another advantage is that the country makes its decisions about allocating savings in the full glare of public scrutiny, not in bank loan committee meetings behind closed doors. When all borrowers submit their applications for credit to the market, and when every lending decision is visible to many market participants, observers will be able to track how the country is allocating its available supply of capital.

A country's capital-allocation institutions can do their jobs well or badly. When they do their jobs badly, they can take the savings of an entire nation of frugal people and waste them, allocating the savings to one useless project after another. When they do their jobs well, they can work with a small amount of resources and allocate those resources to highly productive uses. The resources that a country's financial system allocates can include money from abroad, because a well-functioning national system can attract resources from abroad. A well-functioning capital-allocation process can catalyze real economic growth and can catalyze more growth than the nation's savings rate would appear capable of supporting. It accomplishes this not only by allocating capital to activities that are especially productive, but also by starving whole sectors of the economy that are unproductive. When a country's capital-allocation process works the way it should, it can facilitate a virtuous circle of rising savings and productive, innovative investment. Young people with new ideas can get financing and create new waves of employment and prosperity.

Most Americans have become aware that bond and stock markets also put prices on existing assets, and these send signals that direct the workings of a modern, advanced economy. They also know that capital markets gather and process information, and convey their assessment of that information constantly. A country where banks operate in secrecy to make the capital-allocation decisions is at a disadvantage, because it is more likely to give too little money to innovative projects, scare away foreign portfolio investors, and send discouraging signals to young people and cause them to emigrate.

Americans are more aware than people in other countries of the catalytic effect that well-functioning national stock and bond markets can have. Outside the United States, opinion leaders often seem complacent about the capital-allocation process in their countries. They put first priority on raising productivity in manufacturing and improving export performance. They do not seem to believe instinctively that the capital-allocation process can create wealth directly. Consequently, they do not fully acknowledge the entire array of effects that a country's capital-allocation process can have on its real economic growth and on the wealth of its citizens. They rarely see the untapped potential for issuing securities in their own countries. They often do not acknowledge that those securities could have a higher value than the depressed local market prices of businesses and real estate would indicate. They find it hard to visualize local family-owned businesses as corporations with shares trading on stock exchanges, and with bond financing instead of bank financing.

Countries outside the United States are under pressure to fix the defects in their national financial systems quickly. Many countries still rely too much on banks and are not moving rapidly enough to expand their local markets for corporate bonds, debt securities of other sorts, and common stock. Every country's institutional arrangements evolved differently, and the lingering effects of those differences now look ominous and potentially decisive. Outside the United States, some astute people are now seeing the capital-allocation process as the new prime mover of wealth creation; the old prime mover was technology, particularly technology in production. In the past, countries sought to be world-class producers, particularly of more sophisticated goods, and nervously counted the number of patents their scientists obtained, the number of academic publications, and the number of Nobel prizes they scored. These used to be the key drivers of wealth.

The Asian crisis of 1997 dethroned the old recipe for prosperity. The Asian Tigers suddenly stumbled. Growth in the Tiger countries turned negative. That was bad enough, but people lost faith in the myth, and that was worse. Along with the Asian Miracle had been an all-encompassing and seemingly authoritative explanation for it. Success was built on a foundation of social cohesiveness, hard work, discipline, and teamwork. The rest of the world, and particularly the decadent, fractious United States, could not compete. Then, in an embarrassingly short time, the Asian Tigers stopped being budding superpowers and turned into caricatures of competitiveness. Almost overnight, they turned into high-tech sweatshops, churning out memory chips and Game Boys as slavishly as they used to churn out toys and cheap clothing.

This chapter discusses how financial assets got to be so important and so valuable, and how they have become the catalyst of economic growth. The transition began when small investors in a few countries acquired legal protections, and after that they could buy financial assets without fear of fraud. As small investors learned that they could rely on the new protections, financial assets became desirable, and their growth began its rapid ascent. Financial assets then superseded the old forms of wealth. The narrative in this chapter discusses several watershed events of the past decades. These events have revealed that countries now need well-functioning national financial systems and cannot easily achieve prosperity if they pay attention only to manufacturing and exporting. These events also have revealed that financial assets can grow very rapidly, much more rapidly than the productive capacity underpinning them. Growth can be solidly grounded, or it can be illusory if the national financial system supporting it is defective. This chapter first discusses failures, then reviews the phases of the United States' success. It notes how flaws in national financial systems undermined the Asian Miracle in 1997 and triggered the Russian default in 1998. It shows how the United States during the period from 1933 onward was laying the foundation of a more resilient, better-policed financial system.

Shining the Spotlight on Financial Infrastructure

To begin the discussion of national financial systems and the defects that some have, a good starting assertion is that the Asian Tigers were undone by defects in institutions that they had considered insignificant. Their stock and bond markets were never a big part of the Tigers' success story.

Local commercial banks were the dominant players in the national financial systems of the Asian Tigers. The national financial systems in those countries were only supposed to gather funds from the frugal, hardworking masses and allocate the funds to the industries in which the country was going to make its biggest gains in competitiveness. There were stock markets in each country, and some of them had dizzying booms and busts, so to a casual outside observer the local stock markets looked like independent institutions allocating capital according to their own assessments. In reality they did achieve some independence, and they did allocate some capital, but they were too small and clubby, and not enough people took them seriously. The banks and the government planning ministries had bigger roles in allocating capital. Until the crisis broke out, most people assumed that the banks were allocating capital well.

Each Tiger's capital allocation process supposedly worked in support of the country's economic strategy. Wise men like Lee Kwan Yew in Singapore would oversee the allocation decisions, and the money would all go to the best uses. There was a lot of money to allocate, so big, capital-intensive projects could be financed. The projects did not have to pay off quickly, because Asian savers were willing to take the long view. They were not flighty and did not press for quick gratification.

Then the news broke that Asian banks had made speculative loans. Many loans were to build office towers and five-star resorts, not for semiconductor foundries. The credit-allocation process began to look less and less objective and technocratic. The vices of self-dealing and enrichment had crept in.

How could banks in such highly organized, disciplined countries make so many bad decisions about allocating credit? The search for answers began, and it had not gone on for very long when the world had to face another financial crisis.

The Russian default of 1998 drew more attention to capital markets, financial intermediaries, and their institutional underpinnings. What impressed people first was how much damage a little thing like a default could do. The effect on Russia's real economy was only a fraction of the total damage. The entire global financial system seemed to go into convulsions. The junk-bond market in the United States went into gridlock for weeks. Alan Greenspan had to use his powers to line up a bridge loan for the ill-named hedge fund, Long Term Capital Management. After the initial shock had passed, people began asking themselves more searching questions, beginning with the obvious one: How could a country as rich as Russia, which was quickly making progress toward capitalism, have such a grossly defective financial system? Before the default, Russia's emerging financial system bore some resemblance to England's around 1650, or Amsterdam's around 1570. Financial houses took deposits, discounted bills, and took care to build their reputations for solvency and probity. A frontier atmosphere existed, and the rules for depositors and investors were to be well diversified, alert to rumors, and skeptical when a financial house asserted it was solvent. Legal institutions were slowly evolving, and people were optimistic that legal safeguards would be in place sooner or later. Of course, there was also a central bank, and some nascent attempts at a regulatory framework, but there were also disturbing stories about gangsters, oligarchs, and bogus audits. Outsiders could wonder about some of the stories, but the general tone was optimistic, and most people believed that Russia was on its way to building a modern financial system. Meanwhile, the rates of return were astronomical.

Then came the default and the shocking revelations. The most shocking was that the Russian Central Bank's dollar reserves had been systematically overstated, and not by mistake, but by a fraud that was concealed in a very clever way. The fraud was like a very elegant check-kiting scheme. Only a few experts at the Russian Central Bank could see the whole operation and knew how few dollars the reserve really held. And even those dollars were being looted!

Plundering a central bank is beyond the pale. Even skeptics and cynics were shocked. Banks can collapse, corporate executives can line their pockets with kickbacks and sweetheart deals, and lawyers can defraud hapless widows, but these are routine infractions dealt with in routine fashion, and they have no power to shock. But nobody is supposed to mess with a central bank. Central banks are the ones that come to the rescue when a country's financial system faces a threat. They are like the fire department, and plundering a central bank is like stripping the fire engines and selling the parts, including the hoses and ladders, and then siphoning the gasoline. It shows a breathtakingly callous disdain for the welfare of society and it reaches a level of gangsterism that other financial crimes do not approach.

Plundering a central bank destroys the credibility of a nation's entire financial system for a long time. An independent, objective, and well-managed central bank is one of the most fundamental pillars on which national financial systems depend. Countries that cannot create an independent central bank and defend it from all improper interference have no hope of having a well-functioning financial system, and should abandon all efforts to issue local currency. If they persist in issuing a local currency without having an independent central bank, people who have a choice will not willingly hold that currency. In countries lacking independent central banks, many local citizens prefer to conduct all their financial affairs outside the country.

Stock and bond markets rest on many pillars. Some of the pillars might seem unnecessary, but when they are missing or subverted, the market can crash. The few countries with adequate institutional foundations for their stock and bond markets have arrived at that happy state of affairs after long and costly histories of trial and error. There were panics, scandals and suicides, and finally success. Success in creating well-functioning financial markets is a temporary triumph and is always vulnerable to the next clever ruse. To sustain the success requires constant vigilance and checks and balances so that the markets will survive the shocks that bombard them and the scoundrels who seek to derail them for their own gain. Many countries have tried and failed to set up fully functional stock and bond markets. Many made bona fide efforts and almost succeeded. Others only went through the motions and stopped as soon as they had a facade in place that was fancy enough to fool foreign bankers.

Countries did not have to put high priority on developing really sound financial systems until recently. Quite correctly, they put more priority on developing physical infrastructure such as ports, bridges, and a national electric grid. There were priorities like technology parks and new laboratories for the universities. During that phase of their development, they left the local stock and bond markets in the hands of a few local wealthy families or business groups. Those well-connected people had been managing the local markets for many years, and many countries trusted them to continue.

Now the cost of this neglect is becoming obvious, and it may be too late for many countries to recover. The magnitudes of financial assets have suddenly ballooned. The few countries with well-working financial markets are rapidly creating the overwhelming majority of the financial wealth in the world, and their citizens are piling up preemptive ownership positions of it. The frugal, hardworking people outside these lucky few countries are falling rapidly behind in the competition that now matters most. Their high savings rates do not help them much, as they lose ground to the profligate, gratification-seeking Americans.

Financial infrastructure is the new requirement for competitiveness. Solid financial infrastructure, in the countries where it exists, has put fistfuls of cash in the hands of many people who did not have much before. It has put in motion many new businesses. Many observers may wonder how such big changes could have arisen from such apparently minor wellsprings as the legal underpinnings of financial markets. But that is where the big changes have originated. Let us see what the beginnings of the rise look like. That will give insight into what the growth elements of the rise are, what the new wealth consists of, and what it implies.

Growth Pattern of United States Financial Wealth 1960–1980

The United States put in place some of the foundations of its current financial superiority during the Great Depression. The U.S. stock market before the Depression was as rigged and treacherous as other stock markets. After the Depression it had more protection against manipulation and insider trading, but the market did not boom until the 1950s. Memories of the Depression made people wary, and most did not have enough extra money to give the market a serious look. Nevertheless, the protections were there and were becoming stronger. Still, in 1960 most Americans held a very conservative mix of financial assets. To see how much difference two decades made, consider the transformation of financial asset holdings in the United States in 1960 and 1980. This two-decade period preceded the really steep growth that began in 1982. The U.S. financial system in 1960 was traditional, and it was only beginning to show the departures from tradition that made it into the prime mover and driving force in the economy. By 1980, the U.S. financial system was larger, differently structured, and ready to flex its muscles.

In 1960 total financial assets were a much smaller percentage of annual output than they are today. Total debt of all types was only about 130 percent of gross national product (GNP).[1] This meant that every sort of financial institution was a less important part of the economy than it is today. For example, savings deposits at all federally chartered U.S. depository institutions were only $160 billion.[2] In that bygone year, there were state-chartered savings banks, and they had deposits too. So, your grandmother's passbook savings account may not be included in that total, but even so the figure looks surprisingly small. Liquid assets, an aggregate that statisticians at the Federal Reserve tracked, were $398 billion at that time.[3] Liquid assets included cash, checking accounts, savings accounts, and certificates of deposit; it was a good indicator of all the financial assets that people could use quickly without paying severe penalties. The job of tracking financial aggregates became harder with each passing decade, but in 1960 a clear demarcation still existed between liquid assets and other assets. People did not have home-equity lines of credit or any other innovative financial products that allowed them to access their fixed assets to get ready cash easily and quickly. Of course, in 1960 there were sophisticated financial products like tax shelters, and rich people had fancy products like lines of credit collateralized by common stocks. But, for most people, the fear of debt still lingered, so they took care not to push their luck. The post-World War II economic boom still seemed vulnerable, and they worried that the economy might slide back into depression. They held a fairly simple mix of financial assets, with emphasis on safety, and they used as little debt as they could.

For comparison, U.S. GDP that year was $527 billion, and gross private savings was $84 billion.[4] This provides an idea of how small the public's total holdings of financial assets were. Savings accounts were only about 30 percent of GDP, and only about twice as much as annual savings. Total U.S. stock market capitalization was $335.3 billion in 1960— relatively small, although a larger percentage of GDP than savings deposits, and much larger than it had been at any time since the Depression. Corporations also were cautious about using debt. U.S. corporate debt in 1960 was only 26 percent of GDP.[5] The high corporate income tax rate and favorable tax treatment for interest expense did not entice corporations to use more debt until later.

People in the United States used to feel skeptical and cynical about the integrity of financial institutions. In many countries people still do feel that way, and in others, growing trust is a recent phenomenon. To show how recent this emergence of investor confidence has been, I report what a Spanish colleague told me in Spain in 1991. Spain's financial system at that time had some similarities to the U.S. financial system of 1960. It had already gone through reforms and restructuring, but nevertheless, Spaniards in 1991 were still skeptical; they did not believe that their national financial system had really changed from the way it was in the bad old days of the Franco dictatorship. The dictatorship had ended only 16 years earlier, so Spaniards in 1991 had fresher memories of bad times than Americans did in 1960.

My colleague was concerned because I talked a lot about the Spanish stock market in the first few weeks I was working in Spain. I was quite interested, and intended to buy some shares as soon as I knew more. My colleague warned me that I did not know how different that stock market was from the American one. He told me lurid stories of distorted financial reports, offshore slush funds, and directors who slept through board meetings. He said that when the companies have a good year, they hide some of the profits, and then show them later when they've had a bad year.

By 1991, many of the companies listed on the Madrid Stock Exchange had already discontinued these practices and many others had never engaged in them. My colleague knew that, but he also knew that I was too willing to jump in and start trading.

Americans in 1960 were wary about investing in the stock market, but not for the same reasons the Spaniards were wary in 1991. Americans were wary of another generalized collapse like the Great Crash of 1929. Spaniards in 1991 were wary that they did not have enough inside information about any particular stock to take the risk of buying it. Some stocks were safe for widows and orphans, and everybody knew which ones those were. Those stocks paid large dividends and their prices did not move much. There were also growth stocks that were suitable for young professionals to buy. The stocks that were tricky were takeover candidates, and there were a lot of those.

The U.S. stock market in 1960 was a vibrant institution. It was completely transformed from the clubby, manipulated beast that it had been in the 1920s. By 1960 it had become the showcase of the new high-tech growth companies that emerged after World War II. Ordinary people could buy stocks and make capital gains. Younger Americans believed this, and put aside the fear of Wall Street their parents had instilled in them.

This willingness to buy common stocks and other riskier securities opened new possibilities for innovation in the U.S. financial system. By 1980 the U.S. financial system was beginning to launch products with new features. There are many kinds of securities besides stocks and bonds, and many types of financial services firms besides banks. The American financial system began to offer products superior to traditional ones. Regulators also began to allow financial services companies to offer products nationally instead of requiring them to operate only in one state or county. Mergers among U.S. financial services companies accelerated, but there were still tens of thousands of independent financial services firms.

In 1980 total bank deposits and bank loans were larger than had been in 1960, but the big story in the financial services sector was the growth of the rest of the service providers. These "nonbank financial intermediaries" had always existed, but had not been very prominent. These are insurance companies, mutual fund management companies, stock brokerage firms, investment banks, and finance companies. Their total assets grew very rapidly in the United States from 1960 to 1980. Total assets of insurance companies grew from $22.7 billion in 1960 to $197 billion in 1980,[6] and the total amount invested in mutual funds grew from $17.0 billion in 1960 to $134.8 billion in 1980.[7] By 1980, the average person in the United States owned more financial assets, owed more money, and had more relationships with financial services providers.

The shift in attitudes about using debt, owning risky securities, and using financial services was dramatic in the United States between 1960 and 1980 for several reasons. First, the boomer generation was beginning to borrow money, and the World War II generation was saving. The boomers did not fear that the economy would fall back into depression. They feared inflation, which in the late 1970s ran as high as 14 percent a year. The boomers borrowed money despite the slow, erratic economic growth and the periods of recession, stagnation, and high unemployment. Second, the protection schemes for savers and investors improved. The Federal Deposit Insurance Corporation (FDIC) increased the guarantee ceiling from $10,000 to $100,000 for individual accounts. The Securities Investors Protection Corporation (SIPC) put in a guarantee of $20 million for individual accounts with stockbrokers, and then raised that to $60 million. These guarantees convinced savers that it was safe to put money into banks and into stock brokerage accounts. Third, regulatory restrictions on financial institutions began to relax, so they were able to compete for customers. Banks and money-market mutual funds began to compete aggressively for deposits, with marketing campaigns and high interest rates. Savers had previously been wary or indifferent to the advantages of having their money in high-interest deposits, but their attitude changed. They became more aware of the interest income they could earn and less worried about losing their life savings. The 50th anniversary of the Great Crash of 1929 came and went, then the memory of it passed into history. In 1980 the financial services sector was alive with innovation and was signing up new clients and delivering them services that had not existed before.

These transformations set the stage for the gargantuan upward leap that put financial wealth into the dominant position it holds today. The United States moved quickly to take advantage of the potential of financial intermediation in the years following 1980. The U.S. institutional framework met the requirements to support this leap, and the public trusted that U.S. financial institutions would be reliable. This combination of underpinning and trust supported and fueled the enormous leap that made the United States the sole economic superpower. The huge edifice of U.S. financial wealth rests on foundations that were carefully laid and reinforced after many failed attempts. The groundwork took decades to lay, and it does not consist only of laws and institutions. Laying the groundwork also involved building a broad political consensus and making financial assets the centerpiece of the American dream of middle-class prosperity.

What changed from 1960 to 1980 was that American corporations and households were willing to use more debt and take more financial risk. Corporations were willing to issue more securities, and American households were willing to buy them. The change in the composition of financial assets that Americans held shows this. From 1960 to1980 American households continued to save and increased the amounts they put aside. Gross personal savings rose from 5 percent of GDP in 1960 to 7.4 percent in 1980.[8] The well-publicized decline in the savings rate did not happen until later. The big difference was that savers in the United States did not put such a large part of their savings into banks. They directed more of their savings into mutual funds that invested in stocks and bonds. The Boomer generation was already buying new financial products. Over the two decades the total pile of U.S. financial assets grew faster than U.S. GNP, but not very much faster.

Growth of U.S. Financial Wealth Takes Off 1980–2000

After 1980, and especially after 1982 when a deep recession and Paul Volcker's rigorous monetary policy broke the inflationary psychology, Americans embraced financial services more enthusiastically than before. Banks gained deposits and loaned more money to more clients, but could not keep pace with the dizzying growth of the other financial services providers. Americans put money into mutual funds, they bought insurance policies, and they bought common stocks. At the same time they mortgaged their houses, took out second mortgages, increased their use of credit cards, and borrowed to buy cars, boats, televisions, vacations, and anything else they wanted.

The financial habits of Americans and people in other rich countries had always been different, but after 1982 the divergence became more stark. Americans bought common stocks (directly and through mutual funds), pension funds, and insurance policies. For comparison, Japanese households at the end of 1999 still had 54 percent of their financial holdings in bank deposits and only 8 percent in shares. Americans had only 9 percent in bank deposits, 37 percent in shares, and another 11 percent in mutual funds.[9] American corporate managers quickly had to become responsive to pressure from shareholders. Institutional investors had always voted to support corporate managers but no longer could. They had to vote according to the best interests of the shareholders. Takeover battles and leveraged buyouts became daily events, and staid financial newspapers became exciting to read, like serialized thrillers about swashbuckling heroes and pirates.

Older Americans continued to put money into bank accounts, but the growth of deposits slowed further, especially after the stock and bond markets began their spectacular rise in the autumn of 1982. Savers in other rich countries, meanwhile, continued to put money into bank accounts and delegate decisions about allocating capital to the bankers. They did not buy junk bonds or mortgage-backed securities, because those asset categories scarcely existed outside the United States. Takeover battles and leveraged buyouts were rare outside the United States. Control of big companies was not up for grabs the way it was in the United States.

The American savings pattern had a dynamic effect. American savers invested through channels that communicated their wishes to management and put pressure on management to deliver shareholder value. In other rich countries savers invested through channels that subordinated their wishes and muffled their voices. In Japan, for example, underperforming companies continued to get new loans. There was little danger that a corporate raider would take over the underperforming company and restructure it or liquidate it.

Savers in other countries have been slow to assert their power. One explanation is that Americans bought riskier securities, so they had to insist that corporate managers be more accountable and responsive. By comparison, people in other countries were hesitant to embrace risky financial assets. In 1991, after most Americans had already thoroughly hitched their financial destiny to risky, high-growth common stocks, people in Spain were still wary and risk-averse. My Spanish colleague made a point of explaining this difference to me during a series of conversations we had in Madrid. Several of his comments reveal how different the American attitude was compared to everyone else's:

- The Spanish government's economic policies were quite intelligent and successful, the figures on real growth were impressive, and many Spanish companies were making the right investments to position themselves for higher profits in the near future. This did not override the fact that Spain had been a poor country until the dictatorship ended.

- The switch to modern, transparent financial conventions was recent, and most Spaniards were hesitant to liquidate their gold and diamonds and move the money into stocks. Some of them still had money in the mattress, and many others had money in Switzerland.

- Younger, cosmopolitan people were buying new financial products, including mutual funds that invested in riskier common stocks. Many older Spaniards saw this as nothing more than a new fad and not the beginning of a new long-term trend.

- Foreign pension funds were buying stocks on the Madrid Stock Exchange and keeping prices there firm. Those funds began buying as soon as Spain entered the Common Market, and they continued to add to their holdings because the Spanish economy was growing fast, and the funds could tolerate the risk because Spanish stocks were such a small part of their holdings.

- Foreign pension funds would keep buying Spanish stocks until their holdings were fully commensurate with Spain's weighting in the world market. Local risk-tolerant buyers were buying Spanish stocks with the expectation of selling them to foreign pension funds. This was a dangerous game, but it would work as long as the foreign pension funds continued accumulating Spanish stocks.

My colleague was right to insist that as recently as 1991 many older Spaniards were still ultra-cautious, and he was right that foreign pension funds were the biggest buyers of Spanish stocks. In contrast, by that time Americans believed very strongly in the integrity of the U.S. financial system and were buying large amounts of risky common stocks.

America's love affair with financial assets took full flight in the fall of 1982, when the stock market shook itself out of a very long slumber and rallied strongly. The love affair blossomed at a time when the economy had been bumping from one severe recession to another. Inflation had been so bad in the late 1970s that Americans were putting their money into tangibles and collectibles. By 1979 every man in American had rummaged around in the attic looking for his childhood collection of baseball cards, because they were worth thousands of dollars. The financial pages were full of ads for rare coins, oriental rugs, and investment-grade art.

Then, after the recessions of 1980 and 1982, the inflationary psychology broke. The shift in sentiment was quick. Tangible investments lost their appeal. Americans who had put their faith in collectibles, gemstones, gold, and real estate during the 1970s turned away from these old standbys and came back to financial assets. They shook off the skepticism they had felt about the stability of the world financial system and stopped questioning the prudence of investing in financial assets. The commodities boom ended in April 1980 when the silver market crashed. By 1981 some investors were starting to buy bonds. Then, in August 1982, the world financial system suffered another body blow as the third world debt crisis broke out. The 1982 world financial crisis was severe, but Americans shrugged it off. Less than two months later the U.S. stock market took off, and Americans turned to buying financial assets aggressively. The baseball card collections went back into the attic. By 1985, collectibles were out of fashion and most Americans no longer questioned whether they should put all their faith and all their savings in the U.S. financial system. They were on the way to having a larger and larger percentage of their total net worth invested in U.S. financial assets, and in the houses that an increasing percentage of them owned. They did not seek much international diversification, and they used debt without worrying about how they would pay it back.

A second driver of America's love affair with financial assets was the tax exemption for retirement accounts. By 1980, an adequate retirement had become part of the social contract in America. Voters really expected to retire and live well in their declining years, and they communicated that expectation to politicians. The burden on the Social Security system would be too great if financial assets lost their value again as they did during the Depression. The average American could safely infer from those facts that U.S. financial assets would retain their value from 1980 onward. Therefore, it made sense to accumulate U.S. financial assets. And it also made sense to pay attention to rates of return, guarantees, and tax status of each investment vehicle.

As the 1980s continued, the average American's faith in financial assets grew stronger, and Americans became more and more dependent on financial assets retaining their value. When there were fluctuations, they hit people hard. The U.S. stock market crashed in October 1987, and I saw the effect on the day of the crash. I taught a late afternoon class at a site on Route 128, Boston's famous Technology Highway, also known as the Silicon Necklace. The students worked at high-tech companies and had professional-level jobs. The course, ironically enough, was on investments. They drove from their offices to the campus and parked in the large lot in front of the building where the class was. For the half-hour before the class started I sat outside the building on a bench facing the parking lot. October can be very pleasant in Boston, and the afternoon was sunny, so I sat on the bench and sipped a cup of coffee. I was not sitting there to watch the students arrive. The crash had shaken me, and I was gathering my wits and trying not to look as shell-shocked as I felt.

Then the students began to arrive. It was like watching a 1950s movie about zombies in slow motion. They got out of their cars with stiff movements, like elderly people instead of the twentysomethings they were, and began to walk toward the building. They looked catatonic. Their eyes were glazed, and their steps were uncertain and shuffling. They walked past me without seeing me, and instead of stopping at the cafeteria, continued straight into the classroom. Some of them had tears trickling down their cheeks, but they made no effort to brush the tears away.

Their lives were shattered. The crash had hit the people in my class harder than almost anyone else. They all had stock options, and were looking forward to cashing them in. Their options had been worth $50,000 or more in the morning, and in the afternoon were worthless. Their companies' stock prices had dropped far enough to wipe out the value of their options. These young professionals knew a lot about the stock market from working on Route 128. They knew the stock prices of volatile little companies like the ones they worked for were going to take a long time to recover. At that moment it looked as if the companies would be unable to raise more funds to fuel their growth, so the young professionals had to give up hope of getting the promotions and raises they expected before the crash.

A few minutes after beginning the class, I gave up. The group was too distraught to pay attention to anything except the personal calamity each had suffered. I tried for a few minutes to get them to talk about the crash, and the chances for a quick rebound, and that engaged some of them for a while, but the rest just sat there looking vacant and distressed. I ended the class early and let them go home, but some stayed, as if they had nowhere to go. I sat with them, and we talked quietly for about an hour. Then we all went to our houses and hoped for a rebound.

America's prosperity was not as completely tied to the stock market in 1987 as it is in 2003. The students I worked with on the day of the 1987 crash were the vanguard. Their lives danced to the ups and downs of the stock market because they were in high tech. The stock market put quick value on the discoveries and innovations their firms made.

U.S. policymakers acted promptly and decisively after the 1987 stock market crash. The Federal Reserve provided liquidity to brokerage firms and banks to prevent the crash from triggering a cascade of bankruptcies. The Federal Reserve's actions saved the U.S. financial system from a meltdown that would have been worse than the one that began in 1929. The policy of rescuing the financial system was new, and to hard-line traditionalists it condoned excesses and shielded high rollers from the consequences of their own hubris. According to the old view, it would have been prudent to crush speculation, and to "wring out the excesses" that build up during speculative periods.

Americans saw, instead of the outdated punitive policy, an economic policy based on pragmatic comparisons of magnitudes, not on moralistic and vindictive reflex responses. Speculation, despite its unpopular image, performs an important role, even in simple production-based economies.

In an economy with a huge amount of financial assets, the role of investment and speculation is pivotal: Investment in financial assets and speculation are central to the value-creating process. They are mainstream, legitimate activities and add value as surely as manufacturing, mining, or construction do. They need support, protection, and sponsorship. Pragmatic policy must focus on the financial magnitudes and assess how those magnitudes will be affected. Asset values are much greater than annual production and fluctuate much more than macro aggregates like output and employment. The fluctuations that can occur in asset values can frequently be an order of magnitude larger than the fluctuations in annual output. Because volatility is antagonistic to economic growth, it follows that fostering moderately rising asset values deserves to be the main goal of economic policy.

The Federal Reserve's actions, however, could not help the students I was working with on the day of the 1987 crash. Their options did not come back to life, and most of them had to work several more years to reach the same level of prosperity they had before the crash. The distraught students could have recouped their losses if they had borrowed money and bought stocks aggressively the morning after the crash. Investors who shrugged off the trauma and went back to the stock market became the new opinion leaders.

A third reason for America's love affair with financial assets is that new checks and balances came into effect. In the United Kingdom there existed a tradition of the securities industry policing itself. According to that view, the people in the securities business were fiduciaries, and they were supposed to take seriously the trust the public placed in them. The United States tried the same approach, but the Great Crash of 1929 discredited self-policing. After 1933 official U.S. policy went to the opposite extreme. There was never again to be a moment when the American public depended solely on any individual's sense of duty and word as a gentleman. The presumption now is that every person in the securities business is an imperfect human being whose high principles are too likely to fail in the presence of large amounts of money. Threats of criminal penalties, large fines, and jail sentences now deter vacillating fiduciaries. Small investors need the Securities Exchange Commission and the full powers of the criminal court system to protect them.

Experience since 1933 has shown how necessary these protections are. The U.S. securities markets attract every sort of scoundrel, swindler, embezzler, and thief. The full force of the protective shield that the United States has so carefully erected is sometimes not enough to keep small investors from losing their savings. There is a never-ending stream of new ways to subvert the shield. Nevertheless, the track record of protecting small investors became good enough to build trust.

The legal protections for small investors who put their money in mutual funds became particularly strong. The legal structure laid down in a 1940 law is a good illustration of checks and balances that safeguard small investors' money in the United States. Mutual funds have trustees, and their fiduciary responsibility is to protect the money that people invest in the funds. The trustees do not manage the fund, and they do not hold the securities that the fund owns. They designate a manager who chooses the stocks in the fund but never has possession of them. A custodian holds the securities on behalf of the investors in the fund. Auditors verify the fund's accounts on a regular basis. The structure looks complicated and redundant, but it does well protecting small investors from fraud and embezzlement.

The track record indicates that the setup works. There have been very few irregularities in the accounts of U.S. mutual funds, and no cases of any embezzlement causing the investors to lose money. Investors have occasionally lost money when the manager bought stocks or bonds that performed badly. But, if the manager bought securities that were outside the category stipulated in the fund's bylaws, the directors of the mutual fund management company frequently chose to reimburse the fund for the losses.

Small investors who bought shares of mutual funds in the United States structured in this way have had protection from the traditional hazards of investing in securities. They had experts making their choices for them, and the full force of the U.S. legal system protecting them from every abuse. The returns they earned, in consequence, were high. There is a debate regarding how good the experts were, and whether the fees were too high. Both debates are healthy and serve to keep the mutual fund industry from becoming complacent. But the main point is that the fees have been a bargain compared to the safety the mutual fund mechanism provided them. Many small investors would not have dared to invest in common stocks directly. The effect was to create an "equity culture" in the United States that many other countries are now trying to replicate, and to enlarge and stabilize the demand for common stock, including initial public offerings and secondary offerings. This allowed rapidly growing U.S. companies to grow more quickly. If they had not been able to sell new issues of common stock, they would have had to limit their growth to the rate they could finance with debt and internally generated funds alone.

Conclusion

The United States built a strong and resilient national financial system, and this system fostered the growth of the huge pile of American financial assets that Americans and foreigners now own. The United States laid the groundwork over a long period of time, beginning with the epochal reforms of 1933. Those reforms swept away the old vices of conflict of interest, self-dealing, opaque accounting, and insider trading. They ordered that the playing field must be level, and set in motion mechanisms to assure that it stays level. This assurance is what makes the United States' pile of financial assets stable and substantial, and gives the United States its financial clout in world affairs.

Other countries are trying to copy the United States' success. They are consciously and intentionally reforming their national financial systems, and their efforts are already producing real, lasting prosperity.

Many countries still have defective national financial systems. Chapter 5 begins with stories about three bad ones.

5 Three Defective National Financial Systems and Attributes of a Better One

From the picture window of the 12th-floor Manila apartment, I could see half-completed buildings. They looked like tall luxury apartment buildings, and the bright tropical sunlight made them stand out. I could see a wide swath of the neighborhood. In all directions I could see half-completed buildings. Most looked as if they were going to be luxury apartment buildings, like the one I was in. A few looked as if they were going to be office buildings or shopping centers. There were also luxury houses with lawns and gardens of brightly colored flowers. Every house was surrounded by high walls. Some of the houses were in rows, each facing the street and each surrounded by walls. Some of the fanciest homes had guardhouses by their main gates. I could see expensive cars parked in the driveways and garages, and gardeners and maids working in the gardens or inside the houses.

The usual weekday pedestrians were on the streets, and an assortment of small trucks, bicycles, and cars passed by. What was surprising was that nobody was working on the half-completed buildings. The small trucks were mostly delivery trucks. As I watched, two trucks stopped and the drivers got out and took groceries, flowers, and dry cleaning to the luxury houses.

At the time, I was a college student on vacation. My father was working there and knew the Philippines well because he had lived there as a child. He had returned there to work less than a year earlier. He was the president of the local affiliate of a multinational oil company. This was my first visit, and it was the first time I had been to a really poor country. I was excited about seeing the Philippines and interested in understanding why the country was so poor. The Marcos regime had only been in power a couple of years, and the regime's international image was still passably good. The scandals and years of repression were yet to come.

Ramon, the driver of the car sent to drive me to my parents' house, spoke well and seemed highly educated, considering that he was a driver. Later, I learned that he had a university degree in electrical engineering and his job as a driver was the best he could get.

That afternoon, knowing my curiosity about the economy, my father took me for a drive through parts of Makati, a rich suburb of Manila. In a bustling commercial section, people pushed heavily loaded carts, others maneuvered motorcycles, and many people talked vivaciously in small clusters on the sidewalks in front of the shops. The shops appeared to be doing a bustling trade. My father enjoyed driving me to places where we could look at construction projects or docks where ships were unloading their cargoes.

"Has there been a recession here, or is the economy doing well?" I asked. I had no basis of comparison. I saw a few people who looked middle class, and many others who looked very poor.

"Well, things aren't bad these days," he said. "The area we are in now is pretty prosperous. You'll have to see a bit more of Manila, and then you'll have an idea of what things are like here."

I thought he was going to say that there were cycles of prosperity and recession, but his answer was not in those terms. He seemed to be thinking of some permanent normal order of economic life in the Philippines.

We drove past a block of empty lots, with a half-completed apartment building in the middle of the block. There were walls around it, and it was about 15 stories high. The structure looked finished to me, but there were no windows—just openings in the concrete walls where the windows would go. I could see in the lobby, and there was no furniture. An opening in the wall indicated where the elevator doors would be, but there was no elevator. The building was a shell. Concrete rubble and empty bottles and cans littered the area that would be the parking lot. Standing in the sun next to the building was an armed guard.

"What's the guard doing there?" I asked. "The building looks like there isn't anything for him to guard."

"There's always something somebody could take," my father said, without specifying what any thief could possibly want from that site. "Also, you're expected to have a guard."

"But the guy hasn't got anything to do except stand there in the sun and bake," I objected.

"You're right. But there's probably a chair in there where he can take breaks and have a smoke."

"Then why doesn't he sit in it? Nobody's trying to take anything. He doesn't have to be walking around looking so vigilant."

"The owner might come by," my father said. "The guard wouldn't want the owner to see him sitting down on the job."

The guard had a job, and I was already starting to see that jobs were chronically scarce in the Philippines. The guard was putting on a good show in case anybody would notice. He was not posturing to deter thieves. There was nothing at the building site to take, but he was acting as if there were. He was making sure he would keep his job, and that the owner of the building would trust him to guard other places in the future.

We drove by another half-finished building. This one looked really abandoned. It did not have a wall around it. Instead, it was standing alone in a field where weeds grew among the rocks and bits of concrete. The weeds were tall.

"How come there are so many half-finished buildings around here?" I asked. "From the apartment I could see eight or ten in every direction. This one looks like it's been half-built for a long time."

"Well," he smiled, "you tell me why there are so many unfinished buildings. You're studying why underdeveloped countries are so poor. Let's see if you can figure it out."

"I don't see why they would build the structure and then not finish the building," I said. "That seems like a waste to me. Why not line up the financing and do the whole thing at once? Why start it and then stop building it before it's finished?"

"You're on the right track," he said. "Financing has something to do with it."

"You mean the builders start construction without having the financing all arranged?" I asked.

"Some builders might," he said. "But you can bet most got a construction loan of some sort before they started." He was going to make me puzzle out the local economic game.

"Are you saying the banks give commitment letters and then don't honor them?" I said.

"Yes, that happens, but it would be unusual," he said.

"So, the builder starts the building, and then his bank shuts off the money before the building is finished. Does he run out of money himself, so he can't dip into his own pocket to finish the building?"

"You've lived in countries where the currency is stable," he said. "Suppose I remind you that real estate is a hedge against inflation."

"Oh, the developers start construction on the buildings even if they don't have the financing all lined up in advance," I said.

"That's right. They get as much financing as they can, and then they start, even if it's not enough," he said.

"And to get that financing they have to put in some of their own money too," I said, leaning forward in the seat.

"Yes, but mostly they pledge land and other buildings they own to the bank," he said. "Banks here lend mostly against land. The rich families have land and buildings. That's for prestige and social standing. The way to make money here is in commerce. There are people here who have gotten rich in commerce. They have most of their money invested in stuff like canned goods and rice that turns over quickly," he went on. "But they can't really be upper class until they own real estate."

"So, after a person has made some money in commerce, he eventually reaches a point where he's got some extra cash and doesn't use it to buy more inventory," I said.

"Yes, the business they're in sometimes has all the inventory it needs. The guy who has just worked his way to being wealthy wants his son or daughter to marry into one of the top families. So he buys some real estate, and then develops the real-estate business as a sideline. That gives him a better chance of getting into the right country clubs."

I had noticed that the shops we drove past were full of goods. They had row upon row of canned goods and huge bins full to the point of overflowing with rice. Those shops did not need more inventory.

"And this is the best use they have of the extra cash?" I said, leaning back in the seat.

"Especially if they can get a bank loan to cover part of the construction cost."

"Wait a minute," I said. "Somebody in business has some extra cash. Why not invest it in some other business? Why pour it into putting up a building when there are plenty of half-finished ones standing around already? And without even having enough money lined up to finish the building?"

He smiled at that. "You've figured out that most of the owners of these buildings aren't people who specialize in real-estate development. Most of them are in some other business. Like wholesale trading, or maybe they have a few retail grocery stores like the ones we drove by a minute ago."

"And those businesses sometimes have extra cash," I said.

"Yes, because the markups are good and the inventory turns over pretty fast."

"The markups are good even though there are a lot of them, all with the same stuff, but they don't compete and push the margins down."

"No," he said. "They don't get into price wars, and they don't diversify into somebody else's business."

After a minute or two, I said, "So, every industry here is an oligopoly."

He laughed. "That's a fancy word. Let's just say the business people here don't step too hard on each other's toes."

"Okay, but I still don't see why they take the extra cash and sink it in a building. Real estate around here doesn't look like that good an investment. There have to be other ways of buying prestige."

His explanation had reminded me of something I had read about England around 1835. The millionaire bankers in the financial district wanted titles and social status, so they encouraged their children to marry into the aristocracy.

"Around here there aren't many ways of moving up the social ladder," he said. "The real aristocrats here are people who trace their lineage to Spain. They have the land grants from the King of Spain that they got centuries ago, and they still control the sugar plantations. The people who got rich more recently are mostly overseas Chinese. Some of them have only been here eight or ten generations."

"Sounds like the newly rich guys haven't got much hope of moving up that ladder. Maybe they should define a new ladder." I said.

He laughed again. "Oh, they've got pretty good chances. Nobody around here has such pure origins as they would have you believe. So, a little more mixing isn't necessarily impossible. Just expensive."

I looked again at the half-completed buildings. "Seems like there are a lot of newly rich people trying to impress the aristocrats. What are there, a couple of dozen guys trying to become aristocrats?"

"Oh, not that many! All these half-finished buildings probably belong to five or six guys."

"What? They're building this many buildings that the economy doesn't need just to show off? That sure is a waste if it doesn't work, because they must be losing money."

"Who says they're losing money?"

"How can they not be losing money? They're putting half the construction cost into the building a couple of years before the market needs the building. Then they are paying interest on that money for a couple of years before getting any of it back."

"What if sometimes the rate of inflation is higher than the interest rate?"

That shut me up for a while. If the developers could borrow money at an interest rate that was lower than the rate of inflation, they would make money on every building even if they started it much too soon. The cost of construction would rise, so the value of the construction that was done earlier would go up. Timing wouldn't matter. I said, "So, they build the buildings with whatever money they can borrow, and then inflation drives up the market value of the building."

"And they take their own cash out by overbilling for the construction materials," he said.

"They put up cash just to satisfy the bank?" I said.

"The bankers aren't stupid. They know the game too. They make the developer put up some cash and a whole lot of collateral so they won't be financing 100 percent of the construction cost."

"But the banks end up financing 100 percent of the construction cost after all, because the developers take their cash out by overbilling for the construction materials."

"You're right. Otherwise, the banks would be financing more than 100 percent of the construction cost."

"Then, after there's some inflation, the developer sells the building for a big profit and the bank recovers its loan," I said, "And the developer can sell the building even if it's only half-finished."

"You're starting to understand," he said.

We drove on. After a while, I said, "So, what we're looking at aren't half-finished buildings. They're piggy banks that belong to rich people."

"That's it. And most of the money in those piggy banks is borrowed."

"By the time the rich people repay the money, they'll be returning less purchasing power than they borrowed," I said.

"That's because the government keeps interest rates down."

"The country doesn't need this many buildings in this part of town! There won't be enough tenants for all these apartments! They needed to invest the money in other projects." I thought for a minute, then said, "But why isn't there even more overbuilding? Why doesn't every vacant lot have a half-finished building on it?"

"Not just anybody can get a loan. You've got to be pretty well connected. It helps to be related to the family that controls the bank."

"So, real-estate speculation is a game only the rich can play," I said.

"Yes, only the rich who are favored clients of a bank," he corrected me. "It wouldn't work if everybody did it. That's why it's such a sign of having arrived. You can drive a nice car and flash a roll of money, but you're not going to have people around here think you're really rich unless you have the banking connections to play this game." He looked at the half-completed buildings. "This looks like a lot of overbuilding, but I've seen worse," he said.

"Sooner or later somebody has to want to rent the space," I said, thinking out loud.

"Yes, when the buildings that are finished are filled up, then one of the developers finishes one that was left unfinished," he said.

"And then rich foreigners rent the apartments and the banks get paid back that way," I said.

"The banks always get paid back. They take enough collateral from the borrower so their loan is never at risk," he said. "That's why they turn off the money sometimes. When the borrower has taken out all the bank wants to lend him against the collateral they're holding, they don't write any more checks."

I was silent as we drove another block. "So, that's what you meant when you said the borrower doesn't have all the financing lined up in advance but goes ahead anyway."

"Okay, pretty good," he said, after we'd gone a bit farther. "Not bad for someone who just got here and is still running on Boston time. But there's one thing you're not seeing. Why don't they put in the imported equipment, stuff like the elevators, until they're about to finish the building?"

"You're right! None of the buildings have elevators. Shouldn't those go in pretty early in the construction?"

"Sure they should," he agreed. "Keep thinking and you'll figure out why they put them in toward the end."

"The elevators cost money," I said.

"What kind of money?" he asked.

"Dollars?" I asked.

"That's right. They pay pesos for most of the construction materials but some of the stuff they have to use is imported," he said.

"And dollars are hard to get?"

"Not hard to get. Just expensive."

"Can't they get dollars from the bank?"

"Not easily. There is always a scarcity of dollars here. To get them at the official exchange rate you have to go to the Central Bank."

"And that's not the same as the bank where you've got the preferential status," I said.

"Right. When your request gets to the Central Bank, somebody at the Central Bank might ask why you should get the dollars when there are so many requests for dollars to pay for imports that the country really needs. Like antibiotics or tractors."

That made me feel better for a second. But I was still upset about the overbuilding. It looked as if the country's scarce savings were being invested in buildings the country didn't need, just so that some rich guys could move closer to the top of Philippine society. I was willing to believe that their investments in real estate were profitable, but the profits were not coming from making an investment when the economy needed it. The profits were coming because the borrowers were getting the loans too cheaply. If the interest rates on the loans had been high enough, the developers would have lost money, and some of the developers might not have built so many buildings such a long time before there was demand for them.

"Now you're going to tell me the developers use their influence to get the dollars ahead of other people who have a more pressing need for the dollars," I said.

"I don't want you to feel too bad about the way this place works. But you wouldn't want to scrutinize too closely who gets dollars and who doesn't." After a pause, he said, "You've also got to keep in mind that the Central Bank is just one source of dollars. Any time around here when you want some serious amount of dollars, you go to Hong Kong. There you can get all you want, but they're more expensive."

"The developers go to the Central Bank first to get the dollars cheaply if they can. Then if they don't succeed, they get them some other way, and have to pay more pesos to get the dollars?"

"Yes, it's like that," he said. "The real stunt is to borrow pesos here and sell them to somebody in Hong Kong for dollars, just before there's some local crisis here. Then the black market price of dollars shoots up."

I thought about that for a while. "In that case the developer would sell the dollars to get pesos, use the pesos to pay back the bank, and have a big profit on the foreign exchange transaction. Then the developer would forget about finishing the building until later."

"Yes, it's better to finish the building during one of those periods when dollars are easy to get" he agreed. "It's a bad idea to pay extra to get the dollars, and then use them to buy the imported fixtures to finish the building."

"Anytime there's a hiccup in the foreign exchange market, do all the construction projects stop?"

"Most of them."

We headed toward home. We drove in silence while I thought about the way credit was being allocated in the Philippines.

As we approached the house I said, "What a system! The government holds down interest rates, so the middle class who put money into the banks get less interest than they should. Then rich guys borrow it to build buildings the country doesn't need, and make a profit anyway because of inflation. Those rich guys get dollars to buy the imported fixtures. If there's a currency crisis and they find they can make more by selling the dollars in the black market, they don't import the fixtures to finish the buildings. So the buildings stay unfinished longer."

My father laughed, "But it's all worth it if their daughter marries the aristocrat."

"Oh, my gosh!" I said. "Don't let me forget that! The developer gets voted into the country club too!"

We reached the driveway and my father let me out. I looked at the two gardeners in our front yard, and thought of the driver with the electrical engineering degree, and the guard working hard to protect the half-finished building where there was nothing to steal. "No wonder jobs are so tough to get here," I said.

Twenty-two years later I was in Lima, Peru. More precisely, I was in a hotel in Miraflores, the suburb between Lima and the Pacific Ocean. Its name means "look at the flowers" in Spanish, but I didn't see any extraordinary amount of flowers. I did see dozens of half-finished buildings. All of them looked like the ones I'd seen in Manila, but taller—twenty stories or more. The apartments in those buildings were going to be spectacular after the buildings were finished; they all had balconies and panoramic views—some of the Pacific, and some looking inland toward the center of Lima. Many of the buildings had big "For Sale" signs hanging from the 20th floors.

It was frustrating being in Peru at that time. The Shining Path guerrillas were terrorizing the whole country, including Lima. Alan Garcia was president, and had about a year and a half of his term remaining. He was a great orator, but by then people were tired of hearing him, and wanted economic recovery. The currency had many zeroes and two different names. Cab drivers would explain that bills with 2 on their faces and others with 2000 on their faces were really the same amount of money. Then they would politely ask for dollars, any small amount that I happened to be able to spare. The U.S. embassy made me change hotels and kept calling me to come in for a briefing. All they were going to tell me was that my life was in danger—not exactly a revelation, because everybody had already told me several dozen times each day I was there.

The neighborhood had once been very attractive, and would be again, but at that time it looked slightly down at the heel. I walked around and saw the pretty houses, nice restaurants, smart shops, and majestic hills rising out of the Pacific. The neighborhood was on a bluff overlooking the water. Far below where I walked there was an impressive pier with an ornate Victorian-style pavilion at the end of it. I wanted to walk down to it but there was no obvious road down, and I had been warned not to take taxicabs.

With nothing else to do and an hour of daylight remaining, I went into one of the boutiques. The owner was glad to have a customer. The shop did not have much merchandise, but what it had was very stylish and well made. The owner was an elegantly dressed woman who sounded highly educated. I immediately saw what I wanted, a dark green alpaca sweater for my wife, but saw an opportunity to find out what the owner thought about the current economic situation.

"This is a very pleasant district," I said, after telling her I was looking for a sweater for my wife.

"Yes, you should see it when the economy is doing better," she replied.

"Are things as bad as people say?"

"I'll say! Nobody has any money to buy nice things. This was a rich neighborhood. Can you tell?" she said.

"Yes, I can certainly see that this is normally a rich neighborhood, but the hard times are affecting everything, even the buildings in this neighborhood. Still, there are some very nice old houses, some of them with wonderful architecture, and rose bushes in the front yard. And that pavilion at the end of the pier! That must be really nice."

"Well, I hope something will work pretty soon. We're having blackouts, and some items that are always available are starting to run out. The other day the local grocery store didn't have any chicken! And to think this used to be the most important city on the whole continent," she said.

"Well, there's a lot of new construction going on, so that should bring some prosperity," I said.

"New construction?" she asked. "Where?"

"All these new apartment towers around here. There are a bunch of new towers between here and the edge of the cliff. They start about two blocks from here. I mean over there." I pointed west and a bit north.

"Oh, you mean those buildings," she said. "There's nothing happening with those. Work on those has been stopped for a while."

"Do you mean there's some problem like a strike or something wrong with the permits?" I asked.

"No, it's the banks. The banks aren't funding any loans, even the loans that were arranged months ago," she explained. "You've only been here a couple of days, right?"

"Right, but people have told me a bit of what's going on. It's something with the banks, but I don't know what, exactly," I said.

"Well, at the beginning of Garcia's term lots of people were optimistic, and so they put money in the banks. Also it's illegal for them to own foreign bank accounts or foreign currency, so they didn't have much choice. Whenever they had any extra money they put it in the local private banks. But the businesspeople were wary of inflation. They didn't borrow the money except to invest in stuff that would benefit from inflation."

"The businesspeople didn't do the usual thing like borrow money to buy imported consumer goods like color TVs?"

"They couldn't do that here," she said, "because right from the beginning Garcia said he wasn't going to allocate much foreign exchange to pay the foreign debt, so foreign lenders stopped lending and exporters started leaving the dollars outside the country. Shortly after he was in office, it became too hard to get dollars to buy stuff like that. That hasn't been an available strategy."

"Instead the businesspeople borrowed local currency and used it to build luxury apartment buildings?" I said.

"Right, they were able to get construction loans at interest rates that turned out to be much lower than inflation."

"It seems their speculation worked pretty well. What happened then?"

"You must have heard that the government forcibly took over a few of the oldest and most powerful commercial banks just a couple of days ago?" she said.

"I saw the confrontations on the TV news and in the newspapers almost as soon as I arrived, but I arrived in the middle of the whole furor, so I don't know what provoked the takeover."

There had been footage of a tank driving into the business district of Lima and aiming its cannon at the facade of one of the oldest commercial bank buildings in the country. Troops had gone into the building and into the office of the bank president, and had ordered the president to leave the bank and turn it over to a government-appointed administrator. The confrontation was between uniformed soldiers brandishing automatic weapons and the bank president dressed as usual in a business suit in the bank president's office. The bank president remained seated behind his desk and refused to leave, so the soldiers picked him up out of his chair and carried him out of the bank and into the street. They made sure he did not go back into the building, and after standing around him for a few minutes in the street, they led him away at gunpoint.

"You're probably wondering what that was all about," she said. "In your country you don't have that sort of thing."

"Not like that," I said. "The army doesn't do it. Federal marshals would be the ones to do it, and believe me, bank presidents do get removed in my country, just like here."

"In your country the takeover wouldn't be of the whole commercial banking system. It would be a takeover of a bank where there was embezzlement or where the president was making too many aggressive loans and putting the depositors' money in jeopardy. Here it was a clash between the commercial bankers and the President of the country. The President wants the banks to lend to projects that he says are high priority, not the kind of projects they always have financed in the past."

I noticed that she no longer said the President's name. The name is easy to pronounce, but she avoided saying it nonetheless. I thought for a few seconds.

"So, the confrontation was really about who sets the lending priorities, the President of the country, or the presidents of the private commercial banks."

"That's what the confrontation is about," she said. "We have always had private banks here. But they don't lend money to projects that help all the people. They lend money to rich people, and the rich people get richer. That's always been one of the biggest problems in this country. The banking system doesn't give access to credit to everybody, and also it doesn't finance the projects that would do the most good. So some governments intervene, like this one is doing. They usually don't go as far as they did this time. After they intervene, the loans go to projects that the private bankers wouldn't finance. This government has been fighting with the private bankers for over a year now. It wants them to lend according to social priorities."

"Sounds like the debate in a lot of countries. Mexico nationalized the banks in 1982, for reasons just like those," I said. "There must be projects around here that would satisfy the criteria of both the private bankers and the government."

"There must be what?" she said.

"Loans that would be for projects the country needs and would be profitable," I said.

"I'd like to see a few of those." she said.

"They're not as rare everywhere as they are around here." I laughed. But my laugh was forced, and it echoed in my mind, taking me back to the day in my youth when my father and I had driven around the Makati district in Manila looking at the half-completed buildings. There was an eerie similarity between the district I was in and the one I had been in years earlier.

The Peruvian shopkeeper was sophisticated and articulate, and her remarks remained on my mind for the rest of my stay in Peru. The question that kept buzzing into my consciousness was, Did that country ever have a social contract? Had it ever been a nation, in which every member of society felt a sense of shared destiny? Or had it always been so completely stratified that the different strata lived their lives without awareness of what life was like in the strata below, and without any sense that all the strata had to do well for the country to succeed economically? To me it seemed that all the Peruvians had was proximity to each other, without rapport or camaraderie. They all inhabited the same geographical area, but scarcely acknowledged each other's presence. They could pass each other on a congested sidewalk without bumping into each other, but without showing any other sign of seeing each other. If that was the case, every interaction would be a point of friction, and the friction would from time to time lead to conflict. Their financial system would have to break free of the country's thematic conflicts if it was ever going to allocate resources properly. It would have to work on different principles and make allocation decisions that were both productive and profitable.

The next time I saw a district of tall, half-finished buildings was January 1994 in Caracas. I was there with a group of students who had not traveled much, and we were on a 10-day visit that would take us to several parts of Venezuela. We started our stay in a downtown hotel. Almost immediately after arriving I went to look for a grocery store. Within a block I found a suitable-looking store and went in.

The food items were all displayed on shelves, and I picked up a small shopping basket as I entered. Quickly I found crackers and a small can of evaporated milk. As I thought of things I should get while I was there, I began to notice that there were some items that should have been on the shelves but were not on display. I was running low on disposable razors, but none were displayed. There was also no instant coffee. I approached the man at the cash register. A few customers were standing around, but they were not buying anything.

"Perhaps you can help me locate the instant coffee," I said. "I haven't been here before and I don't know what shelf it's on."

The retailer looked uncomfortable. "I'm sorry, the instant coffee is all gone," he said.

"But normally you have it?"

"Yes, but I haven't stocked it for months," he said.

"And throw-away razors? I always like to have a few of those in my briefcase, and I'm running out, so I though I'd pick some up here," I said.

"Those you can probably get at a pharmacy," he said, again looking evasive. By now all the other customers were watching.

Something was wrong, and I thought I knew what it was. I thought there were price controls in effect, so the goods were available only at prices above the posted maximum prices. "I'm an American tourist," I said, as if that were not already obvious, "and I've just arrived here in Caracas. I checked into the hotel over there less than an hour ago." I pointed to my hotel a short distance away. "I'm so new here I don't know what anything is supposed to cost. I haven't had time to change any money or anything." I pulled out a $10 bill. "I was going to ask if you would take dollars as a favor. That way I could get these items without having to change money at the hotel. You know how long that takes, and anyway they give a bad exchange rate."

The man at the cash register was unmoved. "I'm sorry I can't help. I don't have instant coffee anymore here, and you can get disposable razors at a pharmacy," he said.

I hesitated, trying to conceal my surprise. "I'm sorry to be so new here," I said. "I guess I just don't know what sorts of stores sell those sorts of things here."

One of the other people who was near the cash register saw I was about to leave. "Hey," he said, "I bought some instant coffee at another store that still has it in stock, and I have it right here." Magically, a small jar of Nescafé appeared in his hand. "I'll sell it to you so you won't have to look for it. The disposable razors, I'm afraid, you'll have to go find somewhere else."

I gave him the $10 bill and he gave me the jar of instant coffee. Then he pulled a thick roll of bills out of his pocket and added the $10 bill to it, and peeled off a couple of bills of local Venezuelan currency and gave them to me. "Sorry about the razors," he said, "but there's a pharmacy around the corner and you can probably get them there."

I thanked him, took the local currency and the instant coffee, and left the store. As I put the local currency in my pocket, I noted how much he had given me, and did the currency conversion calculation in my head. He had charged me about $4.50 for the instant coffee.

After that strange beginning, my stay in Venezuela became stranger still. The economy had a facade of modernity and normality over a reality of profound social alienation and contradictions. There had been a coup d'état attempt nearly two years earlier and an impeachment, but there were no external signs of any smoldering discontent around the hotel. The hotel had a high vacancy rate, but there could have been many explanations for that. Then I went on a city tour with the group of students and some local businessmen. When we arrived at the fashionable part of the downtown, we saw a dozen or more huge buildings, all 30 stories at least, that were half-finished. As in Manila and Lima, the structures were complete, but lacked windows and other fixtures.

"Looks like somebody overestimated the demand for downtown office space," I said to one of the local businessmen accompanying us.

"Yes, you could get that impression." He laughed.

"You mean these construction projects weren't all started by local business families and financed with local bank loans?" I asked.

"Well, some of them," he answered. "But a lot of these were financed with drug money." In the ensuing days I learned that "drug money" was the convenient local explanation for any investment that did not make sense.

"You mean that Colombian drug lords are putting money into Venezuela?" I asked. Colombia and Venezuela have an uneasy relationship and have had many conflicts over the years. Colombians had higher status than Venezuelans until Venezuela became rich from oil. After the oil money began to flow, rich Venezuelan families hired Colombians as household servants, chauffeurs, and gardeners. I doubted that Colombians would pour large amounts of money into investments in Venezuela, especially immobile investments like office buildings in a district that was already overbuilt.

"Yeah, sure."

"But why would they do that?" I asked. "They must have plenty of other ways of investing cash that are easier to manage and more profitable. They can't be making any money on these buildings."

"They don't have to make a profit on these buildings," he said. "They are just investing here because they have so much money they don't know what to do with it."

"Has there been much inflation here?" I asked.

"Yes, there has been, especially since the coup d'état attempt. Before that there were government regulations putting ceilings on the interest rates banks could charge on loans. Sometimes, a well-connected borrower could get a construction loan at a fixed interest rate."

"Sounds like it would be too good to pass up," I said.

"Yes, and a lot of people had the idea of building in this section. It's the new hot location, very much in fashion," he said. "In fact that's where we're stopping."

The bus pulled up in front of one of the largest office buildings. The front of the building at street level was finished. Above the street level the building was still an unfinished shell. We got out of the bus and went into the air-conditioned lobby. There were expensive carpets, and uniformed doormen standing by looking helpful. A very well-dressed young woman greeted us in English, "Welcome to Caracas. Let me show you the museum's new displays." They were a series of works of art and posters showing Caracas at various times in history. In a glass case was a model of how the building would look when it was finished. The model of the building included the name of the architectural firm that designed the building, and it also showed the name of the bank that had arranged financing for the construction. It was a prominent local bank.

"Looks like this building has local financing," I said to the business-man who had sat next to me on the bus.

"Well, this one, yes," he said. Then he gave a quick wink. "But if it really were drug money, do you think they would tell?" He paused. "No, of course not! They would get some prestigious bank to front for the real source."

The question might have stayed on my mind, but a short time later something even more extreme caught my attention. The next stop on our itinerary was an ultramodern shopping mall. It looked brand-new and the fixtures were all of the highest quality, of the sort you would see in a wealthy suburb in the United States. Stainless steel and chrome were everywhere, and the entire mall was air-conditioned. The group got off the bus and immediately began to fan out inside the mall. There were stores selling every expensive consumer good you could buy in any rich capital city. One of the students was delighted to find an automatic teller machine, and many of us went to it to take out money. Then they started buying T-shirts, beach towels, and newspapers and magazines in English.

That night, after a late dinner, I went to my hotel room and turned on the local TV news. There had been a run on a bank that afternoon. We had not seen it because our bus did not happen to go past the main office of the bank. The news showed people milling around outside the bank and police struggling to keep order. The announcer was saying that after the bank closed in the afternoon, people kept milling around in front for sev-eral hours. Government auditors were rumored to have entered the bank in the early hours of the afternoon and were rumored to be still inside. Meanwhile, the president of the bank was rumored to have left the coun-try. The news broadcast showed several private jets taking off after dark from a local airport. Private jets arrive and leave all the time in Caracas, but there was something ominous about the situation.

The next morning I went to the hotel lobby early and asked people at the reception desk what was going on. They feigned ignorance and also said that the local papers had not arrived. I went out and walked a block or two until I found a newspaper kiosk and bought every different local newspaper the vendor had. I took them back to the hotel and read them over breakfast.

There indeed had been a run on a bank, and the bank was a big one. It was called the Banco Latino and had 1.2 million depositors, a very large number for a country that had fewer than 20 million people. It also had an offshore affiliate in the Cayman Islands, and the affiliate was unable to meet the demands for withdrawals.

Later that day the group went to the ultramodern mall again. As before, the students made a beeline for the automatic teller machine, but this time they came away empty-handed. The machine appeared to be in good working order, but was no longer giving out money. Several of them tried, in case the first one had exceeded his credit limit, but none got any money. They asked me what was wrong with the machine.

"I don't think there's anything wrong with the machine," I replied. "The whole Venezuelan banking system is what's wrong."

"What do you mean?" one asked.

"There was a run on a bank yesterday," I said.

"There was? You mean they have those here too?" another asked.

"Here too, and worse than in the United States, because there aren't as many backup arrangements to keep the panic from spreading."

"Don't they have deposit insurance here?" asked one of the students.

"They do, but I heard this morning that half of the guarantee fund was deposited in the bank that had the run yesterday."

"So what?" asked another of the students.

"I don't know how big the guarantee fund was in the first place," I said, "but if the rumor is true, it's effectively only half as big now, because half of it is deposited in the bank that had the run. About midmorning I heard that several banks didn't open today, and there are government auditors in the one that had the run. Then, by lunchtime, all the others had closed because they couldn't deal with the crowds trying to get their money out."

"Will the government guarantee the deposits?" asked another.

"Most likely," I said, "but not today, and probably not for the rest of our stay here. First the auditors will have to sort out what happened. In the meanwhile it looks as if quite a few other banks are going to fail too. This mess will take a while to shake out. If any of you need cash, we'll have to start asking how you can get some—maybe a trip to American Express, but it's probably mobbed right now. The best thing for now is just use credit cards."

"If all the banks are closed, how are we going to be able to use credit cards?" asked one of the students, an American.

"The retailers will just take an impression of your card on one of those blank vouchers that every retailer used to use. They'll have you sign the voucher, and then they'll send it by courier to Miami and present it there. That way they can circumvent the banks here. They've got to have a way of turning credit card receipts into dollars in Miami."

One of the students from a third-world country said, "That'll mean the retailer will be able to evade taxes on those sales."

"True, and it's probably illegal for them to transact credit card sales without passing the sales through the local banks. But today and probably for the next few weeks they won't be able to pass the sales through local banks. They'll probably keep on selling merchandise any way they can."

"Tax evasion isn't a serious crime here the way it is in the States," said one of the Venezuelan businessmen.

"How will the tax authorities arrive at a figure for sales that went through banks in Miami?" asked one of the American students.

The Venezuelan businessman and I looked at each other. The Venezuelan spoke first. "They won't," he said. Several people in the group looked around the mall. It had not been very busy the day before. On this day, when everybody in the city was talking about the banking panic, there were people there, but not very many, and most of them were not buying anything.

"How can they let something like this happen?" asked one of the Americans. "One bank failure shouldn't stop the whole system."

"It's not going to be just one bank failure," said the Venezuelan.

"What were the bankers doing?" asked one of the Americans. "Taking the money out the back door in suitcases?"

"Not quite," laughed one of the Venezuelans. "Thieves here are higher tech than that. They loaned it to companies they controlled and to sham companies that existed only on paper in places like Panama and the Cayman Islands. The money didn't leave in suitcases. It went out by wire transfer."

Across the main lobby of the mall, we noticed a shopkeeper closing up his store front. For the first time we noticed that the store next to him had not opened that day. One of the students was standing close enough for me to hear him say, "This is what we came to see?"

The Era of Financial Assets Begins

There have been two watershed moments in economic history, and the third is happening now. The first two were the agricultural revolution, which happened from 12,000 to 9000 B.C., and the industrial revolution, which happened from A.D. 1780 to 1830. The third is the financial-asset revolution, and that began very recently and is quickly consolidating its transformation of world economic affairs.

The financial-asset revolution had several false starts before it began in earnest. The false starts were surges of financial assets that collapsed. The collapses were caused by breakdowns in the financial system or in the links between the financial system and other parts of the social organization. One reason for the collapses was the lack of regulatory vigilance. Another reason was that every country's financial system used to include too many organizations susceptible to collapse. Several types of organization are susceptible to collapse, and one is the typical, classic-style commercial bank. A type much less susceptible to collapse is the modern-style mutual fund. In the financial systems that collapsed, there were too many banks and not enough institutions that are more resistant to collapse, like modern-style mutual funds.

The idea that one type of financial institution is more susceptible to collapse than another type may not be familiar, but it is very important. Many of the financial collapses of bygone years were bank failures run amok. Usually, one bank failed, and that brought down others with it. The United States has had its full share of bank failures, but since the Federal Reserve System came into existence in 1913, the United States no longer has banking panics of the sort it used to experience. Nevertheless, individual bank failures continue to occur in the United States. The Asian crisis shows that banking crises are still going on, and still causing severe losses and setbacks to the well-being of the countries where they happen. The Venezuelan crisis that began while I was in Caracas was only one example, and not the worst, but it did become very severe. Fifty-six financial institutions closed, and those accounted for almost 50 percent of deposits in the country. People had to wait for their money, and the direct cost to the Venezuela government in bailout funds was $11 billion. Also, at least $10 billion left the country during the period of the crisis as nervous Venezuelans changed their local currency into dollars and then sent the dollars to the United States.[1] The Mexican banking crisis in 1995 was larger and more costly, but the worst since World War II in terms of cleanup cost was the Chilean crisis in 1982.

There have been hundreds of examples of banking crises and failures, and collectively they show that the incentives bankers operate under can cause the bankers to take actions that lead to ruin. The flaw in the typical, classic-style commercial bank, and in other financial institutions that are prone to collapse, lies in the fiduciary relationships within the financial institutions themselves, and vis-à-vis their clients. Many countries have learned this after suffering through panics and collapses.

The main point this chapter tries to make is that the *design*, not the *individuals*, is the cause of financial collapses. Certainly in every collapse there have been scoundrels and embezzlers, but there also have been paragons of integrity. The point is that in a well-designed financial institution, and in a well-designed national financial system, there are checks and balances. These design features create built-in stability, so when scoundrels get into positions of authority, the damage they do does not spread. A good test of a national financial system's stability is whether healthy financial institutions survive when an unhealthy one crashes.

Today there are national financial systems with built-in stability. The U.S. system is an example of one that has developed built-in stability. These new-style national financial systems have some superficial similarity to the old-style financial systems prevailing in most countries. The old-style systems have many of the same types of financial institutions: banks, insurance companies, stock brokerage firms, and mutual funds. The difference is the relative size; in the new-style systems, mutual funds, pension funds, and insurance companies have a large role, and commercial banks have a smaller role. Mutual funds, pension funds, and insurance companies have more built-in stability than a classic commercial bank does. That makes the new-style financial system more stable and resilient.

Built to Fall Down

Whenever anyone manages money that belongs to other people, bad things can happen. For centuries countries have struggled to implement enough checks and balances in their national financial systems to ensure the safety of their savers' funds. Countries have also struggled to give the right incentives to the people who manage money.

After a financial collapse, it becomes clear that the rules of behavior allowed a divergence to form. The objectives of some financial institution managers diverged from the objectives of the depositors who put money into those institutions. In many types of financial institutions this divergence forms easily.

The term "divergence of objectives" may not seem judgmental enough. After a collapse, writers use phrases like "market integrity" and "failure of oversight" to explain and condemn what happened. The victims and losers use stronger words, like fraud, embezzlement, self-dealing, and arrogance.

The following pages give a brief explanation of two important tasks financial institutions must carry out successfully. I then provide two simple reasons why classic commercial banks have chronically performed those tasks badly, then suggest that modern-style mutual funds perform both tasks more successfully. These brief explanations shed light on larger issues: why financial assets have so often ballooned and then collapsed, and why financial systems everywhere have so often channeled capital to people who should not have it and to projects that should not receive financing. This chapter suggests that countries can set up national financial systems that are solid and resilient. This is a tantalizing suggestion because if there is a way to set up a national system that can support an asset boom without collapsing, the country that sets it up first will become the dominant financial power, and other countries will be at a disadvantage.

Already, a few national financial systems are more stable than any system has been in the past. These financial systems have created financial assets that have given their owners overmastering power and influence in world affairs. Some of the assets will keep accruing interest and dividends, and will withstand downturns and shocks. Their aggregate value will rise to magnitudes large enough to dominate world affairs.

Two Tasks

In the centuries since financial markets first appeared, there have been many types of financial institutions. These include several kinds of banks, insurance companies, stock brokerage firms, mutual funds, venture capital companies, pension funds, and many others. Each type can be rated according to how well or badly it performs two important tasks. The first task is to stay in business, protect the money entrusted to them, and meet their obligations as they come due.

The second task is less obvious but also very important: to transmit pressure to perform. All types of financial institutions distort the depositors' priorities to some degree. Some do better than others in the little-noticed but pivotal task of transmitting priorities.

This point about transmitting priorities may seem obscure, but it is a key determinant of a country's growth. A country's savers may be willing to tolerate risk, but if the country's financial institutions are very conservative, risky projects will not get financing.

To illustrate how a financial intermediary can distort the priorities, and to show how the design of financial intermediaries can have serious flaws, I look at two defects of a typical classic-type commercial bank.[2] The classic commercial bank takes in deposits and makes loans. It charges more for loans than it pays the depositors. Banks of this sort have existed in Europe and elsewhere since A.D. 1100 or earlier. The classic commercial bank endures despite its design defects. I look at only two of those defects among many that have been identified. These two hopefully are enough to indicate why a well-designed national financial system should have many different types of financial institutions in addition to commercial banks.

Two Defects

In recent decades there has been a long technical debate about the design of the classic commercial bank. This debate has arrived at the conclusion that managers at classic commercial banks are subject to many conflicting incentives and pressures that create biases and make classic commercial banks intrinsically vulnerable to breakdowns. For the sake of brevity I look at only two of the design defects and counterproductive incentives that plague classic commercial banks. A full discussion of the defects and why they are intrinsic to the nature of the classic commercial bank would take hundreds of pages because there are many, and some are subtle. The two described here are easy to see and clearly damaging.

The first defect is that the typical classic commercial bank does not gain enough from really good investments and loses too much when it makes a bad one. This fact makes the typical commercial bank's lending decisions very conservative most of the time. This fact is easy to see if we note that when the bank makes a successful loan, all it recovers is its principal and interest. Considering that the bank had to pay the depositors to use their money, and pay its staff and fixed costs, the bank's net profit on a successful loan is only about 1 percent of the amount of the loan. When the bank makes an unsuccessful loan, it can lose much more than that. In the worst case it can lose as much as 100 percent of the loan amount.

This point shows why commercial bank lending officers are usually so conservative. If a loan is a failure, the bank may recover nothing from it and will have to make as many as 100 successful loans to recoup the loss. This highlights a glaring divergence of objectives. A bad loan is not anywhere near as damaging to society at large as it is to the bank. There is always some waste in any process for allocating capital. That is true in all economic systems, but the allocation process should not be judged according to how little it wastes. Instead, the criterion should be how productively it allocates the scarce resource. There are always risky projects that offer high potential, and it is important for some of those risky projects to get financing. For that reason bad loans can be a healthy sign if they indicate that society is backing its young people in risky new ventures.

The typical bank's aversion to loan losses explains why the banks I saw in the Philippines and Peru preferred to lend against real estate or other top-quality collateral. That preference is damaging to economic growth, because it biases banks toward lending only to borrowers who can give collateral or strong guarantees. That preference is what makes bank lending policies a barrier to social mobility; the rich can qualify for loans and the poor cannot, regardless of the merits of the proposals each may put forward. The preference does not come from the personalities or class origins of the bankers; it comes from the operating characteristics of the commercial bank. The preference goes a long way toward explaining why there were so many half-completed buildings in the Philippines and Peru, and why the counterproductive lending policy that I observed appears so often.

The built-in conservative bias is a big reason why every country should have other types of financial institutions in addition to commercial banks. In every country's financial system there need to be some financial institutions that make risky allocation decisions. The U.S. financial system has many more of these risk-taking institutions than do the Philippines, Peru, and Venezuela.

The second defect is occasional inducements for commercial bank lending officers to act recklessly. The technical term for these inducements is "moral hazard." One of the inducements that has received press coverage is deposit insurance. According to many experts, deposit insurance causes depositors to become complacent. If the bank begins lending recklessly, the depositors often turn a blind eye because they face no risk of loss. In that sense deposit insurance induces reckless behavior, but it is only one inducement among many.

Lending officers at classic commercial banks face many temptations, and sooner or later some officers succumb to one temptation or another. The most obvious temptation is to embezzle the depositors' money and take it out the back door in a suitcase. This happens often enough, but is not the cause of most bank failures, and it is also easy to prevent.

The next most obvious temptation is the one that causes most of the damage: to loan money to businesses that in one way or another are in the family. There are many variants on this theme, and some of them have a long pedigree and pretensions to respectability and legitimacy. In an example of the most blatantly unsound version, an individual gets control of a commercial bank and gradually loans the entire loan portfolio to businesses that he controls. In most banking crises, there is at least one bank that some rich man has turned into his personal petty cash box. Sooner or later one of his businesses is unable to repay the bank, and the whole patchwork of affiliates faces a liquidity crisis. The controlling person faces the unappealing prospect of losing all the businesses. The alternative is to place the bank in receivership after ordering all the businesses he controls to default on their loans. That is the alternative that gives him the best chance of keeping most of what he had before the liquidity crisis began.

The Banco Latino crisis in Venezuela, the debacle that I happened to witness, was an extreme example of what happens when a bank falls victim to this temptation. This would have been a run-of-the-mill collapse, and might not have triggered a banking panic. The unlucky detail was that about half of Venezuela's deposit guarantee fund was deposited in the Banco Latino. That turned the failure into a full-blown collapse of the entire country's financial system. The Venezuelan deposit guarantee scheme had built up a portfolio of financial assets that might have been large enough to maintain confidence. But when people learned that the deposit guarantee fund was, in effect, half gone, they decided that their deposits at other banks were in danger, and they lined up to withdraw them.

Why is it so dangerous when a bank lends money to a business controlled by the same people who control the bank? The danger begins from the moment the borrower submits the application. Because the loan is going to be approved, the borrower may skip some of the paperwork, and the bank's credit analysts may skip the usual careful review of the loan proposal. The danger grows after the loan has been made and the borrower falls out of compliance with the ratios in the loan agreement. The bank does take immediate action, as it would if the loan were to an unrelated party.

In one variant of this popular but defective arrangement, the bank becomes the center of a group of businesses that a wealthy, powerful family controls. There were banks like this in countries as different as Indonesia and Ecuador, and there still are many banks like this in other poor countries. Depositors put money into the bank, knowing that it is going to be loaned to one of the family's businesses or another. They rely on the family's acumen and influence. If anything goes wrong, they rely on the prestige and connections of the patriarch to line up a bailout. Sometimes there is no bailout.

Deliver Us from Temptation

The brief look at design defects of commercial banks makes it clear that bank lending officers would have to be philosopher-kings to do their jobs well over long periods of time. Luckily, new kinds of financial intermediaries exist, and some do not suffer from as many design defects. I will look at one of these, the modern-style mutual fund, to see if its managers have incentives that are less distorted, and if they face fewer temptations.

Managers of mutual funds do their jobs in the glare of full disclosure and intense scrutiny. Every decision they make to buy or sell securities becomes public knowledge within a few weeks. Journalists make a good living writing newsletters commenting on the portfolio decisions these managers make. This disclosure and scrutiny might sound like adequate protection, but managers can still sometimes feel pressure to take risks that do not match the investors' risk tolerance. To see how this can happen, consider that the costs of running a mutual fund are mostly fixed, but the management company's fee income depends on how much money the fund has under management. Also consider that if a fund is one of the top performers in its category, it will attract more money, and if it is one of the bottom performers in its category, it will shrink as investors pull their money out of the fund. Those considerations are enough to incline a manager who is doing poorly to take risks in hopes of outperforming the other funds in that category. If the risks succeed, the manager survives. If the risks fail, the manager would have been fired anyway. Now add gasoline to the flames. Suppose that the mutual fund management company gives the manager an annual bonus that varies depending on how profitable the fund was from the management company's point of view. This amounts to giving the manager a bonus if he or she can attract more money to the fund. The easiest way to accomplish that is by being one of the top-performing funds in the category.

These temptations are obvious and, with a few glaring exceptions, have been controlled well in the U.S. mutual fund industry and elsewhere also. Apart from the temptation to take too much risk in hopes of having the best performance in the category, the other incentives and pressures on mutual fund managers are much simpler. The manager knows that if share-holders are not happy, they will liquidate. That possibility keeps the manager working hard, but the manager does not become obsessed with keeping the job. The norm in the industry is that the typical manager does not manage the same mutual fund for a very long time. The career path for a mutual fund manager is a succession of jobs. Being fired from time to time is normal. Most managers can get another job. Doing something reckless is worse than being fired because everyone who cares to look will see the reckless act. The manager would have to explain that in every subsequent job interview.

In sum, the managers of U.S.-style mutual funds face simpler and less perverse incentives than the managers of classic commercial banks. The temptations are fewer, easier to see, and less damaging when a manager acts recklessly and causes losses.

Transmitting Pressure to Perform

The modern-style mutual fund is not perfect, but it is much better than a commercial bank at transmitting pressures from shareholders to corporate managers. The mutual fund manager is a conduit for the aspirations and frustrations of the people who put money into the fund. An individual who buys 100 shares of a company cannot expect to have much influence on management. But if that same individual puts money into a mutual fund and the mutual fund then buys 100,000 shares of the company, the individual's voice becomes stronger. The mutual fund manager speaks on behalf of the small investors and also on his or her own behalf. If the fund buys 100,000 shares of a company and the managers of the company then do something selfish, they hurt the small investors and they hurt the mutual fund manager too. The mutual fund manager will call up and berate them, and threaten credibly to sell enough of the company's shares to depress the price. In that sense the mutual fund mechanism agglomerates and amplifies the voices of small investors, and the mutual fund manager acts as the mouthpiece.

For comparison, consider how much pressure there is to perform in a financial system where commercial banks are the dominant source of credit. The bankers monitor loans for compliance with ratios that are stipulated in the loan agreements. As long as the borrower stays in compliance with the terms of the agreement, there is no pressure from the bankers. Then, if the borrower falls out of compliance with the terms of the agreement, the bank can accelerate the remaining payments so that they are all due immediately. The borrower therefore faces no pressure except negative pressure: avoid defaulting on the terms of the loan. Borrowers who stay within the terms of the loan agreement get no day-to-day pressure from the bank. That is why the managers of many companies prefer not to list their shares on the stock exchange or raise money in public markets. Instead, they borrow from banks and use borrowed money sparingly. If they underperform, they do not receive constant phone calls and pressure from reporters, stock market analysts, portfolio managers, and empowered shareholders.

Modern-style mutual funds transmit the investing public's preferences and desires in another way that is very important for promoting economic growth. The mix of loans that a society gives should match the mix that society desires to give. The mix of loans should not be too conservative or too risky. Every society includes people who are risk-tolerant and others who are risk-averse. In the aggregate, these diverse attitudes toward risk would cause society to give a mix of loans that would include some longer-term risky loans. In a national financial system consisting mostly of banks, the mix of loans would not include as many long-term risky loans. The mix would be too conservative because commercial banks are risk-averse. Banks can have only a limited amount of long-term loans outstanding, and savers might wish to make more long-term loans than that. And banks can have only a few risky loans, and almost none that looked risky from the start.

Conclusion

Countries can now aspire to have financial systems that resist collapse and allocate capital to its most productive uses. They can also have systems that transmit savers' preferences and put pressure on corporate mangers to perform up to their potential. Many countries do not have systems that perform satisfactorily with regard to those criteria.

The Philippines, Peru, and Venezuela had defective national financial systems at the times when I happened to see them. The United States has a system with many more built-in checks and balances. A good system is now a bigger advantage than it was in the past. Financial power accumulates rapidly when it is resting on a solid base, and its reach extends to decisions in all parts of the world.

If the U.S. system is already good, and many others are still defective, the question arises whether all the savers in the world should invest in the United States. If all of them could earn high yields by doing that, it would be rational for them to bypass their national financial systems and put all their money into the U.S. system. Chapter 6 addresses this question.

6 Is It Workable for Everyone to Invest in the United States?

The rate of return on investment in U.S. stocks and bonds since 1990 has been much higher than the rates of return on stocks and bonds in other countries. The dollar has also been strong for much of this time period, during which the United States has successfully attracted inflows of savings from many foreigners. Also, most Americans have chosen to put their savings into the U.S. financial system instead of investing abroad. This chapter addresses why U.S. financial investments have performed so well. It then examines whether all the world's savers can put their money into U.S. financial assets and continue earning high, stable returns.

The discussion begins by showing that the U.S. stock market performed much better than the productivity growth of U.S. economy would justify, and then gives an explanation for the stock and bond markets' superior performance. The chapter then shows that Americans ratcheted upward their aspirations as they saw the gains from securitization, and want securitization to continue and keep delivering gains. Next, the chapter sets forth a numerical illustration showing that all the savers in the world will not be able to get the returns they need if they put all their money into U.S. stocks and bonds. This result motivates the major assertion that the rate of return on stocks and bonds outside the United States will have to be higher and steadier than it has been since 1990. Portfolio investors who put money into non-U.S. markets, and especially into emerging markets, will have to be more successful in getting their fair share of the returns. Since 1994 they have not done well enough and so they have been wary of investing in non-U.S. markets and especially wary of investing in emerging markets. That has consequences for economic growth and especially affects the real growth rates of the emerging countries. Portfolio investors will press to get higher returns on their investments in the emerging countries. The methods they will use to get their fair share of the returns are a theme in later chapters.

Yields on U.S. Financial Investments Take Off

After 1980, U.S. investors poured money into mutual funds. The amount invested in U.S. mutual funds rose from $17 billion in 1960 to $134 billion in 1980, and then mushroomed to $6,965 billion in 2000. The growth from 1980 to 2000 included $4.5 trillion of new purchases and $2.3 trillion of interest, dividends, and capital gains reinvested. The average annual compound growth of the total amount including new purchases was 20.6 percent.

The years from 1990 to 2000 were even more impressive. The total amount in mutual funds rose from $1,065 billion to $6,965 billion, and the growth consisted of $4.04 trillion of new purchases and $2.5 trillion of interest, dividends, and capital gains reinvested. These figures show how dramatic the 1990s were compared to the 1980s. Mutual funds became an important savings vehicle in the 1980s, and then in the 1990s their performance overshadowed previous accomplishments.

The 1990s was when many Americans realized they could invest and make returns greater than what banks were offering on savings accounts. This fact raised their hopes of lifting themselves into the leisure class, and it also allowed them to save less. Savings as a percent of GDP in the United States fell from 7.3 percent in 1990 to 1.2 percent in 2000. Meanwhile, the rate of return on financial investments in the United States was high. A widely cited index of common stocks, the Standard and Poor's 500 stock index (S&P 500), rose at an average compound rate of 11.3 percent from January 1, 1990 to December 31, 2001.[1] This broad-based index includes shares of large companies in all sectors of the economy. It does not give special emphasis to technology stocks, so it tracks the rate of return that a person with a diversified portfolio of common stocks would have earned. That index is more broadly based than the NASDAQ index that rose to giddy heights in the first quarter of 2000 and then fell so sharply. The 12-year period includes the entire decade of the 1990s and the first two years of the new century. It includes two recessions and the biggest U.S. stock market rally of the modern era.

The dramatic performance of financial investments was not the result of a quantum leap in the return on investment in the underlying real economy. This might surprise people who heard enthusiastic comments about a New Economy. Indeed there may be a New Economy, but the underlying rate of return has not been any higher than it was in the old one. There has been no major interruption in the long downward slide in return on physical capital investment in the United States. To see this, let us examine a precursor of the rate of return: annual private investment relative to annual real economic growth. These two macroeconomic aggregates in the United States were approximately in the ratio of three-to-one in the 1950s and 1960s, meaning that investment of $3 in one year would increase GDP by $1 the following year. That ratio got worse in the 1970s; in that decade it took $4 of new investment to make the GDP rise by $1. Then the ratio got worse in the 1980s, and stayed almost as bad during the 1990s. In both those decades it took about $5 of new investment to make GDP rise by $1.[2]

From 1982 onward, the stock market headed upward much more strongly than the real economy. The bond market also rose strongly. There are adequate conventional explanations for the surges in bond prices and for the real-estate boom that took off in the mid-1980s. The victory over inflation explained the bond rally. Real-estate prices went up because mortgage financing became more affordable. Real estate had been a defensive investment in the 1970s as a hedge against inflation. From 1982 to 1986, real estate's positioning in investors' minds shifted. It became a leveraged, tax-advantaged vehicle to deliver capital gains.

Conventional explanations were not as adequate to explain the stock market rally. The stock market rally was very strong, and took many people by surprise. There had not been a rally like that for decades, and almost from the very beginning it looked different from the occasional half-hearted rallies of the 1966–1982 period. There was not much evidence to support the view that the United States was beginning a new era of above-normal growth. At the beginning of 1983, the U.S. economy appeared to be having a normal cyclical recovery. The stock market rally showed more strength than the underlying real economic growth justified. That was the first harbinger of the really big changes in the making.

Priorities Shift to Raising Returns on Financial Assets

The rate of return on financial investment remained much higher than the rate of return on investment in real productive assets after 1983, with brief interruptions. By 1990, the United States had become an economy focused on financial assets and had shifted its focus away from production. U.S. economic policy continued to put priority on process innovation and investment in new machinery and equipment, but the top priority became raising the rate of return to holders of financial investments, particularly long-term bonds and common stocks.

What caused the massive rally in prices of common stocks, bonds, and real estate was a confluence of favorable conditions. The obvious ones were fiscal reform and victory over inflation. But the biggest change was that shareholders began to call the tune. Prior to the 1980s, shareholders had no organized advocacy at the macroeconomic level, and no awareness of their clout as a pressure group. They had worked effectively at the level of individual corporations, but not at the level of influencing national economic policy. The public consciousness did not recognize shareholders as an interest group. The media mistakenly lumped shareholders together with rich people. The average voter did not know that shareholders were suffering, and would probably have remarked that they could cry on the shoulders of their friends at the country club. Yet shareholders had endured 16 years of mediocre returns, from the stock market peak in 1966 to mid-1982.

Then shareholders staked their claim as mainstream, middle-class voters with a legitimate need for adequate returns. Their numbers grew as millions signed up for 401(k) accounts. They gained power in the 1980s and more in the 1990s, and they used their power. They cracked the whip over corporate managers and they influenced Congress to give better treatment to shareholders and to the companies they invested in. Corporate managers embraced the goal of creating wealth for shareholders, and became more adept at taking only those actions that would raise their stock price, and rejecting other actions. For example, they optimized their use of debt, took advantage of accelerated depreciation, and bought back large numbers of their companies' own shares.

The rise of after-tax corporate profits is one indicator of the sea of change that shareholders were able to accomplish. Congress helped with tax cuts, accelerated depreciation, and tax credits for new capital investment. Corporate managers also helped by placing high priority on making profits. The priority rose, and other objectives became less important. Prior to the mid-1980s corporations had articulated other objectives besides raising profits and stock prices. Corporate profits averaged 5.3 percent of GDP for the 1970s and only 4.7 percent for the 1980s, then rebounded sharply to 5.9 percent of GDP for the 1990s.

The jump in corporate profits was impressive, but it does not show the true magnitude of the improvement that corporations achieved. To see the full magnitude, it is necessary to include depreciation along with after-tax profits. Depreciation is an expense that reduces profits. So, when Congress passed rules allowing faster depreciation, corporations could shield more of their profits from taxation. The figure that captures the full magnitude of the jump is the sum of corporate after-tax profits plus depreciation. That figure rose impressively from 9.9 percent of GDP in the 1950s to 10.8 percent in the 1970s, to 11.5 percent in the 1980s, to 12.8 percent in the 1990s.[3] U.S. corporations managed to raise their annual stream of profits plus depreciation by almost 3 percent of the country's annual output over the span of five decades, and by fully 2 percent in two decades. This shows the success that shareholders and corporations had in imposing their priorities on the country. Their success helped fuel the stock market rally. Their success also confirms that they achieved legitimacy as a mainstream interest group in the United States.

There is more evidence that shareholders gained clout as an interest group in the United States during the 1980s and 1990s. Companies and shareholder groups lobbied for lower taxes on corporate profits, and Congress approved. The Treasury stopped collecting so much of its total takings from corporations and got more of its tax revenues from other sources. During the 1950s the corporate income tax accounted for 28.6 percent of federal tax collections. In the 1960s the figure dropped to 22.2 percent, then to 16.7 percent in the 1970s. In the 1980s and 1990s it was around 11 percent. That is a big drop, and is one more reason why common stock prices rose so dramatically beginning in the fall of 1982. Shareholder empowerment helped corporations keep more of their profits, and shareholder empowerment caused corporations to use those extra dollars to reward shareholders.

The results were spectacular. The U.S. stock market rally from 1982 to 2000 is one of the broadest and most powerful on record. Other countries are in awe of this success and are trying to deal with the power and the threats it presents. They want to replicate its power without falling victim to the volatility that accompanies the power.

Americans Raise Their Aspirations

Americans are always quick to embrace new trends, and they joined the new fad in large numbers. More than half the households in America got a free ride up the staircase of prosperity as their retirement accounts and houses rose in value. Millions more got carried from the upper middle class into the swelling ranks of the truly wealthy. A huge number of people discovered that they did not have to work anymore. Some jumped to that conclusion before they had accumulated enough financial assets, and later had to retrench. But tens of millions of others who were still working discovered that they no longer had to save. Their household net worth was rising enough each month, and they could foresee that they would have enough with what they had saved already.

Americans shifted their aspirations upward. Previously, they had aspired to earn a high income, but as the boom went on, many of them thought of accumulating a pile of financial assets and joining the leisure class. The boom proved that millions of people could accomplish that, and motivated many Americans to set early, opulent retirement as their goal.

After the boom cooled off, Americans remained optimistic about the potential for another boom. They believed that another boom could begin as soon as the country had purged the excesses and repaired the institutions that had failed. They did not lose faith in the country's ability to repeat its success.

America is quick to recognize failure, cut its losses, liquidate, and then move onward. The segment of the American middle class that lost the most was in a position to return quickly to a middle-class standard of living. Many people who owned risky stocks on margin lost those stocks but managed to keep their houses. Many of them kept their jobs, or got other jobs that were almost as good. Bankruptcy lost its stigma in the United States, and more than one million people filed for personal bankruptcy in the United States both in 2000 and 2001.[4] The bankruptcy law sometimes allowed people to keep some assets, particularly those they held in accounts that creditors cannot reach, like insurance policies. For many Americans who lost when the frothy sectors of the stock market came down, the setback was just a bump in the road. They dealt with it like a hangover after a wild party. They shook it off and began rebuilding their battered personal finances.

The 1982–2000 stock and bond boom added a new component to the American dream. Many Americans believe they can reasonably expect to accumulate a pile of financial assets. As stock prices sagged, Federal

Reserve policy tried to keep the flagging asset boom from declining too sharply. The Federal Reserve cut the short-term interest rate over and over again, trying to lower the cost of money so that borrowers would be willing to take the risk of borrowing once again. The Federal Reserve's interest rate cuts were not only an attempt to keep economic activity from sliding into recession. More importantly, they were an attempt to maintain the market prices of financial assets and real estate. When earlier booms ended, the aggregate value of financial assets was not so large in proportion to annual output, so the monetary authorities would stand aside and let asset prices fall. The old thinking was that a steep drop in asset prices would facilitate the "creative destruction" of the capitalist renewal process, so it would have been imprudent to slow the decline.

Federal Reserve policy in 2001–2002 showed that America's economic priorities have shifted. Asset prices were high by historical standards, but the Federal Reserve acted to keep them high. The Federal Reserve's aggressive stimulus policy signaled that it will try to protect the wealth of asset holders. Too many American households now own homes and common stocks and are too vulnerable to capital losses. The Federal Reserve now takes steps to prop up the value of the financial assets and real estate.

There is a more sobering reason why the Federal Reserve takes steps to hold up the prices of bonds, real estate, and common stocks. America's savers need to earn high, stable rates of return on their investments. If the rates of return they earn on their financial assets are low and erratic, millions of Americans will not be able to afford the retirement they are planning.

The New Mechanism for Creating Wealth in the United States

During the boom, Americans got a good look at how quickly the American financial system can create wealth. They saw a wealth-creation process that was more powerful than the old wealth-creation process. The old process was a slow accretion of real productive assets.

The new process for creating wealth that Americans saw is securitization. Chapter 1 gave an example, and here is another. Suppose that there are two businesses. The larger one is listed on a U.S. stock exchange and its shares trade at 20 times earnings. The smaller one is not listed. The larger one buys the smaller one by issuing new shares and exchanging those shares for 100 percent ownership of the smaller business. This creates value, and part of the value accrues to the shareholders of the larger business and part to the former owners of the smaller business.

The larger business was earning $10 million a year after taxes and it had 10 million shares outstanding before it acquired the smaller business. The earnings per share of larger business was $1, and its stock price was $20. The smaller business was earning $1 million a year after taxes. The larger business offers 700,000 of its shares for 100 percent of the smaller business, and the owners of the smaller business accept the offer.

After the acquisition the larger business has earnings after tax of $11 million a year, and has 10,700,000 shares outstanding. The owners of the smaller business have 700,000 shares of the larger business. It appears that they sold their business for $14,000,000. That is 700,000 times $20.

That assessment is too pessimistic, however. After the acquisition the price of the larger company's shares rises. Its earnings per share rise from $1 to $1.03. Note that $11 million divided by 10.7 million is $1.03. If its price-to-earnings ratio (P/E ratio—market value per share divided by earnings per share) remains at 20, its stock price rises to $20.56. That increase is a gain for the larger business' shareholders and for the former owners of the smaller business.

The shareholders of the larger business gain because the shares they own go up. The former owners of the smaller business find that the stock they got is worth $14,392,000, not $14,000,000.

There are many reasons why this transaction creates value. One is that merging the two businesses improves the stability and viability of both. Another is that the earnings per share of the larger business grow, and another is that the shareholder base grows, and the potential trading volume of the shares increases.

The biggest reason why this transaction creates value is that the owners of the smaller business sell it for a price lower than what it becomes worth as part of the bigger company. The merger transforms the small business into securities that are worth more than a cash buyer would have paid to buy the entire small business.

In the wealth creation process that Americans saw, securitization adds value to assets that already exist. The investment bankers take the raw material, namely privately held businesses or other productive assets, and transform them into securities that fit buyers' needs. In 1980 there were many productive assets and businesses in the United States that were suitable raw material for securitization. There were sectors of the U.S. economy that did not have a very big presence in the stock and bond markets.

These sectors had many small- and medium-sized businesses that operated profitably but had not issued securities to the public.

The wealth creation process that Americans saw used mostly U.S. raw material. They saw the wealth-creation process slow down in 2000 before it had transformed all the raw material in the United States into securities. They wanted to get the process going again so they could get more profits from it. Americans grasped the key fact that millions of them would not have to work and more millions of them would not have to save, provided that the wealth creation process would get going again. They saw when the process gets going again, it will transform the raw material that is still available in the United States, and they also saw that there is much more raw material available outside the United States.

An Upper Limit to the Financial Wealth-Creation Process in the United States?

The U.S. financial wealth creation process securitized the raw material that was most readily available, but did not transform every asset and every income-producing property that potentially could have served as raw material. The wealth-creation process did not operate uniformly across all sectors of the economy. In some sectors it did a complete job of transforming raw material into highly valued securities. In other sectors it skipped some assets, and those have not yet been transformed into securities.

This section addresses how close the United States has come to running out of assets to securitize. If there are many more assets in the United States suitable for transformation into securities, savers everywhere in the world can continue to invest in the United States. The United States would be able to deliver high rates of return, comparable to the rates it delivered from 1990 to 2001. Americans would not have to invest abroad, and foreigners would be able to invest in the United States and earn high enough yields.

If securitization in the United States is approaching an upper limit, the wealth-creation process will have to use assets outside the United States as raw material. That would mean that U.S. savers will have to invest outside the United States and foreigners will not be able to achieve their objectives by investing all their savings in the United States. The answer to this question determines how much pressure U.S. savers will put on foreign countries. In many foreign countries there are obstacles to securitization, and U.S. savers have so far not exerted much pressure to remove those obstacles. The following calculations indicate that U.S. savers will press for those obstacles to be removed so that the securitization process will gain access to more raw material outside the United States.

The easiest way to determine whether securitization in the United States has reached an upper limit is to inquire if the total market value of U.S. assets reached a theoretical maximum. Paul Samuelson, the noted economist, wrote that the market value of a country's capital stock should be in the range of two to five times its annual output.[5] With U.S. GDP slightly higher than $10 trillion, this would imply that the value of all the capital assets in the country could not rise much higher than $50 trillion. In the first quarter of 2000, the value rose to approximately that level. And in the worst days of mid-2002, it was not very far below that level. That data indicates that securitization in the United States approached the upper end of Samuelson's range. Next we need to examine Samuelson's range to see whether it really is an upper limit.

The question of whether U.S. asset values are approaching an upper limit is really important for America and for the world. If U.S. asset values can rise much higher than $50 trillion, for example to $100 trillion, without inflation, American savers will be able to achieve the rate of return they need by continuing to invest at home. They will not have to buy large amounts of foreign securities, and they will not have to press foreign countries to give equal treatment to incoming foreign portfolio investment, or to allow securitization. Middle-class savers in foreign countries will also be able to buy U.S. stocks and bonds and earn high, stable rates of return. If instead $50 trillion is an upper limit, American savers will have little choice but to buy foreign securities. Before they do they will have to exert influence on foreign countries so that those securities will yield high, stable returns.

U.S. Department of Commerce figures give annual estimates of the value of capital assets in the United States. These figures show that a defined category of U.S. capital assets were worth $16.8 trillion in 1990 and $23.7 trillion in 1996, and $29.6 trillion in 2000.[6] These figures cover fixed reproducible tangible wealth and do not include four important components of the $50 trillion: the value of going concerns, intellectual property, human capital, and land. A going concern is usually worth more than its equipment, buildings, and inventory. Intellectual property is an important component of the U.S. capital stock and needs to be included in this discussion. Human capital is normally excluded, but in this assessment some of it should be included because it constitutes part of the value of common stocks. Many companies are worth much more than their tangible assets, and one reason is that they have excellent employees. The value of land in the United States should also be included. If we include these components, the total asset valuation would be close to the $50 trillion figure.

To see whether the $50 trillion valuation could rise to $100 trillion, we must determine which asset categories can be worth more. We are asking which assets can be worth more in constant dollars (adjusted for inflation), and we are assuming that inflation in the United States will be very low. Obviously, if there is a hyperinflation in the United States, the assets could be worth $100 trillion, but that would not be satisfactory for investors because they need the securities they buy to yield more in purchasing power terms. We are also assuming that there will be no sudden surge in output; output will continue to grow at 2 or 3 percent per year. Having made those assumptions, let us look at each asset category to determine whether it can easily be worth much more than the level it reached in 2000–2001. Real estate cannot be worth very much more, because the amounts that people can pay for housing or for office space cannot go up very much unless salaries go up. Bonds cannot go up very much because inflation and interest rates are already low. More bonds can be issued, because there are many assets in the United States that have not been pledged. But investors need capital gains if they are to make high returns, and they will not get big capital gains from bonds. It appears, therefore, that if the total value of U.S.-based assets is to rise from $50 trillion to a much higher number like $100 trillion, new common stocks will have to be issued, and existing common stocks will have to go up. The aggregate value of common stock is the easiest category to raise, and the only category that can deliver the high returns that investors need to make if they are to have enough in their retirement accounts without increasing their rate of savings.

The answer to whether U.S. asset valuations can exceed Samuelson's range of two-to-five times GDP is now before us. The answer is yes, assets in the United States can be worth more than five times GDP, but the valuation of common stocks would have to rise farther above its historical range and then would have to remain well above that range. Common stocks have already risen above their historical range and would have to rise more. For the three years following the stock market peak in the first quarter of 2000, the P/E ratio of the S&P 500 stock index remained above 21. Most of that time it was trading above the maximum P/E ratio of 23 that index reached in 1966, the peak year of the 1950s and 1960s bull market.[7] It is notable that the U.S. stock market was drifting for those three years well below the levels it reached in 2000. The U.S. stock market's high valuation held up through the three bad years after the first quarter of 2000. There are conventional explanations for this, but still it is impressive to see the U.S. stock market drifting at levels above what used to be the highest levels it reached at cyclical peaks in the past.

Can U.S. stock prices rise even higher? U.S. economic policy now takes stock prices into account, and maintaining high stock prices has now become an unstated goal of U.S. economic policy. There are, however, more actions the U.S. government could take to raise common stock prices. The following are a few actions the U.S. government could take that would raise common stock prices and spur demand for new issues of common stocks. These actions may seem shocking because they would apportion more of the national income to shareholders and less to other interest groups, including consumers and white-collar workers. These actions are more extreme and high-profile than the steps the U.S. government has taken in the past to apportion more of the national income to shareholders, but these actions are legitimate if holders of U.S. financial assets are the main group that U.S. economic policy is trying to benefit. Here are four policies that would accomplish that aim:

1. Make a more systematic effort to reduce inflation closer to 1 percent per year. This would raise bond prices and stock prices. To do this would require taking several actions the U.S. government is not taking now. One set of actions would be aimed at lowering the prices of commodities. The United States would work harder to undermine OPEC and would remove the trade barriers that restrict cheap food, clothing, steel, other industrial raw materials, and simple manufactures from entering the U.S. market. This would lower the cost of part of the consumer's basket of goods and services. Another set of actions would lower the cost of services by allowing Canadian and Mexican professionals, for example doctors and nurses, to practice in the United States. When consumers are paying less for goods and services, they would then be able to pay more for high-tech goods like pharmaceuticals. The U.S. government would make no attempt to control the prices of prescription drugs because the policy aims to raise the stock prices of pharmaceutical companies.

2. Extend patents and copyrights for longer periods of time. This would increase the value of intellectual property. Of course, consumers would suffer because it would take longer for prescription drugs to be available in generic form. But extending patents would quickly raise the prices of pharmaceutical shares.

3. Give all H visa holders green card status. The H visa holders have a technical skill that is, or was, in short supply in the U.S. labor market. The H visa lasts three years and can be extended for an additional three years. At that point the visa holder has to find a sponsor in order to stay in the United States. Some H visa holders return home instead of staying in the United States. The U.S. stock market would benefit if the H visa holders stay in the United States. They have valuable technical skills and they keep high-tech companies from having to slow their growth because of a lack of qualified personnel.

4. Discontinue the corporate income tax. Then all U.S. corporate profits would be available to pay bondholders and shareholders. The Treasury would need to develop a source of income to replace what it collects from the corporate income tax. Otherwise, the Treasury would have to issue many more government bonds than it does now, and the additional supply of bonds would push bond prices down.

These actions would certainly raise the prices of common stocks and bonds in the United States. The policies might be unacceptable from other points of view, but they illustrate the type of policy the U.S. government could adopt if it wanted to deliver capital gains to owners of financial assets. The effects of these policies would be to raise stock prices, and particularly stock prices of high-growth companies. These companies can be worth 40 times earnings, and then a short time later can be worth 100 times earnings. Their share prices can rise very quickly in response to an improvement in their future prospects.

Total capitalization of U.S. common stocks reached $17 trillion in 2000, with an additional $1 trillion of unexercised stock options. Could this $18 trillion total reach a much higher figure, for example, $40 trillion? It would have to reach that level if the total value of the U.S. capital stock would approach $100 trillion. Obviously, the U.S. stock market could achieve a total capitalization of $40 trillion if U.S. GDP would double or triple. But is a rise of that magnitude possible without increasing the size and growth rate of the underlying economy?

The simple calculation that follows shows that a rise of that magnitude is not quite possible. Suppose that all corporations have sold stock to the public and their average P/E ratio is 28. Next consider that corporate profits after tax averaged 5.9 percent of GDP during the 1990s. Therefore, all corporate stock is worth 28×5.9 percent = 165.2 percent of GDP if 28 is the appropriate multiple. With GDP being approximately $10 trillion,

U.S. common stocks would be worth $16.52 trillion, close to what they were worth in early 2002. Now suppose that the corporate income tax is discontinued, the lives of patents are extended, and H visa holders get green cards. Corporate profits would rise sharply, from 5.9 percent of GDP to a number closer to 10 percent of GDP.[8] If we apply the multiple of 28 to this higher figure for corporate profits, we arrive at the figure of 280 percent of GDP as the value of all U.S. common stocks. With GDP of approximately $10 trillion, common stocks would be worth $28 trillion.

The $40 trillion target is too high. We can take into account the multinationals whose shares are listed on U.S. stock exchanges, and that will add to the $28 trillion figure, but that will not bring the total up to $40 trillion. The only way we would be able to arrive at a total valuation for common stocks of $40 trillion would be if the P/E ratio of the average stock reached 40 times! That is almost twice the 1966 peak of 23 times.

Therefore, Samuelson's range is not a theoretical upper limit, but it does indicate that a practical limit exists. Even if the United States had policies that were entirely aimed at raising the value of financial assets to their maximum attainable limit, and if those policies were more aggressive than the ones mentioned in my example, the market value of the country's capital stock cannot reach $100 trillion while its GDP is $10 trillion. By the time U.S. GDP reaches $12 trillion, the market value of the country's capital stock could plausibly reach $75 trillion. To reach $100 trillion, GDP would have to approach $15 trillion. That would not happen soon enough.

Breaking the Upper Limit to the Financial Wealth-Creation Process

The pivotal question in world affairs is whether the hundreds of millions of people who are saving for retirement can accumulate enough to pay for their retirement in the amount of time they have available. The question is pivotal because it affects such huge financial magnitudes and because of the burden it can place on the younger generations and the fiscal accounts of many nations. The question is also pivotal because savers are becoming a more powerful group in the rich countries, increasingly capable of advancing their agenda and protecting their interests.

The previous section showed that the value of the U.S. capital stock cannot reach $100 trillion quickly. This is important because it means that the world's savers cannot simply accumulate U.S. financial assets and reach their goal. At the beginning of the time frame from 2002 to 2020, there are already as many as 300 million people around the world accumulating financial assets as their means of providing for their retirement, to leave a legacy to their children, and to give to charity.[9] It has been clear for many years that these 300 million people will have to rely on personal savings if they want to retire at 65 and enjoy a lifestyle comparable to what they had when they were working. That fact puts the spotlight on how much they are saving and what rate of return they are earning on those savings. In the aggregate they have not saved enough, and the easiest remedy is for them to earn a high rate of return from now on. The financial assets these savers buy must deliver high annual yields. This disturbing conclusion has implications.

These 300 million people might be able to support themselves on their savings, or might have to draw on the resources of the younger generations and the governments of the countries where they live. The outcome is favorable if the rate of return those 300 million people will earn is high enough. The outcome is sobering if the rate of return is lower. Using a spreadsheet program, it is easy to calculate what the rate of return will need to be. You can vary the starting assumptions, but the result is robust. The rate of return must be high, or there will be a serious shortfall.

If the rate of return is not high enough, the countries where the 300 million people live will face unpleasant choices. The countries will not be able to turn their backs on those 300 million people because they vote, and they outvote the younger cohorts. The political choices regarding the retirement conundrum are already moving toward the center of the national debate in several first-world countries. The remedy so far has been to delay retirement for people over 60. In the United States, the age when workers began to collect Social Security used to be 65. Now it has been delayed to 66 for younger people, and will probably have to be delayed to age 67 or older.[10]

Another remedy is that the savers and their governments take action now to make the rate of return high enough. They can press to make the rate of return on financial investments outside the United States higher than it has been. Savers who bought non-U.S. securities did not, on average, receive rates of return as high as U.S. yields. In some countries the returns were especially low in comparison to the yields those countries could have delivered. The track record since 1990 is striking. Most investors outside the United States would have done well if they had invested in U.S. financial assets for the entire period since 1990. In some foreign countries the returns were so bad that it would have been better to hold greenbacks in a safe deposit box.

There were a few bright spots among the disappointments in the performance of financial assets outside the United States during the period from January 1990 through early 2003. One was European common stocks, which did well in the years leading up to the monetary unification. The disappointments included Japan, which in the first half of the 1990s could at least point to its strengthening currency, but then saw its currency weaken along with its stock market in the latter half of the 1990s. From 1996 onward, Japanese investors would have done well to sell their Japanese financial assets and invest in dollar-denominated bonds. Investments in the emerging markets appeared also to give disappointing results, but a closer look gave reason for optimism. Emerging markets equities rose steeply in the early 1990s, reached a peak in February 1994, and then floundered, with occasional upward moves quickly giving way to declines. Emerging markets debt, however, performed better. Government bonds of many poor countries, including Morocco, Turkey, and India, did well for part or all of this period. Corporate bonds issued in some poor countries also performed well. Those bonds delivered high yields to holders that had enough diversification and cool enough nerves to hold on through the turbulent times. In fact, the yields on emerging markets debt were so encouraging that there is hope that the world's savers can earn high enough yields in the future. The returns on emerging markets debt were volatile, but high enough to deliver the needed yield.

Stocks and bonds issued outside the United States offer encouraging possibilities for higher yields. Many countries already are putting capital markets reforms into effect, so rates of return in those countries should improve. Looking at the other rich countries, there is latitude for prices of financial assets to rise. The exception is Japan, which has already pushed interest rates down almost to zero, and has issued many government bonds and given government guarantees to many private financial obligations. Japan cannot do much more to raise prices of financial assets and probably will have trouble keeping prices from falling. Europe, in contrast, offers good possibilities. European countries, and the companies domiciled in them, have issued a large amount of bonds and stocks, and these appear at first glance to be fully priced. Nevertheless, Europe's economy is not fully securitized, and many of the European securities are not at the highest prices they can achieve. Europe as a whole therefore has the potential to deliver capital gains to savers who buy financial assets.

Emerging Countries as Sources of Raw Material for Securitization

The emerging countries offer the greatest potential for delivering the high rates of return that today's savers need to earn. Emerging countries, and the companies headquartered in them, have not issued very large amounts of bonds and stocks. The economies of the emerging countries are only slightly securitized, and many of the securities they have issued in the past are trading at depressed prices. Emerging countries, and the companies headquartered in them, have not conceived themselves as issuers of securities. If some reconceptualize their economic role and position themselves as providers of capital gains to portfolio investors, they can do very well. They have enough unsecuritized assets to deliver enormous capital gains. Macroeconomic data show that the magnitude of the capital gains the emerging countries can deliver would be large enough to bridge the gap between what the 300 million savers will set aside and what they will need to spend after they retire. Macroeconomic data also show that if the 300 million savers are to earn enough capital gains, the easiest way for them to do that is by investing more in the emerging countries and earning high returns on those investments. The savers will not earn enough by investing only in the United States and Europe.

The world's savers will need to make tens of trillions of dollars of capital gains on their investments in emerging countries during the next two or three decades. The emerging countries have the potential to deliver the needed capital gains, so the question is whether that potential will become reality. This is a pivotal issue.

The emerging countries certainly need to attract capital and have projects that can compete successfully for financing. The past performance of emerging markets bonds has been good enough to attract new investors. Those facts give a basis for believing that the needed capital gains can be achieved. There is also reason for skepticism, however. People who have traded emerging markets stocks and bonds in the past would doubt that the emerging countries will deliver capital gains of the needed magnitude. The emerging countries as a group do not currently place high priority on delivering capital gains to portfolio investors. There are many other priorities that they take into account.

The calculations in this book indicate that some emerging countries can gain by repositioning themselves as producers of capital gains. If several emerging countries focus on issuing well-collateralized securities, they will do well. They will successfully attract inflows of portfolio investment and their economic growth will improve.

Opponents of globalization may react with anger to this suggestion. They might be dismayed at what these computations imply about the future role of emerging countries in the world economy. The emerging countries would relinquish their economic sovereignty and manage their economies with the objective of producing capital gains for 300 million portfolio investors, most of whom do not live in the emerging countries. The emerging countries would use their businesses, buildings, mines, and farms as raw material for securitization. They would be performing a new economic role in the world financial system. Their new role would be as peripheral and subservient as their previous role, but it could be much more rewarding than their previous role. Their previous economic role was as commodity producers or as producers of simple manufactured goods. In the scenario this book sets forth they would actively participate in a production process that creates capital gains. Most of the capital gains would accrue to foreigners, but the citizens of the emerging countries would gain some of the wealth and would benefit from the increased efficiency of their national financial systems.

Macroeconomic aggregates give very powerful support to the idea that the emerging countries can be the source of enormous capital gains. To see the magnitudes, consider that the emerging countries have an aggregate population of 5.1 billion people and an aggregate annual output of $6.3 trillion.[11] The combined outstanding bond issues of those countries total only $4 trillion, and the aggregate capitalization of their 35 largest stock markets totals only $2 trillion. The aggregate annual output is low and the total market value of bonds and stocks is low. In that sense, the real economies of these countries and their financial economies are in a consistent relationship vis-à-vis each other.

The potential for the emerging economies to grow is enormous. If the emerging countries could increase their annual output to $10,000 per capita, their aggregate annual output could then be $51 trillion. Using Samuelson's range of multiples, their financial assets could then be worth between $102 trillion and $255 trillion. That is an immense magnitude, and gives an idea of how much the world would gain if the emerging countries could increase their annual output and foster securitization.

The usual approach to raising output in the emerging countries is to promote exports, invest more in education, and improve institutions. In the usual approach, the real economy leads the way to higher growth. The financial system does not act as prime mover; it plays only a supporting role. The new view is that a country's financial system can play a more proactive and constructive role in spurring growth. It can mobilize capital and allocate capital to projects with high returns. There are trillions of dollars earning low returns in first-world financial markets, and some of that money would migrate to national financial systems of emerging countries if the returns would be high enough to compensate the risk.

Reforming National Financial Systems in the Emerging Countries

Since 1994 the performance of stock markets in emerging countries has not been as dynamic as it was in the years from 1988 to 1993. Since 1994, returns in those stock markets have not been high enough to compensate the risk, and foreign portfolio investors have drifted away. That is part of the explanation why third-world stock markets are so small relative to the size of their economies. If these stock markets were more dynamic, they could raise and allocate risk-tolerant capital and speed the growth rate of output in these poor countries.

These stock markets do not have to be as moribund and marginalized as they have been since 1994. They can deliver capital gains to foreign portfolio investors two ways. First, the shares that have already been issued can rise. Second, new issues of shares can be floated, and then the prices of those shares can rise. Each of these ways will pull in new capital from foreign portfolio investors. This would start a virtuous circle, leading from capital gains to real growth to more capital gains. The aggregate stock market capitalization of 35 third-world stock markets could rise from 30 percent of total annual output of the underlying countries to 100 percent. If, in the meantime, the annual output of those countries doubled, from $6.3 trillion to $12.6 trillion, the stock market capitalization could rise from $2 trillion to $12.6 trillion. That rise would fuel further rises, because at the level of $12.6 trillion, the stock market capitalization of those countries would still be nowhere near its theoretical upper limit.

This book proposes that many emerging countries can pursue a stock-market-led growth strategy. Countries that choose this strategy would implement reforms that would entice portfolio investors to buy common stocks listed on their national stock exchanges. This strategy seeks to tap the potential for raising the market prices of existing financial assets. As prices rise, investors' appetite for new issues of common stock and bonds would awaken. This stock-market-led growth strategy would jump-start the economies of the countries that implement it successfully. It is a feasible first step and can potentially launch countries on a trajectory toward progress. By itself it does not educate billions of people or overcome the other intractable problems that third-world countries face. To implement this strategy only requires disallowing completely the unfair practices that brought the emerging stock markets down after the high-flying days of 1988–1993. From 1994 onward there were too many instances of insider trading, falsified accounts, rigged rules of corporate governance, lax regulation, and weak enforcement. Those vices held back the growth of emerging stock markets.

In many emerging countries local efforts have been made to improve standards of corporate governance and to reactivate local stock markets. At the level of multilateral agencies, the Institute for International Finance "published a code for corporate governance in emerging markets...in an effort to boost private capital flows and protect minority shareholder rights."[12] If these efforts succeed, and international portfolio investors put aside their skepticism and again move money into the emerging countries' stock markets, two good outcomes could occur. First, prospects for the world's 300 million savers would improve. Second, as those savers put money into the emerging countries, the capital inflows might improve living standards for some of the 5.1 billion people living in the emerging countries.

Whether emerging countries succeed in reactivating their stock markets or not, they can become more successful at issuing bonds. The institutional requirements for successfully issuing bonds are not as demanding, and many emerging countries already have the framework in place. Bondholders' claims have priority over other claims, and the legal system has to enforce that priority.

The calculations in this book show that the emerging countries have enough businesses, buildings, and other assets to collateralize the amount of securities that the world's 300 million savers will need to buy. Those securities can yield enough so that the savers will accumulate enough purchasing power to support themselves during their retirement.

Conclusion and Implications

The world's savers will not do well enough if they put all their money into U.S. stocks and bonds. The savers have too much buying power and they would bid the prices of U.S. stocks and bonds up to unsustainable levels. At those high levels the returns would be erratic and the savers would not make enough gains to support themselves after they retire. The savers will have to invest in non-U.S. stocks and bonds, and those investments will have to perform better than they have done since 1990. Emerging markets bonds have done better than other non-U.S. securities and can deliver the needed yields.

Americans can again ride the tide of a financial asset boom. If foreign stocks and bonds begin to deliver high returns, and if foreign countries make securitization a top priority, yields can once again be as high as they were from 1994 to 2000. If emerging countries reform their national financial systems and promote securitization, savers everywhere will benefit, and the emerging countries will increase their growth rates as portfolio investment flows in.

This chapter suggests that there will be pressure to make investments in emerging countries perform up to their potential. Performance to date had given some reason for hope, but there have been many more setbacks than necessary. Chapter 7 looks at individual investment projects in emerging countries to see why the returns have been low at the level of individual projects. It also looks at different ways of structuring the financing so that the returns would be higher.

7 Structuring Viable Ways to Invest in Poor Countries

The number of savers in the world is growing, and the amount of financial assets they buy each month is rising. They buy predominantly stocks and bonds issued in the rich countries. They would willingly buy stocks and bonds issued in the poor countries if those investments offered competitive yields. When the yields are high enough, savers will bid for emerging markets stocks and bonds, will subscribe enthusiastically to new issues of those securities, and will devote a larger portion of their portfolios to those securities. The small total amount of emerging markets stocks and bonds contrasts sharply with the large amount of good collateral those countries have within their borders. This chapter gives some indications why the demand for these securities has been so weak and why the securitization process has progressed so slowly in the poor countries. It describes three projects, shows how their financing was structured, and shows how it should have been structured instead.

In poor countries, business opportunities exist that are potentially profitable enough to offer high yields to prospective investors. Many private businesses in the poor countries earn high rates of return, and some categories of foreign investment in those countries have a long history of yielding high returns. Some private companies have been able to deliver positive returns in the most difficult, corrupt, and unstable countries.

Many projects in the poor countries look promising, but fail. Capital is scarce in those countries, and so it would seem that to compete successfully for capital, projects would have to offer high rates of return. Despite the scarcity of capital, many projects in the poor countries waste capital; too much capital investment is dissipated on projects that do not make economic sense. Many of the failed investments are high-profile white elephants jutting starkly against the skyline of third-world capital cities, or spectacular monuments to ego plopped down in some remote area of jungle. Others are less conspicuous but wasteful nonetheless. Also, many projects that do earn high returns divert the returns to people who did not take any risks and who did not provide the capital. In those cases the people who put in the money do not get enough returns to compensate for the risks they took.

Local savings and foreign investment are both at risk of going astray in poor countries. Ill-conceived projects and unfair distribution of profits both weaken economic performance and hurt the countries' ability to compete for funds in international capital markets.

The overall pattern, however, is not completely dismal. Many projects deliver needed products and services and reward their investors appropriately, but these are not the subject of this chapter. This discussion focuses on projects that were supposed to make profits and examines how they were financed. It looks at the financial architecture of two failures and compares them to a success. There is much to be learned from these failures; thousands of them dot the landscape throughout the third world. They are incorrectly set up, or poorly executed, or exposed to plunder, and then they languish, leaving embarrassment, disappointments, and unpaid bills. The unpaid bills are added to the country's foreign debt. These projects were intended to generate enough foreign exchange to repay the borrowing country's debts, but they ended up unable to repay their own liabilities. The decisions that led to these fiascoes were supposed to be like decisions that a hard-nosed banker would make, but ended up compromised and torn by conflicting objectives. Poorly designed credit approval procedures and weak control systems allowed these projects to go ahead, then fail. These control systems do not have to be as bad as they have been in the past. The financial architecture of the individual projects can be improved so that yields go to the people who did the work and put in the money, and this chapter shows how.

The failed projects include many that received government-to-government financing and some that received financing from multilateral agencies, but that is not their fatal flaw. The key criterion for success is not the source of financing; it is the structure of the deal. A good design has key requirements. A good design includes guarantees against all eventualities. If a disaster occurs, the guarantees and insurance policies will repay the amounts that have been invested. Many writers have pointed out that a good design also gives the managers and decision-makers the right incentives. A deal that lacks these design features may succeed, but only by luck and if key managers happen to be capable and selfless.

Scrutinizing the incentives of everyone involved is important. Projects that get financing have promoters, and promoters often have personal reasons for advocating particular projects. Many projects that receive funding are especially profitable or advantageous to the promoters, and these may not be the projects that best benefit the investors or the public.

Successful private-sector projects yield profits because the sponsoring firms are careful to acquire and retain control over day-to-day operations. That way, the firms can control the disbursements and monitor performance. They can quickly flag discrepancies and take remedial action.

Recycling Risk-Tolerant Capital

Erratic yields are not the only reason why the total supply of capital for projects in the third world is low. The investments are not recycled fast enough in the capital markets. To see what this means, consider that in the rich countries the financing of an investment project usually changes during its life. When the project is being built, the funding comes from risk-tolerant lenders. These risk-takers buy insurance against adverse events, but still bear more risk than the investors who come in after the project has already been built and is operating successfully. In the construction stage, for example, the initial lender intends to make a very profitable short-term construction loan and expects the owner to repay the construction loan after the building is finished and occupied. The owner repays by obtaining long-term financing from a lender like a pension fund or an insurance company. The construction loan is not supposed to turn into a long-term loan. After the construction lender is repaid with the proceeds from the long-term financing, the construction lender then has cash to lend to the next construction project.

Recycling risk-tolerant capital is essential if large numbers of projects are to be financed. In the rich countries the relatively small supply of risk capital is husbanded very carefully and is allocated to a project only as long as the project is risky. As soon as the project is safe, the financing is replaced with cheaper, risk-averse capital. In the third world this recycling sometimes happens, but sometimes the risk capital remains "locked into" the project for years or decades longer than necessary.

In the rich countries there are experts who liberate risk-tolerant capital so that its owners can reinvest it. They do this by repackaging and refinancing risky loans. They earn their living by taking risky securities and converting them into safer instruments. The best-known example is the U.S. mortgage securitization process. In that business the experts add value by transforming mortgages into very safe bonds. What these experts do has the effect of recovering risk-tolerant capital and freeing it to bankroll one risky business proposition after another. To an uninitiated observer their work looks like the miracle of the loaves and the fishes, as the experts work their magic to fund one new venture after another from the same limited pool of risk capital.

In the third world the miracle of financing one venture after another with the same risk-tolerant money happens much less often. The investment projects usually are not set up to facilitate refinancing. Instead, the initial lenders are repaid from the project's cash flows. If the project succeeds, it can take many years to repay its financing, and if it fails, it never repays. The risk capital is tied up longer than necessary or forever.

The national financial systems in most third-world countries do not offer many opportunities to refinance a project's debt. That is one reason why promoters and entrepreneurs in third-world countries focus on getting a project financed, but then do not think of refinancing it. Also, even after the project is built and operating successfully, it is still risky because of where it is located. That might seem to reduce the possibilities for refinancing third-world projects once they have reached the stage where they are operating successfully.

This is where modern financial engineering can come in and liberate the risk-tolerant capital that is "locked into" the project. The project can be refinanced after it is built. The financial engineer enhances the project's safety with insurance policies, guarantees, and other gadgets of modern finance. The engineer repackages the project's cash flows into safe components and risky components, and sells the safe ones to risk-averse investors. The engineer packages the risky components in ways that allow the buyers to hedge the risk of owning them. In that fashion, the financial engineer quickly recycles all the capital that was invested in the project.

This chapter describes a deal that failed, a deal that succeeded, and a deal that a small investment bank proposed. The structure of each deal was flawed. I explain what the flaws were, then describe a deal structure

that would succeed, and show how the deal structure neutralizes temptations. Next I describe the refinancing possibilities and discuss how the
risk capital can be freed after a short time so that it can finance the next
risky deal.

The Nicaraguan Flour Mill[1]

Many projects in the third world fail when they should have succeeded.
The promoters' intentions are good, and forecasts indicate that the
project's output will be needed. This flour mill project was not like that.
From the country's point of view, it was a bad idea from the beginning.
Nicaragua did not need the project, and, if it had ever been completed,
would have had to subsidize it to keep it operating. The project had no
real purpose but to enrich a well-connected colonel. The project is
instructive because it had a typical life cycle and its deal structure was
classically flawed.

The money for this project came from the Interamerican Development Bank. The project's brief and shameful history took place in Nicaragua during the mid-1970s, when Somoza was in power. The
Interamerican Development Bank loaned $10 million to the Nicaraguan
government for projects in the agricultural sector that would create
employment and improve Nicaragua's balance of payments. The Central
Bank of Nicaragua administered the loan. This meant that the Central
Bank took applications from local businessmen who wanted to borrow,
monitored the disbursements, and generated studies showing the benefits
of the projects to the Nicaraguan economy. The Central Bank was also
ultimately responsible for repaying the $10 million loan.

This $10 million was especially vulnerable to being misallocated or
stolen. It entered the country from abroad with little fanfare. Very few
people knew it had arrived. Local savings are much more conspicuous,
and when a loan officer throws away local savings on projects that are
obviously uneconomic, or lends local savings to borrowers who are not
going to repay, the insult to the community is more palpable and widespread, and the political cost is higher. This money arrived, funded a few
projects, and then was gone, and very few people noticed.

Many people might feel that fraud is prevalent in foreign investment
projects in the third world. This perception is an artifact of the way the
press reports news, and is a misleading way of categorizing projects that
are hit by fraud. Fraud hits projects that do not have checks and balances

to prevent it. Wherever a project is located, it can fall victim to cost over-runs, embezzlement, nepotism, and self-dealing. The Nicaraguan flour mill was a loser not because it was in the third world, but because the institutional rules in effect at that time allowed its promoter to use it as the means to his own enrichment.

This deal was very typical in its structure. The Interamerican Development Bank lent $10 million, a large sum of money at the time, to an agency of the Nicaraguan government, and the Nicaraguan government guaranteed the entire loan. The Nicaraguan Central Bank then funded several projects using the $10 million, and a few of the projects failed or were rip-offs from the beginning. A few of the projects succeeded, or at least survived long enough to benefit the target group of poor people. One project, as luck would have it, was successful enough to repay the entire $10 million loan. Unfortunately, the borrower for that project had only borrowed $1.5 million, so that was all he had to repay. That fact gives a first glimpse of the defects in the structure. The successful loans could not compensate for the failures because all the Central Bank could recover was principal and interest. Obviously, if all the projects had failed, the Central Bank of Nicaragua would have recovered nothing from the projects it funded, and would have had to repay the $10 million loan from other sources. But, if four out of five of the projects had succeeded, the Central Bank would still have had to repay part of the $10 million loan from other sources.

This structure, a large loan that funds several different projects, has a design flaw that is not obvious at first. The payoffs of the different projects appear to be pooled, in the sense that the earnings of the successful projects cover some of the shortfalls of the failures. The borrowers agreed to pay the Central Bank of Nicaragua a higher interest rate than the rate the Central Bank had to pay to the Interamerican Development Bank. The individual borrowers, however, were only obliged to repay what they borrowed with interest. The Central Bank did not have any equity in the projects, so it did not have any chance of getting back much more than it put in. In the entire pool of loans, the successes would have to outnumber the failures by a wide margin, or they would not generate enough profit to the Central Bank to compensate for the losers. Nicaraguan taxpayers would have to shoulder the shortfall.

The flour mill project got a $2.5 million loan from the Central Bank of Nicaragua. The project's purpose sounded worthy enough. Nicaragua did not have a flour mill at the time the project was funded, and so the project would import, install, and put into operation the first one in the country. The flour mill would generate employment and save foreign exchange. Nicaragua would import wheat and mill it in the country instead of importing flour.

A well-connected colonel, who was a member of the dictator's clique, proposed the project and submitted the loan application. It moved quickly through channels and the funding was disbursed.

The mill, however, was not needed. At the world level there was overcapacity in flour milling. Data from readily available sources showed that the price difference between wheat and flour was almost always too small to justify the flour mill. For further proof that the mill was not needed, consider that food-aid programs would ship wheat flour to Nicaragua at very low cost. Wheat and wheat flour surpluses were chronic in the rich countries. The imports of wheat flour did not damage the interests of local farmers directly because Nicaragua does not grow wheat. Consequently, there was not as much local opposition to importing wheat as there was to importing rice or powdered milk, both of which Nicaraguan farmers produce.

A further argument against the project was that the colonel had no business experience and did not know anything about flour milling.

The true objective of the deal was to keep as much of the $2.5 million as possible and then default on the repayment. The project proposal argued for buying used machinery on the grounds that it is cheaper and more appropriate for a labor surplus economy. The mill would use local mechanics to maintain the machinery, and so generate employment in the community near the mill. There was an unscrupulous machinery dealer in Puerto Rico who had already submitted a quote for a complete flour mill that supposedly had been shut down and disassembled. The mill machinery and fixtures were going to be transported to Nicaragua in shipping containers. Then they would be transported to the site and reassembled where the mill was to be located. The quote for the used mill was $2 million. The remainder of the $2.5 million loan was to pay for site costs including the shed and the reassembly.

The machinery dealer never bought the used flour mill. The used flour mill may never have existed. Instead, he sent a few containers full of bits and pieces of machinery and scrap metal. There were no blueprints and no instructions how to reassemble the mill. Many of the pieces were broken and did not look as if they had ever gone together.

Rumors circulated in Managua business circles that the dealer had charged $500,000 for this junk, and had kicked back $1.5 million to the colonel's Cayman Islands bank account. The rumors began to circulate a few weeks after the shipping containers arrived at the port in Nicaragua and nobody bothered to come and pick them up. The rumors gathered strength in the ensuing months when the business had not hired anybody to assemble and operate the mill. People found out what was in the containers when curious customs officials opened them and found the scrap metal and broken bits of machinery.

The colonel was never forced to repay the loan and was never charged with a crime. He had more political power than the Central Bank, so the Central Bank staff could not do anything. For the Central Bank staff, the flour mill loan was an embarrassment, but it did not hurt their own personal finances. They had no recourse but to shrug it off and hope the dictatorship would not last forever.

The Blue Jeans Factory

All of the $10 million loan from the Interamerican Development was not stolen. One project that it financed was a success: a blue jeans factory. The blue jeans entrepreneur applied for a loan to buy sewing machines and import denim cloth. He proposed cutting it and stitching it into blue jeans. The output went to export markets and to the local market.

The blue jeans factory was wildly successful. It generated employment, built up Nicaragua's exports, and produced a return on investment in excess of 200 percent per year. The owner of the factory repaid the loan with interest.

The Central Bank, to its regret, could not get any more interest from the blue jeans factory owner, so it did not have enough extra income to fund the shortfall from the flour mill loan. The blue jeans entrepreneur repaid all he had borrowed right on time, and then did not try to borrow any more money for the blue jeans factory or for any other business.

The flour mill and jeans factory projects had the same legal structure. The structure was seriously flawed. Nevertheless, one of the loans was recovered. The rules of business in Nicaragua at that time explain why. There was rule of law of a particular sort, but it did not have much to do with the legal code. The rule was that some people had to repay the Central Bank and others did not. Everybody knew who was in each category, and acted accordingly. The penalties for violating the rule could be extreme. Those facts took precedence in explaining why one loan was lost and the other was collected.

The blue jeans factory owner had to repay because he was not in the privileged group. If he had defaulted, he would have had to go into hiding or exile. Nobody would have believed him if he had claimed to have lost the money. Anybody could pay an accountant to prepare a distorted set of financial results, so getting an auditor would not have saved him. Everybody would have assumed he had stolen the money, and he would have been jailed or killed.

Design Defects

Why choose such shocking examples? Why choose such a difficult environment as Nicaragua during the Somoza dictatorship? The flour mill loan was a sordid little deal, and the Somoza regime fell a short while after it came to light. The blue jeans factory owner sounds like a hero simply because he repaid what he borrowed, but in reality he had no choice. The examples are instructive because they put the subject of deal structure into sharp relief. They shatter the comfortable assumptions that everyone tends to make, and put the deal structure in the spotlight alongside human frailty, greed, cowardice, cruelty, and intimidation.

The flour mill loan was easy to attribute to the miasma of corruption that permeated Managua during the regime of Anastasio Somoza Debayle, the last of three Somozas to rule in Nicaragua. The reason for the loss, however, was much simpler and more general. It goes deeper than the specifics of place and time.

The deal did not have enough checks and balances, and its payoffs were not distributed to all the stakeholders in proportion to the risks they had taken. The penalties for failure were nonexistent in the case of the colonel, or too extreme in the case of the blue jeans entrepreneur. The only control system in place was the good intentions, vigilance, and sense of social propriety of the Nicaraguan government officials. The policy-level staff and lending officers at the Nicaraguan Central Bank were supposed to be competent, scrupulous, and dedicated to their country's well-being. They were, but those attributes were ineffective when it came to preventing the money from being stolen.

The deal's protectors were people who should not have been involved in the first place. Their incentives were consequently inimical to the deal's success. This is not to say that they wanted to deal to fail. The point is that the deal's success or failure was not their guiding consideration. They had to pay more attention to the unwritten rules of behavior under the Somoza dictatorship. They had to keep their jobs and they had to worry about their own standing with the dictator.

As protectors of the $10 million loan, the Central Bank officials faced the classic dilemma of the agent. They had to act in their own interest, and the unfortunate consequence was that they acted against the interests of the greater society. They approved the loan to the colonel knowing he was not going to repay it.

The Philippine Generating Plants

Sixteen years later there was a deal 10 times as big, nowhere near as scandalous, but equally instructive. In 1994 one of the smaller islands in the Philippines needed two diesel generators. These would produce much cheaper electricity than the small gasoline-powered generators in use on the island. A small and unknown U.S. investment banking firm proposed a deal to finance the purchase, transport, installation, and operation of the generators. The generators, each about the size of a school bus, were going to be loaded onto an oceangoing barge and towed from the U.S. East Coast to the Philippines.

The generators would remain on the barge, and if there was any trouble collecting for the electricity, the barge could be towed away to another place where electricity is scarce.

The plan was to sell electricity for $0.25 a kilowatt-hour. This is much more than the cost of generating it, but much less than the $0.40 a kilowatt-hour that it cost with small gasoline-powered generators.

The generators were going to cost $2 million each, and the oceangoing barge was to cost $1 million. All costs, including the cost of towing the barge to the Philippines and a generous provision for unforeseen expenses, did not total any more than $8 million.

The investment bank capitalized the deal at $20 million. This was extreme, and everybody who read the offering circular could see it. The investment bank sought to raise $17 million from investors and claimed it was going to put up $3 million of equity to complete the $20 million.

The investment bankers whispered that some of the extra money was for bribes to get the necessary permits from the Philippine government. The deal involved an offshore holding company, ostensibly for tax reasons, but also to break the audit trail of the bribes.

The offshore holding company helped in another way that the investment bankers did not acknowledge. The offering circular included a letter from an offshore bank confirming that the investment bank held a $3 million certificate of deposit. That was the investment bank's proof that it was ready and able to put in the $3 million of equity. The offshore bank's address was a post office box on an island in the Caribbean.

Investors could see all these points quite easily. The facts were in the offering circular, or written between the lines. Investors were being asked to put up $17 million to pay for an investment that was really going to cost no more than $8 million. The investment bank was not going to put any money at risk unless and until the $17 million had somehow been used up. If the deal went sour, the investors were going to suffer. Despite all these facts investors might have put $17 million into the deal because it was so profitable. The economies of scale in generating electricity combined with the low cost of diesel fuel would easily repay the excessive capitalization. The investors were going to earn 16 percent a year on their money, and they would be repaid in two years. At the end of the two years the investors would get some residual benefits that would raise their return to 30 percent a year for the two years.

The rate of return was so high, and the credibility of the story was so good, that the potential investors were not going to verify the $3 million of equity from the investment bankers. The investors looked at the quotes for insurance policies that were included in the offering circular, and found that most risks were going to be covered, and the quotes were from well-capitalized insurance companies.

No Design Defects?

The Philippine generating plants deal had a much better design than the Nicaraguan loan deals. The first and most obvious difference concerns the people making the decision whether to put up the $17 million. They were institutional investors, and the money they would be investing was not their own, but they would treat it very carefully. For them, rate of return and loan recovery were their primary priorities. They were not under any pressure to lend the money to one borrower or another. They had plenty of deals to choose from. Their job performance ratings and annual compensation depended heavily on choosing profitable investments and avoiding bad investments. In contrast, the Nicaraguan Central Bank officials were not rewarded or punished unless they got into conflict with someone with more political power.

The second point concerns repayment. In the Philippine deal, if the borrower did not repay, the lenders would make a real effort to collect. If there were any problem, the lenders would make a real effort to force the investment bankers to put in the $3 million they pledged. In the Nicaraguan deals, repayment was not an issue. One borrower was not going to repay and the other was. The Central Bank officials would not have to do anything regarding collection.

A third obvious difference is that the Philippine deal was going to operate under American rules. The Philippine legal system was kept as far out of the deal as possible. In the event of any dispute, the matter would be resolved in U.S. courts. The Nicaraguan loans were made under Nicaraguan rules. Once the $10 million left Washington, it was entirely the Nicaraguan government's business. The Interamerican Development Bank was relying on the Nicaraguan government guarantee and had no other protection and no plan of recovery if anything went wrong.

The Philippine deal did have one enormous design defect. The investment bank was raising more than twice what the project cost, and was going to be in a position to take a $9 million profit up front. This fact, which readers of the offering circular could infer by adding and subtracting, caused the investment bankers some nervousness and embarrassment when the investors pointed it out. They would make excuses, but would not say what they were going to do with the $9 million. Investors assumed that some of it would go to pay bribes and the investment bankers would keep the rest.

A Better Design

The Philippine deal's major structural flaw is that the investment bankers get too much profit up front and do not shoulder any of the risk. Although many readers would be shocked at the size of the payoff they get, from a technical point of view the design defect is not that they get $9 million from a $20 million deal. The defect is that the investment bankers get such a large portion of the total payout at the beginning, so their incentive is to raise the money. They do not have much incentive to monitor the deal's progress, or to make sure that the payoffs happen on schedule. They get $9 million up front, and if the deal fails completely, they will have to put in $3 million at the end of the second year. The risk they shoulder is not commensurate with the risk the institutional investors take. The institutional investors put up $17 million and in the worst case might recover only $3 million, or nothing if the certificate of deposit at the offshore bank proves fraudulent. The insurance policies pay in the event of natural disaster or expropriation, but there is nothing in the deal structure that protects against lax management control.

The institutional investors get 30 percent a year if all goes well, and that sounds like a high rate of return. The tempting forecasted return, however, should not make the institutional investors let down their guard and expose themselves to so much risk when they can lower the risk and get more of the payoff. The project would yield much more than 30 percent a year. We can figure out what the total payoff on the $20 million investment will be if all goes as planned and then apportion it differently.

Evidently, the project is going to be very profitable because the Filipinos are going to pay $32 million over two years for an investment that really costs only $8 million. To arrive at the $32 million figure, consider that 30 percent of $20 million is $6 million, and $32 million is $20 plus $6 million a year for two years.

With the total payoff in mind, let us construct a structure more fair to the institutional investors and having more built-in safeguards. Then we will look at how this structure would apportion the gains. Suppose that the investment banker agrees not to take money at the beginning, but instead agrees to be paid on the same timetable as the institutional investors. In that case, the deal could be set up as a corporation with shares. The shares would then be apportioned to the institutional investors and the investment bank. The distribution would determine how the profits from the deal would be paid out. For example, the total deal could be capitalized at $11 million. That would be $8 million from the institutional investors at the beginning, plus the $3 million standby commitment from the investment bankers. There could be, in this hypothetical deal structure, sixteen shares. Each of the eight institutional investors would put in $1 million and get one share. The investment banker would put in the $3 million guarantee and get eight shares. Everyone would understand that the $3 million would be called only if, after two years, there were no other monies in hand to repay the $8 million the institutional investors put in.

With this more fair structure in place, the institutional investors will make a return much higher than 30 percent a year if all goes well. They are also more likely to make a high return, because the investment bankers would have a strong incentive to monitor the project. The project will pay $6 million after one year, and $26 million after two years. The new structure would give the institutional investors half of those cash flows because they hold eight of the sixteen shares. They would get $3 million after one year and $13 million at the end of the second year. Their annual return, therefore, would be 47.6 percent on their investment of $8 million in the more fairly structured deal capitalized at $11 million, and their position would be stronger than in the brazenly overcapitalized $20 million deal structure that was originally proposed.[2]

With this structure the investment bankers would also get much more than $9 million. Because they hold half the shares, they would get $3 million after one year and $13 million after the second year.

Obviously, the more equitable proposed structure is better for the institutional investors and they should insist on a structure like it. They especially must not allow the investment bankers to take an up-front rake-off larger than the $3 million guarantee. The size of the investment bank's up-front fee is important because it influences how much attention the investment bankers will give to the deal once it is funded. The investment bankers do need some money up front to pay paperwork costs, and perhaps to pay bribes, but they do not need $9 million. If they get too much up front, their incentive is to be shills and raise the money regardless of whether the deal is good. If their up-front payment is $2 million or less, they will devote effort to making sure the deal is successful, because if it fails, they will have to pay $3 million at the end of the two years. In a well-structured deal their incentive is to be partners with the institutional investors.

This modified structure also facilitates refinancing. As soon as the barges have made the voyage across the Pacific, the generators have entered into service, and the Filipino customers have begun paying for the electricity, the risk of the project drops. At that point the institutional investors could sell their shares to investors who were not willing to take the risk of the project at the beginning. If all eight of them sold six months before receiving the $3 million payment, and eighteen months before receiving the $13 million payment, let us compute the rate of return the new buyer would make and the rate of return the institutional investors would make. Suppose the institutional investors sell for $11.5 million. They would have invested $8 million for six months and would receive $11.5 million. Their annual rate of return would be 107 percent. The new buyer would make an annual rate of return of 29 percent.[3]

The new buyer's money would have refinanced the risk-tolerant money that the institutional investors put into the project, and the institutional investors would then have their capital back to invest in the next risky project. Note that the institutional investors' annual rate of return is higher than if they had left it in the project for eighteen more months. The new buyer, who was unwilling to participate in the project before the generators were in service, provides capital to the deal for the remainder of its life. The risk-tolerant capital, after the refinancing, seeks its next opportunity, and the relatively risk-averse capital takes its place until the generators are paid off.

You may be shocked that the institutional investors make such a high rate of return, an annual rate of 107 percent, in this example. The new relatively risk-averse buyer makes 29 percent a year for a year and a half. The investment bank, however, probably makes the highest rate of return. The investment bank will get payments totaling $16 million without putting up any money. The investment bank's rate of return is infinity because it puts up no capital. Its rate of return in the original deal structure was also infinity, but it gets that infinite rate of return at the beginning instead of having to wait for it. The modified deal structure keeps the investment bank focused on making the project a success, and that is why it is a better design. Furthermore, the Filipinos are more likely to get cheaper electricity than with the original deal structure. The original deal structure allows too many ways for the investment bank to take its upfront payment and walk away before the generators are anywhere near the Philippines. This is especially true if the $3 million certificate of deposit did not really exist.

You may question what difference the deal structure makes to the poor Filipinos who will pay so much for electricity while wealthy investment bankers and institutional investors haggle over how to divide the huge payoff between them. This is a valid question, and it may seem beside the point to be tinkering with the structure of the deal. The numbers in the offering circular, nevertheless, are as I report them. Somebody proposed the deal, and if it had gone through as proposed, the cost of electricity on an island in the Philippines would have dropped. The deal, if successful, would lower the cost of electricity and increase people's access to it. There was nobody hovering in the wings offering to provide the island with electricity at a more reasonable price. The deal structure makes a difference to poor people living in remote areas over two time horizons. In the short run, if the deal is well structured, the institutional investors will put up the money and the Filipinos will get cheaper electricity. In the longer run, if the deal is well structured, the institutional investors will make profits and will then put more money into similar projects, in which case the cost of electricity on that remote Filipino island will drop more.

Potential Gains from Better Design

The opportunities for investing in infrastructure projects throughout the third world are immense. The total cost of projects that would bring water, electricity, and roads to third-world populations is measured in trillions of dollars. For example, the amount needed to bring electricity to the people in Asia who do not have it, or who are currently using portable gasoline-powered generators, is in excess of $800 billion.

Although the total need is great, the world's capital markets are easily large enough to mobilize enough money to finance all the projects. Yet they do not. Instead, the money stays in the industrial countries, where it finances other projects.

What would it take to mobilize money for infrastructure projects in the third world? There would need to be properly designed deals that distribute the risks and potential rewards fairly among the promoters and investors. Finance experts would need to design these deals using insurance policies to cover specific risks, and then would need to use other techniques of financial engineering to create safe cash-flow streams to mobilize risk-averse investment dollars. Third-world countries can also improve their financial infrastructure, and this will lower the rates they must pay to attract capital and increase the magnitude of capital inflows they can attract.

The Cost of Defective Design

There have been too many bad investments in countries that are still poor, and there are too many defects in their financial systems. These defects are at times more damaging than the individual bad investment projects. A defect in a country's financial system can make good projects into bad investments by depriving the investors of their return. The defect leaves further damage in its aftermath because it scares away investors and curtails access to capital for later projects. To support these assertions, here is an illustration using macroeconomic data from the World Bank. The country is Mexico, and the data cover the period from 1990 to 1999, a time when Mexico experienced a traumatic devaluation, a stock market crash, and then a protracted banking crisis. The data are quite simple. They say that for this period, gross private investment in Mexico grew at 3.9 percent per year, but GDP grew at only 2.7 percent per year. For comparison, consider data for two countries: India, never known for investing its savings efficiently, and Singapore, known for its efficiency. During those same years India's gross private investment grew at 7.4 percent a year, and its GDP grew at 6.1 percent per year. Singapore's gross private investment grew at 8.5 percent per year and its GDP grew at 8 percent per year. To state these numbers another way, Mexico's economy grew 69 percent as fast as its rate of investment, India's grew 82 percent as fast, and Singapore's grew 94 percent as fast.

Many explanations are possible for these differences, and some of those explanations would invalidate the comparison completely. However, taking the data at face value makes it appear that Mexico's allocation of domestic investment was less efficient than India's during that decade, and Singapore's allocation was the most efficient of the three.

All three countries undoubtedly had some bad investment projects during that decade. Mexico's poor performance might have been caused by a number of factors, including some beyond its control. One possible cause might have been that its system skimmed some of the good investments and underpaid the investors who put in the money.

There may also be errors in the data, and some capital may have leaked out of Mexico to safe havens. Third-world countries have chronically suffered capital flight, so some of the money recorded in the gross private investment accounts probably left before adding to local GDP. The true realized rate of return on investment may be high in both Mexico and India if we adjust for rake-offs, over-invoicing, and the other types of chicanery that plagued these countries at various times.

To give voice to the concern that foreign portfolio investors often express, the problem is that too much of the gains went to people who did not put in the money. To state the point in terms meaningful to countries wishing to attract portfolio investment from abroad, the average realized return has to be high enough to compensate for the risk that existed during previous periods.

Pressure for Better Design

Savers everywhere need investments with adequate yields; otherwise, they will not be able to support themselves after they retire. The prospective yield on new investments in emerging countries is high. Nevertheless, these attractive projects, in the aggregate, do not compete successfully for funds. Only a few of them get financing during each time period. These facts generate pressure and create opportunities. The growing demand for high-yielding securities must be met. A way of meeting the demand is to finance projects in the third world and capture enough of the returns to deliver high yields to savers.

There are reasons for hope and for skepticism. Emerging countries are reforming their national financial systems, and savers are intensifying their search for new securities to buy. The main obstacle is that investors everywhere are watching U.S. stocks and are ready to jump aboard if the United States appears to be waking up. The U.S. stock market is large enough and credible enough to pull capital away from any other market, especially the emerging markets. Investors are aware of the past performance of emerging markets securities, so new inflows into emerging markets stocks and bonds will be small until the track record improves. Another obstacle is the low recycling rate of capital invested in successful projects in the third world. The funds for new projects come, in part, from the payoffs from previous projects.

Conclusion

The world took a long, circuitous route before it stumbled on valid rules for setting up national financial systems. Most countries still have seriously deficient systems. The deficiencies are hard for most people to see because they learn about the existing system in their country and then do not question whether it is adequate. They usually do not realize how much their national financial system circumscribes their lives and holds down their wealth. If their national system does not give them much access to credit or many good alternatives to save and earn suitable returns on their savings, they often accept those limitations. They learn what the defects are in their national financial system when there is a breakdown. By then the defects are glaringly obvious, but the time to act has already passed, and the big losses have already happened.

The appropriate architecture of a national financial system, and of any type of financial institution, carefully takes into account the incentives every participant in the system has. Finance professionals handle money on behalf of others, and they face temptations. Many of these temptations are obvious, and most countries have protected their citizens against those. Many temptations, however, are less obvious, and those have come to light more recently. Most countries have not protected their citizens against the effects of those more subtle temptations.

In this chapter we looked at the design defects of three deals to finance projects in the third world. In earlier chapters we looked at national financial systems and banks that acted in counterproductive ways. Several types of financial institutions do not suffer from such severe design defects, including modern-style mutual funds, which are more stable. National financial systems become more stable as money migrates out of commercial banks and into more stable financial institutions. This shift in market share has already happened in the United States and is happening rapidly in Europe.

When a country's financial system works well, it does a better job of protecting the savings it gathers and a better job of allocating those savings and recycling them. A well-functioning financial system is a big part of what makes some countries richer than others. These few countries with the best-functioning financial systems are becoming much richer in several ways. Their financial systems create wealth by repackaging assets and cash flows so that those assets and cash flows are more valuable, and those systems also attract savings from other countries. They recycle risk-tolerant capital quickly, and in that way bankroll more startup ventures than other national systems. They also protect small investors and minority shareholders, and obtain for those investors the return they deserve on their investments. The well-functioning financial systems occasionally waste capital, but mostly on ideas that sounded good at the beginning and not because someone was able to commandeer the capital for a pet project that investors did not willingly support. For those reasons, the well-functioning financial systems become leading sectors, not mere supporting players. They generate employment in the financial sector and accelerate wealth-creation in other sectors of the economy. A superior national financial system can be the basis for a country's economic superiority.

In a country with a superior financial system, the middle class will not have to save as much, because the rate of return they earn on savings will be higher. The country's growth rate will be higher than its own savings would support, because its financial system will attract savings from abroad. Its savers will get some spillover benefits from the inflows as foreign buyers bid up prices of stocks and bonds in the country with the superior financial system.

The examples from the third world show that individual deals must be structured so that all the investors and managers have the correct incentives and receive returns commensurate with the risk they take and the work they do. The design of the deal is as important as the design of the factory, hydroelectric dam, or highway. When the decision-maker is too thoroughly insulated from the oversight and wrath of the people who put up the money, the money often goes astray.

In the Nicaraguan examples, the money came from U.S. taxpayers to the U.S. Congress, went from there to the foreign assistance appropriation, and from there to the Interamerican Development Bank. By the time the money arrived at the Nicaraguan Central Bank, it was far removed from U.S. taxpayers and their advocates. U.S. taxpayers had no idea what happened to it, and no way of holding the decision-makers to account for allocating it poorly. Neither did Nicaraguan taxpayers. The mechanism for assuring accountability lacked a tight link between the funding decision at the beginning and the final reckoning at the end.

In the Filipino deal, the institutional investors were accountable to the middle-class savers who put money into the mutual funds and pension funds that the institutional investors manage. When an institutional investor puts money into a deal, in full knowledge that he or she is going to be out of touch with day-to-day progress toward completion, the investor questions quite closely how the control system and guarantees are set up. The whole question of accountability, including rewards and penalties, is a top item on the agenda. There must be a key person who is responsible for the success or failure of the project, and the investor questions what incentives that person will have to work hard and make the deal a success. Many investment projects in the third world have multiple objectives: job creation, regional development, helping disadvantaged minorities, spurring exports, and others. Consequently, many third world investment projects are hard to design so that the objective of making a positive return will have high enough priority. There are many stakeholders, and each seeks priority. The holders of financial claims often do not have the power to step in if a deal is going sour.

National financial systems in the third world are beginning to reform themselves. Policymakers in those countries now see the importance of having a national financial system built on valid principles. The track record of third-world national financial systems, however, has been erratic. It is pertinent to question whether the reforms are going to happen in time. With each passing day the advantage that rich countries already enjoy becomes greater. Securities markets in rich countries compete successfully for transactions business with securities markets in third-world countries. Investment banking firms in rich countries compete successfully and win big jobs in third-world countries that have local securities markets and local investment bankers. If a big company in a third-world country wants to float a large issue of bonds or stock, its directors frequently choose a bulge-bracket investment bank with a top international reputation that can place the bonds with investors in London, Zurich, or New York. The challenge for middle-income and poor countries is to reform their national financial systems quickly so that those countries can reap some of the gains from transforming their own assets into securities.

Chapter 8 shifts the focus to population trends to see if improvements in national financial systems will translate into worldwide improvements in per capita wealth and income.

8 Population and Wealth

The argument in this book is that per capita wealth is rising and will continue to rise. The billions of people who are not yet enjoying an adequate standard of living will experience a rise in their standard of living. They will increase their engagement with the world economy and the telecommunications network. They will earn wages and salaries, and many of them will begin to accumulate financial assets. These happy events all depend on the rate of population growth. If population growth slows to zero, all these happy events will happen sooner, and the outlook for the most desperately poor people will be better.

In the late 1970s, I was part of a team that spent a week visiting rural businesses in the Dominican Republic. The team was an official mission of the Ministry of Agriculture, consisting of three Ministry staffers and me. Our job was to visit small agriculturally based businesses to see if the Ministry could help them. The week-long trip was successful and rewarding compared to some other trips in which I participated. We chugged around dusty back roads, four of us in a Volkswagen Beetle, and visited one or two businesses a day. All the businesses were tiny and rudimentary; they provided part-time employment for four or five people at most, and none of the businesses had any formal production facilities. One business was really just a middle-aged peasant making grape juice and grape jam in his back yard. While he showed us how he made the juice, chickens ran underfoot. A pig lay in the sparse shade of a scraggly tree across the yard, just a few meters away from the wooden table the man used as a workbench. That was the sort of business we were visiting. When we returned to the capital city we tried to get him some simple machinery to sterilize and seal the bottles he was using.

The most successful business we visited was a small group of women making sugarcane candy. Their marketing plan was to sell the candy from a roadside stand on the main highway a couple of kilometers away. The candy was really good, and they had developed a stable clientele. They made the candy by crushing sugarcane and boiling the juice over an open fire. They crushed the cane using a little crushing mill, called a trapiche, that should have been in a museum. Its rollers were made of wood! It had some spokes coming out of the top for the women to grip as they turned it by hand. Sugarcane has a lot of juice in it, but most of the juice is trapped tightly in the fibers and doesn't come out except under intense pressure. The wooden trapiche couldn't squeeze out much of the juice, and the women complained about having to push the rollers by hand in the hot sun. We tried to get them a new trapiche with steel rollers and a gasoline engine.

The most revealing moment of that trip did not happen while we were visiting these businesses, but while we were asking for directions. We were outside the town of Dahabon, driving south along the Haitian border, about as far as you can get from Santo Domingo without crossing into Haiti. That area was totally agricultural and thinly populated once we were beyond the outskirts of Dahabon. Every couple of kilometers was a sort of village, with a shop selling the few items those people could afford. The area was not absolutely primitive, and the road was fairly good. People had electricity and radios, and one or two houses in each village had television, but only the village shopkeeper had a refrigerator.

We were looking for one of the businesses, which was supposed to be about eight kilometers south of Dahabon, and we needed to ask for directions. We were hot and dusty and hoped to get a drink of cold water while getting directions. We turned onto a side road that ran off into the scrubby, parched meadows, past a stray goat, and soon came upon a ramshackle house. Like most of the houses in that area it was unpainted and had a back yard with an irregular barbed-wire fence. The back yard was hard, bare earth with not a blade of grass in it. A brood of small children played in the yard among the usual assortment of animals, including an emaciated pig that was hardly larger than a stray dog. The woman who lived in the house was standing in the front yard as we approached. We stopped and got out.

One of our team was a woman in her late twenties named Lydia. She was university educated, had been working for the Ministry of Agriculture for a couple of years, and had risen to be head of her section. She was from a small city, but like all Dominicans had close ties to the countryside and was very much at ease in rural areas. She was always the person the small business people addressed, and she had a knack for creating an immediate rapport with them. She was not the senior official in our group, but she took charge on this occasion. She got out, walked toward the woman, and began asking directions. By that time all four of us had gotten out of the car, and the rest of us were standing around at the edge of the road, stretching our limbs and hoping for a drink of cold water. Lydia quickly determined that the woman did not know where the business we were looking for was. Then Lydia did something surprising. Instead of asking for water, she asked the woman how many children she had. We had all noticed the small children in the back yard because there were so many of them.

"Eight," answered the woman.

Lydia frowned at the woman and said bluntly, "Ma'am, you should get yourself planned. You've got too many children and you should get your tubes tied before you have any more."

The woman turned her head away, looked at a spot on the ground some distance away, and said, "I know."

At that point the mood did not seem to allow asking for water, and in my surprise I forgot my thirst. But it was hot, and the head of our team, Jose, asked the woman for a glass of water. She could have refused, because what Jose was asking was above and beyond the local standard of common courtesy, and because Lydia had just criticized her so directly. Jose sensed that she would give him water, after I had already given up hope of getting any, because she seemed like a person who obeyed authority. Jose was right, she was the type who went along submissively with the wishes of any stronger person who happened to be present. The woman took the opportunity to break the spell of disapproval, went inside, and returned with a glass of water for Jose. She waited silently while he drank it. We all watched him drink and nobody spoke. Then Jose gave her back the glass, with a minimal word of thanks, and the team climbed into the Volkswagen and we drove away.

After we had turned a corner, Lydia spoke again. "What a throwback that woman is! You run into people like that out in these really backward places. I thought people as clueless as that were all gone by now, but there still are a few left. She probably never went past kindergarten, and that's with a school in easy walking distance." The others on the team murmured their approval, and we drove on.

The incident made a deep impression on me because it was the first time I had seen anyone confront a peasant woman in the third world head-on and tell her right to her face she should get her tubes tied. The Dominican Republic is a Catholic country, and I had lived there long enough to become completely convinced that the government would never take a stand in favor of family planning. Yet here I was, traveling with an official delegation of government officials, and one of the government officials had practically ordered the woman to get an effective form of birth control. It was also surprising that Lydia was so completely sure that she had logic and reason on her side. She was unmarried and childless, and was traveling in a remote area with married men who were her superiors in the Ministry and who were nominally Catholic. She was the junior person on our team. It would have been normal for the head to do the talking, even when asking directions, and for Lydia to say nothing. Family planning was not the team's mandate, and we did not have any credentials or official status to back up the directive Lydia issued.

The woman could have reacted by deriding Lydia for not having any children, for spurning that culture's traditional feminine ideal and pursuing a career, and for not fulfilling her responsibility as a Catholic woman by procreating as God ordered. She also could have hurled a barb at Lydia by saying that no man had wanted her, or by asking her if she was barren. But the atmosphere surrounding that interchange did not allow the woman to go on the offensive and claim that she was doing the right thing by having so many children.

Lydia really did have authority and reason on her side in that interchange. Her authority did not derive from her position as a government official. The Dominican Republic at that time was not a dictatorship. The government's authority barely reached remote rural areas like the one we were in. Lydia's authority did not derive from her education either. Her authority came from a much more elementary source. She was speaking as one citizen to another. The prevailing view of appropriate behavior had changed in that country. The woman was behind the times, and Lydia was informing her of that fact.

The Dominican Republic at that time was in many respects a typical third-world country. The government in the capital city consisted of thousands of well-meaning people sitting in offices. There were thousands of laws, and at one level of jurisdiction or another, almost everything was illegal or prohibited. All economic activity was very strictly regulated, in theory. In reality, nobody paid much attention to the laws, regulations, or government commissions that regularly met to alter those laws and regulations. Much of the economic activity took place in the informal or underground economy. Very few businesses reported accurate information to the government, and most of them paid as little tax as they could. Nobody went to jail for failing to file reports to the government or for failing to pay taxes.

Birth-control pills were illegal but were routinely available at any pharmacy. The pharmacist had them under the counter instead of on display. The packaging said they were available only by prescription. Most doctors, of course, did not want to put themselves officially on record as having prescribed birth control, so they would simply tell a woman to go to the pharmacy and buy the pills. This meant that anybody could buy them. The pharmacist did not question closely which doctor had advised buying them. There were also many doctors who would perform tubal ligations, but when filling out forms to report the procedure would call it something else. Many times they reported that they had removed the patient's appendix.

When I arrived in the Dominican Republic for the first time about five years earlier and discovered this perplexing hypocrisy, I asked people why the country would have such a policy. I argued that the policy would engender disrespect for the government and, more seriously, would have the effect of restricting access to birth control. Only rich, informed women would know they could get birth-control pills. Women from disadvantaged backgrounds would not know about the pill, or would not know they could get it, and would have more children than they could afford.

"Well, you may be right, but you are getting all excited over nothing," one colleague told me. "Everybody knows about birth control here, and it's really just a question of whether they want to go against the Church."

I didn't want to argue with him, because I liked him, and was still trying to understand how the Dominican Republic worked. His answer seemed completely inadequate. The more I thought about it, the more unsatisfactory it seemed. He was highly educated and had studied statistics and economics, but obviously he had not applied either of those disciplines in answering me. He was supposed to be a positive force in the country, not one more complacent macho man. He probably had not thought about the issue for five seconds, except to wonder why all the foreign advisors who came to the country criticized the country's de facto policy on population, regardless of their areas of expertise. He was just tossing out a casual reply, repeating platitudes that he had heard in some idle conversation with people who were equally accepting of the status quo.

Those experiences in the Dominican Republic were just little vignettes at the time, moments in the colorful tapestry of experience, but they stuck in my memory and later seemed like exemplars and signposts. Even in the 1970s many women in the Dominican Republic were getting a university education. There were many women like Lydia, and their numbers seemed to be growing all the time. On the other side of the ledger were many women like the hapless peasant woman with eight children. There were also many men like my colleague, who did not see that their education was applicable to issues outside the narrow fields they chose to define as their areas of expertise.

The foreign expert could feel hopeful and discouraged by turns. It was fun and uplifting to chug around back roads full of ruts and potholes, in a vehicle not really adequate for the terrain, looking for the small businesses we were trying to help. The Ministry officials were interesting and engaging and were genuine in their desire to help. Many of their relatives were only slightly better off than the people we met on that trip. They loved their country and knew that it could do better economically. They could have avoided going on the trip and stayed in the capital city, currying favor with the higher-ups, but instead they went to the countryside with me. On the other hand, it was hard to delude ourselves that we really were making much difference. We were hoping to create new jobs in businesses that had sprung up spontaneously in that unpropitious environment. In a modest way we succeeded, but at the same time, around every corner, on the other side of every hill, there could be another disadvantaged peasant woman, fertile as the one Lydia had confronted, creating future additions to the labor force who would need many more jobs than our puny efforts could create.

In the intervening years the issue of population remained a central theme in all fields related to economic development and environment. The Dominican Republic's population continued to grow, and its economy lurched from moments of hope to longer periods of stagnation, retrenchment, and cynicism. World population appeared to be hurtling inexorably toward crisis. The signs of overpopulation popped up in more places, not only in the places where every expert had learned to expect them.

Nevertheless, there was hope. Trends in some regions were not getting worse. In fact, there were a few signs of improvement. The main dimensions of the looming crisis remained the same, but the threat of imminent disaster began to recede. The fear had been that the world population crisis would quickly make a profound alteration in the quality of life in the rich countries. That did not materialize quickly enough to keep the population issue on the front pages. The next time the issue burst onto the front pages, it had changed. It was no longer what it had been before, a universally accepted crisis. It had turned into a controversy.

The Controversy: Slowdown to Zero Population Growth?

World population growth is slowing down. At some time in the future world population will reach a maximum. Then it will start to decline. No expert disputes any of those statements. The dispute currently raging regards when world population will stop growing. It also concerns other questions about the world's future population, and what the rich countries' policy toward world population should be. These questions are important to the arguments in this book. This controversy over population projections and their implications has become polarized and has spilled over onto the pages of mainstream magazines. Despite the intensity of the debate, the subject is too central to ignore, so we will take the plunge into the boiling cauldron of controversy and try to arrive at a working assessment of some key totals and the relationships among them.

The first population forecast we need is how quickly the rate of population growth will reach zero and how many people will be on earth by that time. The most widely accepted forecast is that world population, which hit 6 billion in 1999, will reach 9.1 billion by 2050, and peak at 9.4 billion by 2080.[1] To see that experts expect a slowdown, consider that world population grew a bit more than 2 percent, or about 1.2 percent per year from 2000 to 2002. If experts thought that world population would keep growing at 1.2 percent per year from 2002 to 2050, the forecast for world population in 2050 would be 10.9 billion.[2] Because their forecast for world population in that year is only 9.1 billion, they must think that from 2002 to 2050 world population will only grow at an average annual rate of 0.83 percent, slightly lower than the 1.2 percent per year it grew in 2000 and 2001.[3] They also must think that from 2050 to 2080 the average annual rate of increase will be only 0.1 percent per year—almost zero, but still large enough to add 300 million people to the earth's population in that 30-year span.[4]

These numbers show that the annual growth rate of world population is already low.[5, 6] In 1968 it was much higher, above 2 percent per year, and serious forecasters were predicting that world population would reach 20 billion or 25 billion people by the year 2100 or 2200.[7] In reality the growth rate stayed above 2 percent a year for only five more years, and by

2002 the growth rate was about to fall below 1 percent per year.[8] If we take a very broad overview of the controversy about when the growth rate will hit zero, it might seem like a typical academic debate—intensely important to the combatants but of little practical importance to everyone else. It would be a mistake, however, to dismiss the population controversy as an academic debate; this controversy really does matter. The difference between growing at 1.2 percent per year and growing at 0.83 percent per year seems tiny when we express it in terms of annual percentage increases, but when we express it in terms of how many more people there will be by the year 2050, the difference is much more striking. Using the slightly higher growth rate gives a forecast of the world's population for the year 2050 that is 1,800 million people higher! This difference is huge, equal to a bit more than twice the total population of the Americas in 2000.[9]

The issue is this: What will be the growth rate each year for the period from 2002 to the date later in the century when world population peaks? The correct figure will be lower for each passing year. Experts who think population will continue to rise for many more decades think that the growth rate will drop only a tiny amount each year, say from 1 percent to 0.99 percent, then to 0.98 percent and so on to zero. Experts who think the growth rate will fall more quickly than that project a decline from 1 percent to 0.97 percent, then to 0.94 percent, and so on to zero. These differences sound too tiny for statistical techniques to resolve. For example, you might point out that it would be difficult to compute whether the population of Pakistan grew 2.3 percent or 2.1 percent from 2001 to 2002. The data would not be complete enough or reliable enough for experts to calculate that annual growth rate with such precision. That intuition is correct, but do not go on from there to infer too much. Do not conclude that the entire subject of future population growth is too shrouded in uncertainty, and do not throw up your hands and say that forecasting very far into the future is hopeless. Forecasting is possible because there is so much data. The data are not all about births and deaths, but they are nonetheless relevant. There are data about family size, age of marriage, and how many children women in selected groups plan to have. This large amount of data gives demographers and statisticians insight into future trends.

To see how quickly the population growth rate is slowing down, consider that from 1970 to 1979 world population grew 18.2 percent. From 1980 to 1989 it grew 16.6 percent, and then from 1990 to 1999 it grew only 13.6 percent. Using those numbers alone we can make a straight-line forecast of when the growth rate would reach zero. But should we figure that the growth each decade will be 1.6 percent slower, as it was from the

1970s to the 1980s, or should we figure that the growth rate each decade will be 3 percent slower, as it was from the 1980s to the 1990s? If we use the 1.6 percent figure, it would take about eight decades for the growth rate to hit zero. If we use the 3 percent figure, it would take only about four or five decades for the population growth rate to hit zero.[10]

New information seems to indicate slower growth—even slower than it was at the end of the 1990s. Growth remains high in some regions, but in more regions growth is dropping more quickly than the consensus forecast predicts. To develop a sense of what is happening and to assess the new information coming in, it is useful to begin with a summary of the consensus view. This view was ascendant until a short time ago, when demographers began to notice that the slowdown is happening more quickly than expected.

- Population growth in the rich countries has slowed almost to zero. It would already be negative, but immigration keeps it slightly positive. In the near future it will turn negative even with immigration.
- The forecasted increase in world population will happen almost entirely in the poor countries.
- The poorest countries will experience the largest percentage increases in population from 2002 onward.

All these statements are still broadly true, but are becoming less true. Already there are interesting exceptions to some of the statements, and it appears that the number of exceptions will grow. What the statements do not say is that new information is altering the panorama as the slowdown becomes more widespread. The new pattern of slower growth is happening in many countries at once, including middle-income countries and poor countries. As of mid-2001 the Population Reference Bureau reported that there were 14 countries experiencing negative population growth and nine others with growth at zero.[11] This negative growth would spread to many more countries soon because their growth rates were barely above zero as of mid-2001. Entire regions are projected to experience population declines. Eastern Europe is projected to have 14 percent fewer people in 2050 than it had in 2001, and southern Europe is projected to have 16 percent fewer.

The new information indicates not only that the slowdown is spreading, but also that the areas with declining population will experience steeper declines than the consensus forecast predicts. That is not the only surprise in the new data. A bigger surprise is that in some middle-income countries population growth is quickly slowing toward zero. In the past the prevailing pattern was that population growth was highest in the poorest countries and lowest in the rich countries. That pattern still holds, but the populations of several middle-income countries are projected to grow more slowly than the U.S. population after 2010 or 2020. Among the middle-income countries whose rates of population growth are projected to slow down quickly are several that used to have very high rates of population growth. For example, Brazil's population grew an estimated 1.5 percent in 2001, but is expected to grow only 44 percent between 2001 and 2050, implying a compound annual average growth rate of only 0.75 percent per year for that future time period. Cambodia is a similar and more extreme case. Its population grew 1.7 percent in 2001 but is expected to grow only 38 percent more between 2001 and 2050, implying a compound annual average growth rate of only 0.66 percent per year after 2001, more than one full percentage point lower than its 2001 growth rate.[12] Turkey, Sri Lanka, and Indonesia all display a similar pattern of high population growth tapering rapidly toward zero.

If the world population stops growing as soon as the new data indicate it might, there are implications for the debate over what policy the rich countries should follow. The scenarios described in this book add fuel to the debate, though that is not their main purpose.

Implications of the Population Slowdown

The slowdown has already provoked a heated debate about whether the multilateral agencies and national governments still need to make family planning and population control a top priority. One side argues that the problem is fixing itself. Viewing the problem in the aggregate, they make the case for benign neglect. The other side responds that it is not correct to view the problem in the aggregate. Countries still exist in which the average woman is having eight children and does not have enough resources to care for them properly. Billions of people still live on $1 or $2 a day, and it may be years or decades before the benefits of economic advancement reach them all. In consequence, advocates on that side argue that it is as important as ever to deliver family-planning services to this disadvantaged cohort, so that these impoverished people can gain some control over their fertility.

Unfortunately, this debate has always been divisive, and has often become tangled with issues of religion, race, immigration, and national identity. These hot-button issues easily flare up into political conflicts and are part of the backdrop against which governments set policy. There have always been people who thought it was morally wrong to interfere with others' fertility. Some called it imperialism, and others called it an affront to natural law. Now comes this new statistical evidence, and every partisan in the debate must react to the evidence. The level of emotion and the intensity of past controversies make the whole matter of population policy hard to conduct.

The argument in this book is optimistic with regard to the outlook for the well-being of poor people in poor countries, and it is more optimistic about their children's prospects for having better lives than their parents did. The argument might appear to give a huge amount of ammunition to the advocates of benign neglect. The computations in this book show that the bottom half of the world's population, and indeed the poorest fifth, will soon gain some of the advantages of economic engagement. These computations are straightforward numerical projections done with aggregate data. The projections show that wealth per capita will rise unless there are major disasters. There are also calculations showing that all available labor in the world will someday be absorbed, and that a labor shortage will begin to appear, at first in North America and later in other places. The calculations show that the distribution of income and wealth will become more skewed, but do not show that the poor will become poorer. On the contrary, the calculations indicate that the poor half of the world will become absolutely better off. Their standard of living will rise. This is not to say that their relative standard of living or their relative wealth will improve. The richest 10 percent and the richest 1 percent of the world's population will continue to become wealthier at an accelerating rate.

If these forecasts are accurate, average wealth per capita is going to rise, and the day will come when everybody in the world who wants a job will have one. Those results appear to support the feasibility of a policy of benign neglect. Population in the poorest countries will keep expanding, but eventually will stabilize, and then decline. In the meanwhile, income and wealth per capita in those poorest countries will rise. Everything will come out all right in less than a century. These forecasts might appear to undermine the justification for the proactive policy.

Nevertheless, there are very hard-nosed justifications for the proactive policy. The biggest justification, according to the arguments in this book, is that the rich countries need conditions in the poor countries to improve more quickly. The rich countries need the poor countries to become more suitable receptacles for investment, particularly portfolio investment. The poor countries need to become credible issuers of securities. They need to show that they can deliver high rates of return to foreign portfolio investors. If those countries are struggling to educate millions of children and to provide growing populations with basic necessities of life, they will not be able to prioritize policies that protect the value of locally issued financial assets. They will be vulnerable to inflation and financial collapse. They might fail to build a sound financial infrastructure, thereby allowing their financial institutions to be hijacked. If they allow that, they will not be able to deliver the consistent high yields that foreign portfolio investors need to earn.

There is another hard-nosed justification for a proactive policy to ensure that the slowdown in world population growth continues. The rich countries have struggled to find politically acceptable immigration policies. European countries have witnessed the rise of nationalist political parties. These parties seize on immigration as a gut issue and do well with it in elections. They argue that immigrants take jobs away from native-born citizens. In North America, nationalist parties have not done as well, but immigration is an issue that both major parties have wrestled with. If the population growth rate in the poor countries slows down, there will someday be fewer people trying to find their way into the rich countries.

Another motivation for a proactive policy is to ease pressure on forests, fresh water resources, cropland, and ecologically sensitive areas. People in rich countries need these resources to remain intact. The rich countries can take action to protect these resources from destruction in the future. It is dangerous to expose these resources to the damage that impoverished, uneducated people can do to them. Some scientists argue that the world is dangerously close to upsetting its ecological balance. They argue that the world's environment could fall into a death spiral and become uninhabitable for humans. If they are correct, protecting these resources would be essential for maintaining the ecological niche that humans inhabit.

Causes of the Slowdown

World population growth has slowed for many reasons. Listing these reasons and discussing them provides insight into why the slowdown has been faster than most experts anticipated, and will also show why it might continue accelerating. Several reasons for the slowdown have been in effect since the 1950s or the 1960s, and other reasons have been in effect only since the 1980s. The list is not exhaustive, but is complete enough to illustrate the forces that influence reproductive behavior.

- Population programs have a history dating back to 1912 in the United States and 1950 or earlier in the emerging countries.[13] The United Nations made quality of life one of its target indicators, and that put family planning on its agenda. These programs have emphasized prenatal and postnatal care, nutrition, and immunization. They help parents in poor countries overcome feelings of fatalism and helplessness. They reduce infant mortality, and as a higher proportion of newborns survive past age five, these programs show parents that they do not need to have so many children. These programs have not succeeded completely in controlling infant mortality; in 1997, infant mortality in the poor countries was still 65 per 1000, and in the rich countries it was only 6 per 1000.[14] Funding for these programs has been dropping as the rich countries cut their foreign-aid budgets. During the Clinton presidency, the United States cut foreign aid from 0.2 percent of GDP to 0.1 percent of GDP.[15] When Bush became president in 2001, he suspended U.S. funding for international family planning programs.[16] Big improvement in access to birth control is one of the population programs' accomplishments; increase in access without these programs would not be as great.

- Television and rural electrification reached more and more people in poor countries from the 1960s to the 1990s, when average overall fertility fell from six children per woman to four. The images on television show women who have been able to gain control over their lives; they are glamorous, educated, powerful, have money, and do not have many children. In many poor countries, television now reaches more than 95 percent of the population; it influences the decisions that women of childbearing age make.

- Women in poor countries have rapidly obtained access to education, and their level of education has risen sharply. This gives them opportunities that they did not have before in the job market. Their economic contribution to the household can now be greater. The amount they can earn working outside the home has risen, and at the same time, the economic contribution that children can make to the household has diminished.

- In farming, children used to be able to add value after reaching the age of six or seven. Now the value of children as farm laborers has declined. Grain prices worldwide have been declining since the 1970s. The profitability of farming has been too low to be a motivation for having children.

- Disease and epidemics are not a prime determinant of the population slowdown. Data indicate that the slowdown would have happened without any changes in the mortality from disease. The AIDS pandemic is tragic, and has cruelly cut short the lives of millions of people. Certainly the AIDS pandemic has made the population slowdown a bit more marked in some countries, and if not stopped, it will have a bigger effect. But it is incorrect to attribute the worldwide slowdown to AIDS.

Scenarios of Population and Wealth

How quickly can the world's privately owned wealth rise? Fixed assets like physical plant, equipment, buildings, and infrastructure do not increase much faster than 2 percent per year. Production and distribution become more efficient, logistics improve, and there are technological advances, so the value of output can rise more quickly than the amount of equipment employed. The annual value of output can rise 3 percent per year. There is also inflation of around 2 percent per year, so the dollar value of output can rise by 5 percent per year. This is 3 percent per year of real increase plus 2 percent per year of inflation. These figures make it appear that privately owned wealth cannot rise much faster than 5 percent per year.

For the past few decades, however, privately owned wealth has risen much more quickly than 5 percent per year. It has risen at an annual rate of 11 percent or more.[17] How can privately owned wealth rise so quickly when the underlying physical assets rise so much more slowly? The reason for this big difference is that the value of an asset depends greatly on the structure of its ownership. In general, an asset is worth more if a corporation with shareholders and bondholders owns it, and it is not worth as much if a sole proprietor owns it. The world's privately owned assets used to be owned mostly by sole proprietors. Now corporations with shareholders and bondholders own a higher proportion of the world's privately owned assets than before. The reasons why an asset can be worth so much more, or so much less, while having the same outward appearance and while producing the same output, are central to the argument in this book. Securitization creates value, provided that securities markets exist and function properly.

This section puts forward a simple forecast of how much wealth will exist in future years and compares that to how many people will exist in those same future years. The annual growth rate of the world's wealth that we use for this simple forecast is 8 percent per year—less than the 11 percent mentioned previously, but high enough to show the power of growing wealth. The 8 percent annual growth rate is easy to achieve if more and more of the world's productive assets are securitized. The annual rate of inflation for the wealth forecast is 2 percent. These annual rates determine how much the projected dollar value of privately owned wealth will be, and how much its value in purchasing power terms will be. The forecast then compares the projected figures for the total amount of wealth to scenarios for world population, and then computes trajectories for privately owned wealth per capita.

The beginning value of privately owned world wealth is $153 trillion in 2002.[18] This figure includes the current value of bonds, common stocks, other financial assets, and all the privately owned assets that do not belong to corporations with listed shares. Using the annual growth rate of 8 percent, Table 8–1 gives the forecast for the dollar value of world wealth in selected future years, and also the value in inflation-adjusted dollars, using 2002 as the base year.

Table 8–1 Forecasts of Value of Privately Owned World Wealth

Year	Trillions of Current Dollars	Trillions of 2002 Dollars
2002	$ 153	$ 153
2010	283	242
2020	611	428
2030	1,320	758
2040	2,850	1,343
2050	6,152	2,378

Now compare this simple forecast of total privately owned wealth to world population. These calculations use three forecasts of world population. The first one is the forecast from the U.S. Census Bureau. It is slightly more conservative than the one from the Population Reference Bureau. The Census Bureau forecast is used here as the "consensus" forecast, and it predicts that world population reaches 9.1 billion by 2050. The other two forecasts are called "slower growth" and "much slower growth." They are simple projections of 2002 population; in each, annual growth slows down more than it does in the consensus forecast. In the slower growth forecast, world population growth hits zero in 2050. By that year world population would have reached 8.3 billion. In the much

slower growth forecast, world population growth hits zero in 2040 and
then declines slightly by 2050. In that scenario world population peaks at
7.8 billion in 2040, then declines to 7.7 billion by 2050. Table 8–2 provides the three forecasts of world population.

Table 8–2 Three Forecasts of World Population in Billions, 2002–2050

Year	Consensus	Slower Growth	Much Slower Growth
2002	6.2	6.2	6.2
2010	6.8	6.8	6.8
2020	7.5	7.4	7.3
2030	8.1	7.9	7.7
2040	8.7	8.2	7.8
2050	9.1	8.3	7.7

With these forecasts of total privately owned wealth and total world
population, the next step is to divide each figure for population into the
corresponding figure for wealth and compute forecasts for wealth per capita (see Table 8–3). There are three forecasts, using the three world population forecasts. All figures are adjusted for inflation, so they are
expressed in 2002 dollars.

Table 8–3 Forecasts of Wealth Per Capita for Three
Population-Growth Scenarios

Year	Consensus	Slower Growth	Much Slower Growth
2002	$ 24,677	$ 24,677	$ 24,677
2010	35,588	35,588	35,588
2020	57,067	57,838	58,630
2030	93,580	95,949	98,442
2040	151,724	160,976	169,231
2050	261,319	286,506	308,831

These calculations show that wealth per capita will more than double
before 2020, then rise by five or six more times between 2020 and 2050.
This rapid growth is already corrected for inflation. If it were not, the
numbers would show an even more spectacular rise. The growth is real in
the sense that the people who own the wealth will be able to convert it

into cash and spend the cash. The projected increases in wealth per capita will occur provided that wealth grows at the predicted rate, and provided that world population grows according to one of the three scenarios. If wealth grows more erratically, or if there are major wars or natural disasters, wealth per capita will not rise as quickly.

This optimistic projection is a continuation of what has been happening since 1980, when wealth per capita was so low that there was not much reason to talk about it. At that time there were wealthy people, as there had always been, but most people had little or no wealth and did not think of themselves as having a strong vested interest in the stability of the world financial system. Their interests did not coincide with the interests of the wealthy. Since that year, however, hundreds of millions of people have acquired bonds and common stocks, and they are now very aware of what those assets are worth, and are wary of any threat to their value. This fact has transformed geopolitics. Moneyed interests always exerted influence, but now "moneyed interests" include huge numbers of middle-class people. Also, since the end of the Cold War there has been only one superpower, so geopolitics no longer has détente as its main theme; now the focus is to control religious and ethnic struggles and to raise the level of prosperity.

Chapter 9 begins with three experiences of labor shortages in a country that had always seemed an inexhaustible source of labor. It then goes on to pose the question whether there will be a worldwide shortage of labor in the coming decades.

9 Rising Wealth and the Impending Labor Shortage

The idea crept into my mind slowly that a worldwide labor shortage could develop. It did not occur to me all at once, and at every step of the way it had to overcome preconceptions that years of education had formed and experience had reinforced. The first glimmers of the idea occurred to me while I was having lunch with my colleagues Javier and Jesus in Mexico City in 1993. We were at an upscale, successful restaurant, and there were not enough waitresses. This fact was very obvious, and we talked about it during the lunch. Throughout the third world, service people are always standing around waiting to help anyone with money. Restaurants in poor countries are usually overstaffed, but this one was not.

The shortage of waitresses stayed on my mind because I couldn't explain it. For me the shortage was like the prices of big-ticket items in Costa Rica in 1982. It kept bothering me, like a piece of a puzzle that doesn't fit, and I couldn't put it out of my mind until I understood it.

The shortage of waitresses at that restaurant persisted. In the years following 1993 I went to Mexico often, and always asked if there was still a shortage. My colleagues told me that the shortage was still severe and was becoming worse. During those visits to Mexico I had several experiences that reaffirmed what I had observed in 1993. Those experiences kept pushing to the forefront of my mind the new idea that a worldwide labor shortage can develop. Finally, I gave up fighting against the idea and gave it the status of a tentative hypothesis. This was a big concession, but

I had to let the idea in. The experiences I had in Mexico were compelling and kept bombarding me with evidence that a labor shortage was beginning to appear. I recount these experiences briefly in this chapter to show the way the evidence kept forcing itself on me.

✳ ✳ ✳

The restaurant was crowded, and the diners all were ordering drinks, wine, and full meals. Conversation was spirited and enthusiastic, and across the patio one florid man was laughingly loudly. The tables were outdoors, under awnings, and separated from the street by potted plants in large concrete pots.

The restaurant had an official name, but nobody called it by that. Everybody called it The Cowgirls Restaurant. It is in Mexico City, in a district with nightclubs, tourist shops, hotels and restaurants. It is close to the stock exchange, the downtown, and the old central plaza, and it is a good place to go for lunch. My colleagues Javier and Jesus had invited me, and we were enjoying the very pleasant weather as we sat at an outdoor table.

The restaurant is known for its waitresses. They dress as cowgirls of the Old West, with palomino leather skirts, brown riding boots, white blouses, and chic little palomino leather vests. They wear Stetson hats with the side brims turned up, and they keep the hats smartly in place with rawhide drawstrings that they tie under their chins with sliver brooches. They are all tall, slender, and glamorous, like fashion models ready for a photo shoot. The theme could be an advertising campaign in glossy travel magazines for a dude ranch in the American Southwest that affects a period style from around 1950.

Despite their fetching outfits and their carefully arranged hairdos and makeup, these faux cowgirls were waitresses. They were walking quickly, taking orders, and carrying trays of food. They were very busy. When one of them came to our table to take our order, she was pleasant and crisp. She had no time for small talk.

For several moments the three of us looked at the waitresses practically running from the tables to the kitchen and back. They were barely able to keep up with the work. One was trying to push a lock of her hair back into place as she walked swiftly toward one of the tables with a tray of drinks. Our food was taking a long time to arrive.

"What's the story, guys?" I asked. "Why doesn't the owner hire a few more waitresses? The owner must not know much about business."

"I wondered about that myself," said Jesus, "so I asked the owner. He's inside, standing near the cash register, over there by the bar." Jesus pointed to a formally dressed man who looked attentive and slightly nervous. "He says he can't find any more waitresses."

"What is the guy, a cheapskate?" I asked.

"No, that's not it," said Jesus. "If he were worse than the other owners around here, the waitresses would leave after they'd been here for a while. His problem isn't turnover. He can't find any new waitresses in the first place."

"We're assuming he's getting these people from the countryside," I said.

"Yeah, sure, or course. I mean, I think so," said Jesus. "That's where most of these restaurants get their people. Anyway, he said he put the word out, in the usual places, and nobody showed up."

Our food arrived, and we were silent as we ate. We kept thinking about the shortage of waitresses and did not come up with any illuminating ideas. In Mexico City and its environs there were more than 25 million people, and at that time the official figures indicated that hundreds of people were arriving every day from the countryside looking for work.

The three of us couldn't think of a ready explanation. We were all well trained in the conventional doctrines of economic development. We all assumed that the population growth rate in Mexico was really higher than the official estimate. For much of the hour and a half that we were at the restaurant, we were unable to shake off the view that there simply had to be enough unemployed young women to fill the vacancies.

The year was 1993, the fifth year of the presidential term in Mexico. The next presidential election was a year away. The Mexican economy was in one of its boom periods, rolling along at a good pace, creating jobs faster than it usually does. But nobody thought it was creating enough jobs to absorb all the new entrants to the labor force. It never did that, at least not during modern times.

Unemployment exists in most of the world. In the rich countries we view unemployment as an aberration, and we attribute it to a recession or some other factor such as technological obsolescence or a wave of cheap imports. The promise of a job has become part of everyone's birthright in the rich countries. In the middle-income countries and especially in the poor countries, the view is quite the opposite. Unemployment is the norm. People expect to be unemployed, and when they are not, they have some explanation as to how they had the good luck to get a job. The average person expects to have an intermittent string of bad jobs with bad working conditions and low pay. Occasionally, somebody has the good luck to get a job with the government or a multinational company. Otherwise, most people go on as usual, with no stability or permanence in their work situation. In the intervals between bad jobs they expect to be unemployed.

Against this backdrop the waitress shortage continued to puzzle us. "Just the tips should be enough to have people lining up to work here. If one of these waitresses works lunch and dinner, she should be able to serve 15 tables. That should be fifty bucks a day in tips alone," I said after the conversation resumed. "On tips alone she could support the whole village where she grew up."

"No, they wouldn't get that much," Jesus said, deflating my theory. "Most of these guys wouldn't give much of a tip."

"I agree, but this is a place where gringo tourists go," I said. "There'll always be some Yankee who'll leave a tip."

Javier and Jesus both acknowledged this was likely. The three of us lapsed into silence again.

"The women who work here have to be tall and slender," Javier said. "Otherwise, they wouldn't look good in those cowgirl outfits." He was right. There are not many women in Mexico as tall and slender as the waitresses who were there that day.

Waiting tables at The Cowgirls Restaurant was obviously a really good job. We were not making much progress explaining the shortage. We continued to talk about it on the way back to the office, but could not think of a good reason for it at that time.

* * *

The next year the Mexican economy went into turmoil. On January 1, 1994 the Chiapas revolution broke out. That was also the day that the North American Free Trade Agreement (NAFTA) officially included Mexico. In the summer of that year, I returned to Mexico City to work with Javier and Jesus again, and they said that the waitress shortage at The Cowgirls Restaurant was as bad as ever. The economy had the jaded satiety that comes after a loud dancing party has passed its peak but is still rocking and rolling. The presidential candidate had been shot, and his successor had been named; Zedillo had the demeanor of an earnest schoolboy. The rightist candidate, a self-assured businessman, had shredded him in their first debate. Salinas, the sitting president, had many more months to go before he would hand over power, but he was already a lame duck. It was the time in the Mexican six-year cycle when people in high places were stuffing their pockets with both hands. The roar of financial rape and plunder was much louder than it had been a year earlier. The Mexican stock market had begun a long slide that would drop it 85 percent from its peak before another year would pass. On Paseo de la Reforma, the main boulevard that runs through the heart of the city, buildings that had been under construction a year earlier were still unfinished. The pace of work on them had slowed noticeably. The restaurants were as full as they had been a year earlier, and the menu prices were higher.

Two months later, after Zedillo had scored a perfunctory victory in the presidential election, another assassination rocked the country. This time the victim was a top figure in the ruling party that had run the country for more than a lifetime. That assassination reverberated throughout the country. It told everyone who had just come back from vacation to shake off their torpor and get their heads back into the game. There were only about 10 weeks left before the new administration would take over. The assassination stirred the Mexican oligarchy into a frenzy of activity. It was like the gunshot that tells the runners in a long-distance race that the final lap has begun. People in high places accelerated their financial schemes and maneuvers. They borrowed pesos any way they could, giving any guarantee or collateral they had to, and the moment they got the pesos they converted them to dollars and rushed the dollars to banks in Texas, where they put the dollars into certificates of deposit. To take advantage of the FDIC deposit insurance, they were careful not to put more than $100,000 in any single bank. Some had so many dollars, and were in such a hurry to return to Mexico and convert more pesos into dollars, that they did not have the time to go around to enough Texas banks to avoid depositing more than $100,000 in any one bank.

The party ended on December 2, 1994, one day after the new president was inaugurated. Mexico devalued the peso. The government announced it would not maintain the old exchange rate of three pesos to the dollar. It did not try to maintain any new, cheaper rate for the peso. It did not have enough dollars to intervene in the foreign exchange market. The exchange rate gyrated wildly for weeks, and the Mexican stock market went into a sickening plunge.

I visited again in the summer of 1995. The Mexican economy was really and truly a mess. The banks were hemorrhaging losses. Many bank presidents had simply absconded in their Lear jets, and there was a manhunt going on for one of them. The tabloids were full of lurid stories about multimillion dollar swindles, embezzlement, and opulent hide-aways guarded by private armies. Other bank presidents were putting on a good face for the public and making brave statements about soldiering on despite the difficult conditions. The banks were facing the sobering fact that they would not be able to collect many of the loans they had made. They did not gain much comfort from holding mortgages on real estate as collateral, because the land records were spotty, and mortgages were often hard to enforce.

In the summer of 1995, the recession in Mexico looked deep enough to qualify as a depression. Once again I asked Javier and Jesus about the shortage of waitresses at The Cowgirls Restaurant. They both said imme-diately that the shortage was as bad as ever.

"How can that be?" I protested. "There are people begging on the streets. Times here are really tough. That restaurant must have young women lining up to apply for jobs every day."

Javier and Jesus liked to tease me about being a soft touch for beg-gars. "There are always people begging on the streets in Mexico City," said Jesus. "They find the pickings especially good where rich, naive grin-gos like to walk. You are probably just seeing them in front of your hotel."

"You're right, they are always there," I agreed. "But this time they look desperate. I talked with one, a young woman with a small baby, and she said she had ridden two hours on the bus and had not yet gotten enough to pay the bus fare." I was determined to convince them that this time the beggars were really desperate.

"She probably rented that baby," said Javier. "You know some of them do that. And the sob story was probably a pure invention. She prob-ably walked from the barrio where she lives and picked the spot in front of your hotel because she heard there was a really rich, naive gringo stay-ing there who would believe anything she said as long as it was heart-rending enough." Javier and Jesus were both smiling at me.

When we stopped laughing I asked them if they had any new ideas about why there were not enough waitresses at The Cowgirls Restaurant. They offered an explanation that the young women were going north, to Monterrey, Tijuana, and places like that near the U.S. border. Those towns were jumping, as they always do after a devaluation, because North Americans go there to buy all the stuff that's cheap after the devaluation. Besides that, there was NAFTA. Jobs were better in the towns near the U.S. border. That was the best explanation any of us had come up with. The three of us stood there for a few moments thinking about the explana-tion. It answered the question why the recession had not remedied the shortage of waitresses. But it still did not explain why the shortage happened in the first place.

∗ ∗ ∗

The beginnings of the explanation came later, in 1996. I had gone to Mexico City again to work with Javier and Jesus. The trip went well, and the work was interesting and rewarding, and I was so absorbed that I barely caught my plane from Mexico City to Dallas.

After the plane took off, I relaxed and began talking with the person next to me. She was a Mexican pharmacist on her way to a conference in Dallas.

"Business must be good at the pharmacies along the U.S. border," I said. "Prescription drugs are always cheaper in Mexico, but they must be a whole lot cheaper now, with the devaluation and all."

"Yes, and a lot of clinics are operating in the border towns. North Americans go there to get treated," she replied.

"Do you mean older people? Do you get many younger people in those clinics and pharmacies?"

"Yes, sometimes young people go to those clinics from the North American side of the border. Those clinics used to be places where young women went to get birth-control pills without their parents finding out. And abortions too," she said.

"But now they can get them on the northern side of the border?"

"You're right, but something else is happening. The whole pattern of birth control and abortions is changing. You wouldn't have heard this yet because I just found out myself. My husband is a demographer, and he has been telling me about a survey. If it's correct it would be a big new finding. The survey data indicate that population growth in Mexico is slowing down and is already much slower than anybody thinks."

"What you say is consistent with what I've seen in Mexico recently," I said. "Walking around in the city, there aren't as many women with babies, and hardly any that are pregnant."

"Well, I figured you were going to disagree with me, but now I see you are more up-to-date with what's happening in Mexico." After a pause she said, "I'll tell you about the survey. My husband participated in designing it and is working now tabulating the results. What they did was to find women of different ages who are in the same family. Like two sisters, one 30 and the other one 20. That's easy to find in Mexico, so they were able to find a lot of them. They were able to find enough cases so they could exclude the cases where the women were not having similar lives."

"You mean like one of them went to a university and the other didn't?" I asked, hoping she would continue.

"Yes, things like that. Or if their age at marriage was different, like if one got married at 18 and the other at 25. Or if one was still living in the barrio where she was born and the other wasn't."

"So, the idea of the survey was to find women who were as close to identical as possible except that one is older than the other."

"Yes, that's it. They were able to get a pretty good sample, a couple of hundred cases. The sample includes cases from rural areas and urban areas."

"Enough cases so they would be able to tell if there has been a difference between the urban pattern and the rural pattern?"

"Yes, they got that data because everybody thinks there is a difference."

"And is there?"

"Well, they haven't finished that part of the analysis yet. So far they have only computed a few measures for the overall sample. But they're checking those results because they came out so strong." She looked at me to see if I was following her.

"What did they find?" I asked.

"They found that the younger women were having a lot fewer children than the older ones. I mean a lot fewer."

I hesitated. The result was too strong to be consistent with what I had heard about population growth. Birth rates aren't supposed to change very quickly. "What sort of a difference is he finding?"

"Well, of course, the data are like what you always get when you do a survey. A few of the younger women have more children than their older sisters, for example. And some of the canvassers may have made mistakes."

"O.K., fine," I said. "But just on the basis of the preliminary calculations, what does he think?"

"He thinks Mexico's rate of population increase has already fallen below 1.5 percent a year. He thinks it's 1.4 percent now. And if the pattern he's finding is true for the whole country, Mexico will be at zero population growth pretty fast." She looked at me to gauge my reaction. The most frequently cited figure for Mexico's annual population growth that I had seen around that time was 2 percent a year or 2.1 percent.

"There are going to be a lot of very surprised people if that happens," I said.

The possible explanation for the waitress shortage was that there were not really so many young women in Mexico as everyone thought. The most frequently cited figure for Mexico's population growth rate in 2001 was 1.5 percent a year. The figure for 1995 was 1.9 percent a year, revised downward from the 2 percent or 2.1 percent that sources were quoting at the time. That is a huge drop in only six years—an extremely short time by the standards of demography.[1]

One of the best techniques for forecasting a country's population growth is to compute an average number of children each woman will have during her childbearing years. This average is called total fertility, and when it falls as low as 2.2 children per woman, the country's population growth rate falls to zero. The difficulty is in forecasting the total fertility of women still in their childbearing years. The technique is to take a sample of women who are at the end of their childbearing years and note what age each one of them was when she had each of her children. Then the demographer can say how many children the average woman in that group had at each age. For example, the average woman who is now 45 had four children by the time she was 26. That is the starting point. Then the demographer takes a sample of women who are younger, part way through their childbearing years, and sees how many children each of them had at each age. If the average woman who is now 30 had fewer children by the time she was 26, say only two, then the demographer can forecast that the women who are 30 will have smaller families on average than their older compatriots had.

This method is quite good but has some obvious limitations. It assumes that the younger women have their children at the same ages as their older compatriots did. If the older woman had two children by the time she was 20, and the younger woman has only one by age 20, it would indicate that the younger woman will have half as many children as the older did. That is a good inference if the demographer does not have any more information about the two groups of women. But what if all the younger women are getting a university education and none of the older ones did? The demographer can deal with this if there is enough data. If data are available about a group of older women who got university degrees, the demographer can make a comparison of that group to the younger group and get a better indication of how many fewer children the younger women will have.

The problem of forecasting Mexico's population is an extreme example of the difficulty of forecasting total fertility. Women in Mexico who are now 65 years old had an average of seven children each. Women who are now 55 had an average of six children each. Women who are now 45 had an average of only a bit more than four children each. Women who are now 35 are on track to have only a bit more than three children each. Women who are now 25 apparently will have fewer children than that, possibly fewer than 2.5 each on average. Forecasting how quickly this drop will continue is obviously tricky. Two questions determine how slow Mexico's population growth after 2001 will be. One is How many children will the women who are now 25 have? Will they fall short of the 2.5 children each that they are on track to have? The other question is How many children will the women who are now 15 have? Will they have fewer than 2.2 each? It appears likely, because the figure for total fertility per woman fell from 3.09 in 1995 to 2.6 in 2001. At that rate the figure for total fertility per woman would fall to 2.2 by 2006.

Mexico's demographic transition has happened so quickly that it is hard to predict how many children the younger women will have. The lives of younger women in Mexico are profoundly different from the lives their mothers and aunts had. There have been enormous improvements in access to education, which highly correlates with lower fertility. Many women who are now 65 did not go past the fifth grade, many who are now 55 did not go beyond the eighth grade, and many who are now 45 did not finish high school. Mexican women who are now 15 are mostly still in school, and a record proportion of them will get university education. The women who still do not have access to higher education are in the rural areas and in the indigenous communities. In order to predict population growth, it is necessary to know how soon all women in Mexico will have access to higher education, how many will be able to get good jobs, how many will postpone marriage, and how many will move to the cities. The outlook for each of these patterns is positive, so the precipitous drop in Mexico's birthrate will probably continue, and when total fertility per woman in Mexico reaches 2.2, it will probably keep falling.

As my plane approached Dallas I contemplated the data the pharmacist had cited, and I decided that the study her husband was conducting was probably accurate. His sample showed that there had been a steep drop in total fertility. His results also provided an explanation for the shortage of waitresses at The Cowgirls Restaurant. The waitresses were of age to be getting university degrees. They were also the right age to be part of the much smaller age cohort after Mexico's demographic transition took hold. Mexico did not have a "baby boom," but it definitely did have a "baby bust." The waitress shortage happened because of the baby bust and because young women had so many opportunities to do other things besides work at The Cowgirls Restaurant. The baby bust in Mexico was not a temporary "demographic dip" like the one in the United States, and it did not presage an "echo" of a previous baby boom. Instead the baby bust persisted year after year, and there has been no letup in the steady decline in live births each year. So, if there were not enough young women to fill the vacancies at The Cowgirls Restaurant in 1993, there would be fewer in 1995, and many fewer in 2002.

* * *

In March 2000 I was again in Mexico, this time in the resort town of Ixtapa. This lovely town on the Pacific coast of Mexico is an enclave, cut off from the rest of Mexico by physical barriers and by a ring of guards that keep the common people from neighboring towns away. It is a playground for tourists. There is a row of hotels facing the beach, and behind the hotels an assortment of small businesses in a "town" that is well-scrubbed and has no houses. The businesses are restaurants, nightclubs, and shops selling all the trinkets, beach clothes, and assorted gewgaws that tourists buy. There is also an internet café, which I visited several times while I was there, and talked with the employees and the owners.

The owners are a married couple, a man from Canada and his wife from Trinidad. Both are very friendly and enjoyed talking with clients. It was a pleasant place to pass the hottest hours of the day because it was shady and cool.

The employees were also very nice and would talk with me at odd moments. All were well-dressed and pleasant. They all lived in the large town about five kilometers inland and took the bus every day to work and took it home after work. None had more than a few words of English, and they didn't know much about computers either. I asked them some technical questions about the computers or how the telecommunications connections were set up and quickly had to change the subject. They had all gone to local schools, and all had finished high school. They knew how to make sandwiches and how to use the espresso machine. Usually, three were there, but one day there was only one.

The sole employee was a young woman named Jasmine. I asked her where the others were, and she said she didn't know. She hadn't seen them on the bus that morning. She was busy, but emphasized that if I wanted a cappuccino, she would make one for me as soon as she could.

People were waiting to use the computers, so after a while I went and sat with the owner.

"Things are pretty busy here," I said after he invited me to sit down.

"Yes, this is the high season here."

"Pleasant people you get to work here," I said, looking at the kitchen area behind the counter. Jasmine signaled that my cappuccino was ready and put it on the bar. Twenty-five minutes had passed since I had ordered it. I stood up to get it to bring it to the table.

The owner jumped up. "No, don't get up," he said. "You're not supposed to have to get up. I'll get it for you." He was already on his feet, stepping toward the bar. He brought the cappuccino and put it in front of me on the table.

"You're a bit short-handed today," I said. "Are the other folks having a day off?"

"No, I don't know where they are. Usually, when they skip a day of work I never see them again. I've had a hard time getting staff." He shrugged his shoulders to show his frustration.

"The jobs here look pretty good to me. It's nice and cool here, and the customers are pleasant, so why don't they like it?" I asked.

"I can't imagine. I pay more than the going rate, and I still can't get anybody. I get their applications, and then they come here on the bus, and they look enthusiastic. Sometimes they say they'll take the job, and then don't show up."

"You get them to fill out applications?"

"Yes, to find out a bit about them, and to see if they can write."

"Do you require them to know any English, or anything about computers?"

"No, all of them know 10 or 20 words of English, and some of them know a bit more, enough to carry on very simple conversations with the customers. But none of them knows much about computers," he answered.

He was silent for a moment. "They don't have any really exceptional qualifications. The working conditions here are pretty good. I still don't know why I can't hang on to them."

"How do you get applicants?" I asked.

"I advertise."

That was a surprise. I did not believe the labor shortage was real until he said that. We were in a remote area, at least ten hours by bus from Mexico City. The Pacific coast of Mexico south of the Gulf of California has always been poor. It has no plantation crops, no mines, and no oil. It is a very long way from the United States. For most of the previous century you couldn't get a telephone without paying large bribes, and when you finally got one, the service was bad and long-distance calls were exorbitantly expensive. There was no university nearby. Hardly anybody knew much English, and nobody had a computer. So the region was poor. Young people would have to leave to get jobs or to have much opportunity to widen their horizons.

It seemed obvious that people would jump at the chance to work at the internet café. Yet here was indisputable evidence that they were refusing the jobs or abandoning them soon after getting them. I was amazed that the labor shortage would have reached that remote area.

"Maybe they just stay long enough to improve their English, and then they get a better job," I speculated.

"Well, one guy who worked here did get a job as the night manager at one of the hotels," the Canadian said. "But the rest of them, I don't know what they did. There are jobs in the towns around here. That's what I think they do. They get jobs there," he said. "Anyway, that's the impression I get when I go to the radio station to advertise."

"You go to the radio station to advertise?" I asked, really surprised.

"Yeah, newspaper advertising doesn't get much of any response. To get any applicants I have to advertise on the radio."

"So, you go to the local radio station and buy air time?" I was incredulous. The internet café was not a big business. It had only about a dozen computers. The ideal amount of staff would be only three people on duty at a time.

"Yes, the marketing manager there knows me by now. He tells me some of the other companies that are advertising,"

"And lots of other companies are advertising?" I asked, still surprised.

"Yeah, and some of them go to the high schools and recruit that way," he replied.

Advertising on the radio! Recruiting at the high schools! I was staggered. In most of the third world, you never see a sign in the window at a business saying "help wanted." You see many, many more signs saying "no job openings here." To find new employees, it is usually enough to tell one trusted employee that there might be an opening. The next day, or sometimes that same day, the employee will introduce his cousin or his nephew. The cousin or nephew will be wearing his best clothes, nervously hoping to pass the interview.

Conditions in the labor market must have changed. The shortage of waitresses at The Cowgirls Restaurant was no longer the only labor shortage I had witnessed in Mexico. There have been other labor shortages there, but these two I witnessed with my own eyes.

✳ ✳ ✳

The labor shortages in Mexico are likely to become widespread, and to extend to many other places on earth. The trends in place may ultimately lead to full employment of all the people on earth between the ages of 14 to 65 who want a job. This startling assertion is neither utopian nor as encouraging as it sounds. It is a direct consequence of the trends in world population and wealth that have previously been discussed. It is a macro-level forecast that does not indicate the types of jobs that unemployed people in each zone will get. It is a simple forecast, and it depends on several assumptions. It indicates that many unemployed people will get new jobs, especially new jobs delivering services to wealthy people. It is speculative, and it depends on several parameters that could delay the outcome. Nevertheless, the assertion puts the spotlight on two points. One is that wealthy people may spend part of their annual increases in wealth, and as they become elderly, they may spend principal. That spending is in addition to spending from income. A second point is that the supply of labor is finite, and in several geographical areas, labor shortages have already occurred.

This chapter discusses a very simple method for forecasting the demand for new workers. It begins with worldwide magnitudes and uses elementary calculations to gauge how a key relationship, wealth versus labor supply, will evolve in the future. The objective of these calculations is to draw attention to an important fact: The magnitude of financial wealth is now large enough to raise the annual growth of demand for labor.

The outcomes of the calculations span a wide range. Most scenarios indicate a gradual improvement in labor market conditions, with real wages gradually rising in many disparate geographical areas. Pushing the calculations to the extreme reaches the utopian scenario, in which the world reaches full employment as early as 2033, and after 2036, wages everywhere rise in response to shortages of labor throughout the world. In that scenario, stock and bond markets rise every year, and the people who become wealthier spend a high portion of their new wealth on services that are hard to automate.

These optimistic calculations are simple extensions of conditions that have already happened in small areas. Anybody who was in San Francisco or Boston in 1998 or 1999 saw the acute shortage of labor and can easily imagine how those regional shortages could become more widespread. During those years, entire states had unemployment rates of 2 percent. Each state has rural areas and depressed areas, so for the statewide average to be 2 percent, there would have to be an area with no unemployment at all. The conditions that existed in those places looked like aberrations, but if wealth continues growing and population growth continues falling, those conditions will happen again and may spread over larger geographical areas.

Wealth and Demand for Services

When a person's wealth increases, he or she buys more goods and also hires more people to perform services. The questions are What sorts of services will the wealthy people want? and How many new jobs will their spending create?

The services that people hire others to do are diverse. As a person's wealth increases, he or she hires people to do tasks that are burdensome or difficult. Everybody has tasks they would like to delegate to someone else, but those are not always the same tasks. Many wealthy people like to do some tasks themselves, like cooking, gardening, or shopping, although they could afford to hire someone else to do those things. If we take two people who are not wealthy at the beginning and then track the services they buy as they become wealthier, they would not buy the same services in the same amounts or in the same sequence. Nevertheless, there are some services that almost all people buy as their wealth increases. These include domestic services: housekeeping, laundry, dry cleaning, childcare, food preparation, and food shopping. Wealthy people buy other services to protect their wealth: estate planning, tax advice, and portfolio management. There are, in addition, services that wealthy people buy collectively; for example, if they live in a condominium or a gated community, they buy gardening, valet, and guard services through the condominium association.

Some of these services are difficult to automate. Two rich people can share a personal trainer, but a housekeeper cannot clean two different houses at the same time. As wealth rises, the number of jobs for some categories of service workers will rise. If there are unemployed people willing and able to fill those jobs, they will take the jobs, and unemployment will decline. If there are not enough unemployed people to take those jobs, wages of those service-worker categories will rise. If there is immigration, the new arrivals may fill some of the jobs and ease the labor shortage. If a shortage occurs, wealthy people will have to choose which services they really want, because the prices of those services will have risen.

It is difficult to estimate how many new jobs this new spending will create. The new spending is in addition to spending from income. To view the matter in concrete terms, let us consider what one moderately wealthy person might do. This person is a 58-year-old engineer who lives alone in a single-family house in Colorado. He earns $100,000 a year and has $300,000 in his retirement accounts. His retirement accounts have been yielding 10.5 percent per year on average for the past 10 years, and he takes inflation of 2 percent per year into account, so his real rate of return is 8.5 percent. For simplicity, assume that he rents the house and has no other assets. He has just met with his financial planner and he knows that he can begin taking money out of the retirement accounts without paying penalties when he is 59 years old. He decides to hire a housekeeper and a gardener. Both are illegal aliens and want to be paid in cash. The housekeeper comes two days a week and does laundry, cleaning, and cooking. The gardener comes one day a month and cuts the grass, rakes leaves, and trims the hedges. The engineer pays the housekeeper $120 a week in cash and pays the gardener $75 a month in cash. Those payments total $7,140 a year.

What effect does hiring the housekeeper and the gardener have on the engineer's wealth and on his savings rate? His $300,000 of retirement accounts were on track to rise 8.5 percent for the following year net of inflation. That is $25,500 for the year. His retirement savings plan is his only savings. He was spending his entire net pay each month before hiring the housekeeper and the gardener. He contributes $750 each month to his retirement accounts, and his employer matches that with an additional $750 each month. That is $1,500 a month or $18,000 a year. His retirement accounts would rise from $300,000 to $343,500 after one year. That is the initial $300,000 plus the gain of $25,500 on the initial amount, plus the $18,000 contribution for the year. He does not take money out of the retirement accounts to pay the housekeeper and the gardener. Instead he borrows on his credit cards to get the cash to pay them. Because he is now borrowing to spend more on his lifestyle, his savings rate has gone down. His wealth is now rising more slowly.

There are already many people like the 58-year-old engineer, and their numbers will grow if prices of stocks and bonds resume their upward trend. People like the engineer will increase their spending when they see that their accumulated financial wealth is already high enough and is on track to go higher. Their savings rate falls, and some of them spend more than their after-tax income from wages and salaries. The effect of this spending on the demand for labor can be powerful even if they spend less of their annual gains than the engineer did. He spent $7,140 of his retirement accounts' annual capital gains and accrued interest of $25,500.

Because the rate of return on retirement accounts has been positive over long periods of time, wealth owners can expect to have more to spend each year. If nothing interferes, after a few years they would have enough spending power to generate more new jobs in the United States than the expected additions to the U.S. labor force. Of course, there are many forces that can intervene, so other outcomes can also happen.

Spending from Wealth

The amount of stocks, bonds, and other financial assets that Americans own is on track to reach $46.7 trillion by 2008.[2] If at that time the stock and bond markets are performing well, Americans will be accruing an annual wealth gain of $4 trillion. If they spent 10 percent of their annual wealth gain, that would be about $400 billion of new spending. That spending would be in addition to spending from income.

That spending from wealth could have a large effect on the demand for labor. To see the magnitude of the possible spending, consider that if all the wealth holders chose to spend that money paying service workers who had immigrated from Mexico, Central America, and Panama, they could pay $40,000 a year to each of 10 million people. That is more immigrants than those countries have supplied to the United States since the Mexican economic crisis of 1994–1995.

The wealth holders would not spend all that money paying service workers. Nevertheless, the calculation shows that wealth increases in the United States can easily be large enough to generate demand that would have many effects throughout the world economy. One effect could be to create jobs that immigrants would fill.

The unresolved question is What will wealth holders do? They might not spend any of their new wealth, but in the past they did spend some of their increases in wealth. Data from the U.S. stock market boom of 1994–2000 indicate that the average wealth holder spent between 1 percent and 4 percent of his or her wealth each year.[3] If they would continue to spend that much of their wealth each year, the effects would be large, and there is still the question of how they will spend it. They may take a cruise on a luxury liner, and that will generate jobs for crew. They may hire a gardener, a housemaid, or a chauffeur. The statistical evidence indicates that increasing proportions of new expenditures go to buy services. But that does not indicate very precisely how many new jobs the new spending will generate, and it does not indicate the skill classifications that will be most in demand.

There is also the matter of productivity gains in services. The people who get more wealth may increase their spending on services like one-on-one tennis lessons. In that category of services there will not be large improvements in productivity, but in other categories of services, productivity gains are happening at a steady rate. It matters how the wealthy people choose to spend.

Prospects for a U.S. Labor Shortage

The U.S. might experience another period of high employment, and shortages of many skill categories could develop. The computations that indicate this are very simple, as the following illustration shows.

As a starting point, assume that there are 7 million unemployed people in the United States. That is higher than the official figure for February 2003. The higher figure takes into account illegal aliens who are unemployed and other people who do not count as unemployed but who would take a job if they could easily get one. Also, assume that people living in the United States owned financial assets in the amount of $30 trillion. This is probably less than the amount they own as of the first quarter of 2003, but is close enough to serve as a starting point for this forecast. People living in the United States also own other assets, like land and buildings that are not mortgaged, but for simplicity the computations ignore these other assets.

Now, consider what the situation will be one year later if the $30 trillion of financial assets increase in value by 8.5 percent. That is an increase in financial wealth of $2.55 trillion. For simplicity, this increase does not include the annual amounts that these people save and put into their retirement accounts during the twelve months.

Assume that the owners of these financial assets spend 10 percent of the annual increase each year. Also, assume that they spend one-quarter of the money hiring service workers, and that there are no productivity gains in those services. In this case they spend 10 percent of $2.55 trillion, or $255 billion, and they spend one-quarter of that, or $64 billion, hiring service workers. If each new worker earns $50,000 per year, that amount of spending would create jobs for 1.27 million people. This is a large figure, and would only happen if the assumptions are correct. Creating that many jobs would lower unemployment by more than one full percentage point. The calculation shows that if wealthy people in the United States spend part of their holdings, they can quickly affect the rate of unemployment. Of course, if stock and bond prices do not rise, the owners of the financial assets in the United States would not have gains of that magnitude, and they might choose not to increase their spending that much.

The power of wealth accumulation becomes clearer when we consider what happens in subsequent years. After the first year, the $30 trillion goes up to $32.55 trillion because of capital gains and accumulated interest. Then it goes down to $32.295 trillion because the wealth owners spend $255 billion. In the following year the remaining $32.295 trillion goes up 8.5 percent. That means that the wealth owners have new capital gains and accumulated interest in the amount of $2.745 trillion. Of that amount, the assumption is they spend $274.5 trillion. This spending will support the jobs that were created the previous year and new ones besides.

These simple calculations indicate that this new source of spending can spur employment growth in the United States. Spending from wealth may accelerate as wealthy people grow older and contemplate how to spend the time they have ahead of them. It is speculative to forecast when the United States would develop a labor shortage, but without immigration, there could be scarcities of certain skill categories developing as soon as U.S. economic growth resumes its normal pace.

If spending from wealth increases, the effect on demand for labor could become large enough to absorb immigrant workers. Annual increases in wealth are erratic, and sometimes negative, so forecasts of future spending from wealth are unreliable. Nevertheless, spending from wealth is a large and rapidly evolving force in the economy, and worthy of further attention.

The Distribution of Wealth and the Propensity to Spend New Wealth

The previous sections have noted the magnitude of wealth in the world without considering how it is distributed. What follows is a simple numerical illustration showing how much difference it makes how that wealth is distributed.

This example begins with two hypothetical starting patterns of financial-wealth distribution. As of 2002 there were $110 trillion worth of financial assets in the world. In the first hypothetical distribution pattern, suppose that 110 individuals each own $1 trillion of financial assets. In the second hypothetical pattern, suppose that 1 billion individuals each own $110,000 of financial assets. In both hypothetical patterns, these are the only people who own financial assets.

Let one year pass. At the end of that year, 8.5 percent has been added to the value of each person's holdings. In the first hypothetical starting pattern, each of the 110 mega-wealthy people has $1.085 trillion. In other words, each has obtained capital gains and interest income of $85 billion. How much of this $85 billion would each mega-wealthy person spend? In the earlier computations, we assumed that each person would spend 10 percent of the new wealth, in this case $8.5 billion each. That may not be plausible. Mega-wealthy people presumably have everything already, and already buy every service they want. So, they might not spend very much of the new wealth.

Consider what happens with the second hypothetical starting pattern. The 1 billion people that owned $110,000 each now own $119,350 each. That is, a gain of $9,350 each. In this case it is more plausible that each person would spend 10 percent of that new wealth, in this case $935 each. People who have $110,000 of financial assets do not already have everything they want, and are not already consuming every service they want. So, it is easier to believe that moderately wealthy people, who have $110,000 of financial assets, will consume 10 percent of their annual gains.

This simple numerical illustration shows that the distribution of wealth has an effect on the forecast of a labor shortage. The labor shortage will not happen if the people with the wealth do not spend enough of it. It will also not happen if the distribution of wealth becomes so skewed that only a few people come to own all the financial assets and then do not spend a large enough proportion of their annual capital gains.

There is reason to hope that the people with the financial wealth will spend it. They accumulate it, then they become old. They spend it when they stop working. As they age, they need different services, and when they die, their heirs receive their wealth. The heirs are younger and will probably spend more of the annual increase, and perhaps some of the principal too. The heirs do not need to save because they are younger, are still working, and have many years to save for their own retirement. Also, the heirs may not have had every good and service they wanted before receiving their inheritance. In that case, they would spend at a faster rate.

The spending patterns of mega-wealthy people now make a big difference and will make a greater difference in the future, because the world distribution of wealth is already skewed and is on track to become more skewed. That fact may pose a threat to the job-creation mechanism this chapter describes. If very wealthy people consume less and less of each additional dollar of new wealth, the demand for additional service workers may not rise as quickly and will take longer to absorb the supply.

Spending from Wealth and Job Creation

The discussion until now has given hypothetical figures for how much new wealth the owners will spend each year. It is worthwhile to trace how this spending would create jobs.

In introductory economics, added spending goes to buy goods. The new purchases of goods then trigger responses through the backward linkages in the stages of production. The retailer's inventory declines and reaches the reorder point. The wholesaler then gets an order, and that triggers a new order for the factory, which in turn orders more raw materials. Some of those orders generate new demands for employees. In the Keynesian model there is a multiplier effect: The initial increase in spending generates a total increase in GDP that is a multiple of the initial amount. The initial increase is autonomous, and the resulting increases are induced or endogenous.

There are two reasons why this type of process might not generate many new jobs. One is that the multiplier might not be very large. The other is that productivity gains in the goods-producing sector may dampen the demand for new workers. Factories making new appliances can sometimes increase production without hiring more people. Due to these two reasons, it is possible that wealthy people might spend more money on goods without creating many new jobs anywhere. Consequently, if spending from wealth creates many new jobs, those jobs will probably be in services, and in services that are hard to automate.

Will the demand for labor reach remote places and quickly improve the lives of the billions of people living on $1 or $2 per day? The answer is that the demand will reach the most readily available supplies first. Then, when the prosperous zones reach full employment, demand will reach the peripheral zones.

People living on $1 or $2 a day will get little comfort from hearing that they will get jobs, and then will be able to demand higher wages, in just a few decades from now. They are at such great risk that they may perish from starvation or treatable illnesses in a very short time. The computations in this chapter indicate that the long-run outlook for gainful employment is favorable, and that if the poor can wait long enough, they can expect some improvement in their situation. The computations do not indicate that improvement will be very rapid, so no argument in this book should be taken as support for a policy of benign neglect. The world's poor need help right now. They will get some opportunities as wealthy people spend part of their accumulated wealth, but public health, access to potable water, and liberation from oppressive regimes are pressing needs.

An Impending Labor Shortage, Or a Mirage?

Every person now working in a rich country and young enough to accumulate financial assets for a couple of decades can become, in some sense, wealthy. Wealthy in this context means having a large enough pile of financial assets to be able to do things that right now look too expensive. For each person, that may be something different: retire early, travel, have more possessions, take up the violin, give money away, and so on.

The idea that hundreds of millions of people will become wealthy is optimistic but feasible. Certainly, such a high proportion of the world's population has never in any previous generation been able to have so much discretionary spending power. In all past generations the possibility has never existed, or it existed for a brief time before the wealth-creation process came to a sudden and brutal halt. There was always a world war or a financial collapse, or one and then the other. It is customary to predict that this time will be no exception. This time, however, there is a very pragmatic reason to set aside the customary pessimism: There are already hundreds of millions of people with a vested interest. These hundreds of millions of people are relying on the continuation of prosperity, and are relying particularly on their accumulated savings. They need their portfolios to continue growing, and they are the powerful voting blocks in every rich country. They will vote for policies that preserve their dream of wealth accumulation.

Even if wealth accumulation continues, any forecast of a labor shortage is speculative and susceptible to errors. Reviewing the possible errors will highlight the trends and the issues. The first possible error is that the forecasts can overestimate how much wealth will exist. The rise of financial wealth has always been volatile and erratic. Any disaster of sufficient scale can make the financial forecasts go astray.

The second error is that world population growth may take much longer to cease. The consensus among demographers may be too optimistic. The forecast of a labor shortage, however, is not very sensitive to small variations in the assumptions about population growth.

The third error is that there may be big productivity gains in the services that wealthy people buy. The forecast of a labor shortage assumes that services like childcare and hairdressing are hard to automate.

A fourth possible error that would put the forecast in jeopardy is an overestimation of how much people will spend as their wealth rises. The people with rising wealth may choose to ignore their wealth and not spend any more money on services. They may not hire any more people to do things for them, they may not travel and stay in hotels, and they may not spend any of their new wealth on maintaining their physical fitness.

That error may seem unlikely, but there is a fifth possible error: The distribution of wealth will become so skewed that the average propensity to spend from new wealth will fall almost to zero.

Conclusion

The demand for labor appears to be on track to grow faster than the supply. The supply of labor has already been exhausted in many places for periods of time. These sporadic shortages can become more widespread and more prolonged.

This chapter has discussed whether wealthy people will spend some of their annual increase in wealth, and what effects their spending will have on the demand for labor. The possible outcomes span a wide range, from no effects, to large jumps in demand for workers—large enough to absorb all the unemployed workers.

This new source of spending, spending from wealth, has become an important feature on the economic landscape. In the past, total wealth was much smaller and much more inert. The new source of spending offers hope for new gainful employment, but there are several reasons for concern. The process that creates the employment opportunities is elitist. Wealthy people get wealthier and hire more people to serve them. The process is also hard to control. Purely financial mechanisms magnify, transmit, and distribute the wealth. These mechanisms circumvent government regulations and cross national jurisdictions. The new wealth accumulates in the financial centers of the first world and enlists unemployed workers in the third world. In the process described here, demand comes from the center, not from traditional societies developing indigenous, self-sufficient economies. Native crafts do not flourish. Time-honored agricultural practices turn into heirlooms. Village structure disintegrates as young people migrate. The financial mechanism stimulates migration.

Chapter 10 puts forward an argument that prosperity will spread to countries it has not yet reached. The chapter begins with a glimpse I had of the blood business in Haiti in the 1970s, when that destitute country had the most extreme gap between rich and poor that I have witnessed. I then describe a symbiotic relationship that can exist between middle-aged savers in rich countries and younger middle-class people in poorer countries. The symbiotic relationship can work well enough to lift the world's poor out of poverty.

10 Wealth Concentration and Diffusion

In the poor countries there are extremes of wealth amidst the poverty. In Panama I saw a gleaming 20-story luxury apartment building and a shack right against the base of it, with an impoverished family living in the shack. Countless other images made an impression on me, but one was so striking that it stands out in my mind and evokes feelings of despair surpassing all the others. This example was not a scene of undernourished children dressed in rags crowding around a rich person hoping for a few coins; it was a whole country. The country was Haiti in 1974. I visited for a few days and spent a large part of my time trying to figure out what was causing the distribution of income to be so skewed.

What I saw first was the poverty. It was abject and was the worst I had seen. The cab ride from the airport to the hotel was a devastating experience. At the time I was living in the Dominican Republic, and I thought I had seen poverty, but what I saw during that cab ride was an unrelieved panorama of utter destitution. There was a slight improvement when we were about a block away from the hotel, and then we were inside the fence that enclosed the hotel grounds. The scenery changed immediately to groomed lawns, tasteful gardens, and an atmosphere of quiet opulence.

Later that day my friends and I went in a cab to Petionville, up a steep hill to a bluff overlooking the capital city, and during that ride we saw the most obvious reason for the poverty. The country is agricultural but has very little topsoil. Deforestation and overgrazing had removed the vegetation that held the topsoil, and erosion had carried most of it into the sea. The peasants were trying to grow crops on farms that should have been left fallow to recover their fertility.

When we arrived at the top of the hill, we saw the mansions. We could see dozens of them from the road. They looked like mansions everywhere in the third world, surrounded by high barbed-wire fences and patrolled by armed guards. What I couldn't understand was where the rich people that lived in the mansions were getting their money. The country didn't seem to have any surpluses anywhere. There wasn't anything the rich people could have been taking, and there were no businesses that looked profitable enough to support that many people at that high standard of living.

When we arrived at a restaurant with a balcony overlooking the capital city, we saw rich people wearing the latest fashions from Paris. They came in and took two tables for each group. The rich people sat at one table and their bodyguards sat at another. This was fairly typical throughout the third world, but again I wondered where the rich people were getting the money to support their lavish lifestyle.

The answer finally came after I had been there a few days. The source was a guy I happened to sit next to in the hotel bar. He may have been telling exaggerated stories to shock me, or to keep me paying for the drinks, but what he said sounded to me like the truth.

He said that local military officers were selling human blood to hospitals in the States. They used military trucks and medical technicians to go out in the countryside and pay people $1 a pint for blood. They then used military cargo planes to deliver the blood to an airport in Louisiana. They sold the blood for $25 a pint.

The story convinced me because that business would have been profitable enough to account for the money the local rich people were flashing so conspicuously, and because the destitute people in the countryside would have lined up to sell pints of their blood for that price.

Improvement in the Distribution of Income

The world economy is growing, but the growth is unequal. Some regions are poles of growth and others languish and stagnate. Some individuals earn more each year and others struggle to earn as much as they did in prior years. The question is how prosperity and growth will spread to reach all the people on earth. The macroeconomic projections and population projections make it clear that income per capita will keep rising. What this chapter addresses is a way that prosperity can reach the middle-income and poor countries, and how it can reach the poorer people in those countries.

Many well-informed people believe that everywhere in the world the distribution of income is becoming more skewed. It is understandable that they would believe this because common sense and anecdotal evidence indicate that it is true. To put the point in lurid terms, many well-informed people believe the whole world is becoming like Haiti at the time I was there: a few wealthy people living in mansions overlooking the squalid masses, supporting their lavish lifestyles by draining the blood of the poor and selling it.

This ghoulish caricature of inequality is not accurate today and will be less accurate in the future. Trends that have been in place for many years show clear improvement in the distribution of income. Growth in China and India has led to poverty reduction in both large countries. Data for the rest of the poor countries are more mixed, but still show promising trends.[1] According to one measure, world income inequality peaked around 1975 and has been on an egalitarian trend since then. This measure is controversial, and some experts dispute the improving trend.

The evidence will soon become indisputable, however. Poor people in the middle-income countries will gain profitable linkages to the world economy and improve their living standards. Then the rest of the poor people in the world will gain those linkages and benefit from them, and finally even the poorest people in the poorest countries will be drawn in. Trade liberalization and education are not the only forces that will pull these people into closer engagement with the world economy. There is another force that will pull up their standard of living, and that force is the selfish needs of middle-class savers in the rich countries.

A New Role for Poor People in the World Economy

For centuries there have been more people than the world economy needed. The portion of the population living in subsistence agriculture has declined but has not fallen to zero. Subsistence agriculture is the way that people live when they are barely connected to the modern national economy in their home country, and when the world economy has not yet pulled them into more productive activities. Subsistence farming can have bucolic attractions and eternal harmonies, but people do not usually choose it as a lifestyle. They usually make efforts to gain the benefits of modern conveniences and respond to incentives to join the modern economy, if the modern economy can absorb them.

For many poor people in the third world, gaining a foothold in the modern economy has been difficult. These people have traditionally had specific, very limited roles in the world economy. They produced plantation crops or did low-value service work. During colonialism they worked in the fields or as low-skill workers making simple manufactured goods. They did not produce high-valued goods, and they had no bargaining power, so their standard of living was low. They could not consume or save very much because they did not have enough income.

Now there is a new role for middle-class people in the middle-income and poor countries. Their role is to buy securities. They are already buying small amounts of securities now and it is important that they buy larger amounts in the future. The need for them to buy securities will become more pressing as time passes. The people in the rich countries who are buying securities today face a dilemma. There will not be enough buyers in the rich countries when today's savers will be selling. There are not enough young people in the rich countries and the young people will be facing too many burdens. In the aggregate their purchases will be smaller than the amounts today's savers will be selling. If today's savers in the rich countries are going to get high prices for their stocks and bonds, more buyers will have to appear. The new buyers will be the middle classes of the middle-income and poor countries. They are numerous enough to fill the gap, but they do not currently buy enough securities. If their buying can grow fast enough, the rich countries will avoid the looming retirement crisis.

In the scenarios this chapter puts forth, savers in middle-income and poor countries increase their purchases of securities. They buy securities willingly, and their buying supports economic growth and job creation in their countries. They buy several broad categories of securities: top-rated bonds and blue-chip stocks issued in the rich countries, foreign mutual funds that invest in top-rated bonds and blue-chip common stocks, and also locally issued securities (henceforth called emerging-markets securities). They buy these categories of securities to achieve the same objectives that buyers in rich countries do. First they seek safety and diversification. When they have acquired enough safe securities and when they have achieved a comfortable level of diversification, then they start looking for high-yielding securities. They willingly buy emerging-markets securities issued in their home countries after their governments respond to pressures to give local savers better protection and higher yields.

This chapter proposes a solution to the retirement dilemma that the first world faces. In this solution, timing is critical. The rich countries have time to avoid a retirement crisis, but a series of events must happen in rapid succession, and there is not much leeway in the timetable. Savers in rich countries have already bought large amounts of stocks and bonds and are accumulating more each month. If they earn high enough returns on those securities, they will be able to retire without becoming a crushing burden on the younger generations in the rich countries. Savers in the middle-income and poor countries need to make progress on several fronts, and they are not succeeding quickly enough. Their incomes must rise more quickly so that in the future they will be able to buy the securities that savers in rich countries will be selling. They also need better ways of buying top-rated bonds and blue-chip stocks issued in the rich countries, and better local savings products in their own countries. At present they are not on track to increase their buying of securities quickly enough.

This chapter gives two alternative scenarios. The main scenario postpones the retirement crisis, and the grandiose scenario solves the crisis completely. In each scenario savers in the rich countries have a role to perform and are not currently performing it. They must make only minor adjustments in their behavior to perform it. Savers in the middle-income and poor countries have a harder role to perform, and they will be able to perform it only if there is international pressure to enable them. The scenarios indicate magnitudes, rates of return, and rates of growth. The necessary magnitudes of buying are large but feasible. The necessary rates of growth and yields are high. They do not require sustained periods of super performance, but do require steadier progress than has been achieved in the recent past.

The New Symbiotic Relationship between Rich Countries and Poor Countries

The proposed solution spans the next four decades. It postulates that a symbiotic relationship can exist between older savers in rich countries and younger savers in the middle-income and poor countries. Each group faces problems, and the proposed solution remedies their problems. If it works, it will raise living standards for billions of people in the middle-income and poor countries, and will improve the prospects of future retirees in the rich countries.

To illustrate the symbiotic relationship that can exist, consider Jane, a 50-year-old American manager who is saving for her retirement. She has been buying securities at prices that are very high by historical standards. In the future, after she retires, Jane will be selling those securities, and there is a serious risk that she will be selling them at falling prices. There is likely to be a shortage of buyers. The generation of people in the rich countries who are now in their early thirties is not very numerous and will face heavy tax burdens as they move into their forties and fifties. A person in the United States or Europe who is now thirty years old will, according to most projections, not be able to save very much for his own retirement. This means that Jane will not get very good prices for the securities she is buying today unless a new group of buyers materializes to buy the securities when Jane is ready to sell them. This new group of buyers will have to be people in countries that today are middle-income or poor, because the rich countries all have similar demographic profiles.

Savers in the middle-income and poor countries have faced obstacles, and in the aggregate have not been able to do very well. If they are to perform the proposed role, pressure groups must intervene on their behalf and help them overcome obstacles. To see the obstacles they face, consider the example of Pedro, a 29-year-old engineer in Manila. He has a good job and also has a computer shop, and is able to save small amounts from time to time.

Pedro does not put all of his savings in Philippine financial institutions, because he considers them unreliable. He does not want all his savings to be invested in the Philippines because the rates of return have been too unstable, and he also worries that the government might freeze his accounts. He wants to have some of his savings in other, safer countries. He can invest abroad legally, but he does not want to leave an audit trail that will attract the tax collector. He buys dollars from a local money changer and sends them to his cousin in San Francisco. A friend who works for an airline carries the cash for him. The cousin puts the money in a U.S. bank. Pedro is slightly embarrassed about this arrangement, but says he does it because he can't afford to lose the money. He knows that his actions weaken the Philippine economy and strengthen the U.S. economy, and he knows that he is not optimizing his holdings of securities. He would like to have a more sophisticated portfolio, including safe bonds and world-class blue-chip stocks. After he has acquired some very safe securities and has them on deposit in trustworthy financial institutions, he would be willing to buy Philippine securities if those yielded enough and if he felt comfortable he would have enough protection against fraud and dispossession.

The symbiotic relationship works only if hundreds of millions of people like Pedro quickly gain confidence in their countries' financial systems. In some countries people like Pedro are gaining that confidence, but progress is too slow. The proposed solution does not need to involve all the middle-income and poor countries. Some of those countries are wary of exposing themselves to the volatility of world financial markets; they choose to forego the opportunities those markets offer. However, a vanguard of middle-income and poor countries is modernizing their national financial systems and is gaining from doing so. Their success poses a challenge to countries that are reluctant to participate, and the reluctant countries now face a decision.

Details and Difficulties of the Symbiotic Relationship

The proposed symbiotic relationship has several elements, and each is easy to describe but hard to put into effect. Older savers in the rich countries need new high-yielding securities to come into the market so that they can buy appropriate amounts of those securities and obtain the higher yields; they also need buyers to appear in the future when it is time to sell the securities in their portfolios. Younger savers in middle-income and poor countries would like to be able to buy a full range of securities, so that they can construct portfolios appropriate to their needs at each stage of their lives. The potential for a win-win outcome exists, but there are difficulties to overcome.

To see how the symbiotic relationship can work, consider Jane's situation and how she is investing her savings. She has saved $100,000 so far, and holds that in tax-deferred accounts, including her 401(k) account. She is saving $1,500 a month but computes that she will not have enough to afford the retirement she wants at age 65. Her rate of return has averaged only 8 percent. If she can shift $20,000 into bonds that yield 14 percent and also channel 20 percent of her monthly savings into bonds that yield that much, she will achieve her goal by the time she turns 65.

There are plenty of projects in the middle-income and poor countries that can deliver yields of 14 percent to savers like Jane. For example, new electric power plants and toll highway projects in the middle-income countries can deliver yields in that range. There are bonds in the market that give savers like Jane the income from such projects. But Jane does not buy those bonds. Jane does not know about those bonds, and would be wary of taking the risk. She has heard about currency crises and banking collapses in the middle-income and poor countries.

Jane has never heard of Pedro and does not know how important Pedro, and people like him, will be to her in the future. She assumes that when she is 65, there will be enough buyers to pay for the securities she will be selling. By that time Pedro should be one of the buyers, but Pedro is not on track to develop into a buyer.

Pedro does not currently earn enough income to buy the amounts of securities that he will need to buy from Jane. One reason is that he is paying too much for electricity and does not have enough of it. The area where he lives needs a new power plant, but people like Jane do not buy the bonds that would pay for the plant to be built. For the symbiotic relationship to work, the economic growth rate of countries where people like Pedro live needs to rise. Calculations further on show how high the growth rate in those countries must be.

Pedro could buy the bonds himself and then the power plant could be built, but he does not want to take the risk of buying bonds like those. He is still focused on building up an adequate amount in his bank account in San Francisco. The power plant bonds would offer high yields, but Pedro will not be enticed to buy them until he has enough really safe securities and until local financial institutions design and offer securities that address Pedro's concerns.

Jane can take the first step to break the impasse and set the symbiotic relationship in motion. She can allocate 1 percent of her portfolio and 1 percent of her new purchases, to bonds like the ones that will finance the power plant in Pedro's neighborhood. She can afford that risk, because if 1 percent of her portfolio does badly, it will not hurt her very much. If she earns the 14 percent yield, she can then shift another 1 percent of her money into similar bonds. Her action will raise the return on her savings and put her closer to her retirement goal. It will also raise the economic growth rate in regions like Pedro's. If enough people like Jane direct a portion of their savings to emerging-markets bonds and earn high yields, they will accumulate enough savings to retire and will not burden the younger generation in the United States and the other rich countries. Countries like Pedro's will grow quickly enough so that savers like Pedro will be in a position to buy the securities that Jane will begin selling when she turns 65. Those countries will get the power plants, toll roads, and other big-ticket items they need, and their prosperity will improve.

Implementing the Proposed Solution

Middle-income and poor countries can break the impasse by taking the first steps themselves. They do not have to wait for Jane and people like her to act, and they do not need to call a press conference to announce their decision. A country that decides to attract investment from people like Jane would begin by taking several actions that would signal its intentions. These actions are:

- Arrest and prosecute several high-profile white-collar criminals who have violated securities laws, committed fraud, or evaded taxes. This would have a political cost, but the payoff would be large if the country then gains inflows of portfolio investment. Jane herself might not notice, but managers of mutual funds and pension funds in New York and London will.

- Foster reforms so that local business owners will be able to issue high-yielding bonds. Some middle-income and poor countries have already put in place the needed legal arrangements. Others would have to make technical adjustments to their tax codes, banking regulations, and securities laws.

- Allow local savers to buy foreign securities, including stocks, bonds, mutual funds, and insurance policies. This would signal that the country is not going to protect its local financial institutions from foreign competition and is not going to give them preferential access to local savings. It would give local savers the opportunity to build internationally diversified portfolios more easily, and would give them a reason to learn more about securities. It would lay the foundations for an "equity culture" and increase the credibility of locally issued common stock.

- Make conditions for foreign portfolio investors more hospitable. This includes explicitly giving them equality versus local litigants in lawsuits, and the right to bypass the local legal system and opt to litigate disputes in foreign courts.

The next step in the implementation is that some of the business owners in the country would issue bonds. They would hire experts to design the deals and structure the terms of the bonds. The bonds would be designed to appeal to sophisticated buyers in international markets. The projects to be financed would offer high returns. The experts would structure each deal so that there would be accountability and proper incentives. For some of these bond issues, the experts would recommend using credit enhancements, which are guarantees purchased from insurance companies.

After the bond issues have been designed, the business owners would try to place the bonds. They would do road shows to international financial centers, and if they succeed in placing the bonds they would invest the cash.

If the country succeeds in bringing in enough inflows of portfolio investment and raises its growth rate, it will have improved the well-being of its own citizens and also will have begun to solve the retirement dilemma the rich countries face.

The numerical illustrations that follow indicate that the magnitudes of this win-win solution can be large enough to work. Middle-income and poor countries have enough collateral within their borders to issue large enough amounts of high-yielding bonds. Savers in rich countries have enough buying power to buy the bonds, and would willingly buy the bonds if the deals are well designed. The economic growth of the middle-income and poor countries can rise enough so that savers like Pedro in those countries can gradually gain enough buying power to buy the securities that savers like Jane will be selling. Over the relevant time horizon they can eventually buy large enough amounts of blue-chip stocks and high-quality bonds issued in the rich countries to keep the prices of those securities from falling. Those are the components of the win-win outcome. Savers in the rich countries can get the yields they need, and savers in the poor countries can get higher incomes and the safe investments they want.

The numerical illustrations begin with estimates of the amounts of stocks and bonds that rich-country retirees like Jane will be selling each year, and how much the younger savers in the rich countries will buy during those same years. The shortfall of buyers in the rich countries becomes large, perhaps as early as 2008 and more probably by 2010. After that, unless people like Pedro buy enough, the shortfall widens until approximately 2040. The numerical illustrations then continue with an assessment whether savers like Pedro in the middle-income and poor countries will be able to buy enough securities to fill the gap.

The scenarios assume that issuers in the emerging countries will be able to issue bonds but will not be able to issue common stocks until later. Emerging-markets bonds have performed well enough to attract buyers, but emerging-markets common stocks have not. Because of that history, the scenarios assume that issuers in emerging countries will issue bonds. The bonds can include conversion features and credit enhancements. The bond buyers will be experts working on behalf of savers like Jane in rich countries. The expert buyers will be capable of analyzing all the features of each bond issue.

The proposed solution works in three stages. In the first stage, savers in the rich countries buy emerging markets bonds. The cash from savers like Jane earns high yields and also creates jobs and raises real incomes in the middle-income and poor countries. Savers in the middle-income and poor countries lobby for improvements in their national financial system, and for permission to buy foreign securities.

In the middle stage, savers in the poor countries add safe securities to their portfolios and achieve international diversification. They accumulate ultra-safe investments like Pedro's bank account in San Francisco, then they buy safe securities issued in the rich countries. In the meanwhile, they continue to invest in their home countries, in the traditional ways they have always done, and they also willingly buy emerging-markets bonds. They earn low, steady returns on the safe securities and high, volatile returns on the emerging-markets bonds.

In the third stage, savers in the middle-income and poor countries step up their buying and buy enough securities so that during the decades when baby boomers in the rich countries are selling most heavily, stock and bond prices everywhere in the world remain high. Self-interest drives the entire process. The selfish actions of savers like Jane in the rich countries help people like Pedro in the emerging countries. Jane and Pedro work together, without being aware of each other's existence.

For the symbiotic relationship to reach its potential, savers in the middle-income and poor countries will have to buy amounts of securities each year that appear large compared to their current annual incomes. The projections indicate that it is feasible for them to attain the needed levels of income in time to buy enough stocks and bonds to keep the prices from falling.

The Coming Shortage of Buyers in the Rich Countries

The dollar amounts of stocks and bonds that savers in the rich countries buy each month will keep rising for a few more years. Then the dollar amounts stop rising and start falling. There is a debate about when the dollar amounts of new purchases will start falling, but it may happen sooner than 2010 if many of the Boomer generation retire young.

There will be younger workers joining the labor force in the rich countries each year, but there is widespread agreement that these younger workers will not save enough each month. In the forecast given here, there will be excess selling every month from approximately 2010 onward. Excess selling pushes down the prices of stocks and bonds. The need to relieve that downward pressure on prices will motivate people in the rich countries to take action to increase the number of savers in the middle-income and poor countries.

Varying the assumptions does not affect the outcome very much. An important number is the aggregate amount of financial assets today's savers in the rich countries will be selling each year in the future. That figure is the minimum amount that younger savers will need to be buying each year in the future to keep prices of stocks and bonds from falling.

I used a spreadsheet program for the calculations and kept it simple so that it would be easy to tinker with. The spreadsheet indicates that in the rich countries by 2010 there will be about $500 billion more selling than buying, and by 2014 there will be as much as $2 trillion more selling than buying.

This alarming forecast depends on the number of people in the rich countries who will retire each year and the amounts of stocks and bonds they will be selling each year. The main scenario assumes that 15 million people in the rich countries retire every year beginning in 2006. The spreadsheet program allows calculating how many new buyers must begin buying each year to take up all the securities that these retirees will be selling. The main scenario assumes that in the rich countries, four million young workers begin buying securities every year from 2002 onward, and each of them will buy $12,000 a year of stocks and bonds.

Savers in Poor Countries Rescue Rich Retirees?

Evidently, a large number of people in the middle-income and poor countries will need to begin buying securities. The forecasts in this chapter use population and income data to estimate how many people in the poor countries will be able to buy stocks and bonds, and how much on average each will need to buy every year.

The main scenario makes the assumption that savers in the middle-income and poor countries will buy a large amount of top-rated bonds and blue-chip common stocks each year. This amount is $400 billion of stocks and bonds in the first year, and 7 percent more each year after that. This $400 billion figure is much higher than the annual amount of stocks and bonds those savers are buying now, but it is not large compared to the amount they are capable of buying each year. The scenarios assume that savers in the middle-income and poor countries overcome the obstacles preventing them from buying safe, blue-chip common stocks and top-rated bonds.

Can savers in the middle-income and poor countries buy $400 billion a year of stocks and bonds? The figure sounds large but is within the feasible range. In a recent year the output per capita in the middle-income countries was only $2,000 a year, and the output per capita in the poor countries was only $410 per year. This is not as hopeless as it sounds, because there were 2.67 billion people in the middle-income countries that same year. Among those 2.67 billion people were many living on $1 or $2 a day, which implies that there were many, perhaps as many as 800 million, earning $4,000 a year or more.[2] Those 800 million people can and do save much more than $400 billion a year.

This new group of buyers augments the buying power of the outnumbered, overburdened Generation X. In the main scenario the new buying postpones the retirement crisis in the rich countries but does not prevent it altogether; the crisis occurs in 2018 or 2019 instead of 2014. After giving more details about the main scenario, this chapter presents a more grandiose scenario in which the new buyers buy enough to prevent the crisis altogether.

International Diversification for Everyone

Many savers like Pedro in the middle-income and poor countries currently save in old-fashioned ways, like putting their money into savings accounts at local banks or banks in the rich countries. They should stop doing that and start putting their money into mutual funds that yield more and have better protection against loss. They should diversify their holdings internationally so that a single event does not wipe them out. The bedrock component of their portfolios should be some highly rated, very safe securities issued in rich countries. They should add high-yielding emerging-markets securities according to their stage of the life cycle and their tolerance for risk.

Savers like Pedro often go to a lot of trouble to buy financial assets that have more desirable attributes than those they can easily get at home. Many savers in those countries send cash abroad to relatives living in the rich countries. Sometimes they buy dollars or euros and stuff them into the mattress, or keep them in safe deposit boxes. Savers in middle-income countries bear the costs of circumventing rules that prevent them from sending money abroad, and those costs reduce the returns they earn and also discourage them from saving. Local savers in the poor countries need easy, legal ways of obtaining a full range of financial assets, including some that are especially safe, like Swiss government bonds, and some that are slightly riskier, like blue-chip common stocks. If they can get securities like that, they will be able to bring their holdings into line with their preferences for safety and yield. After they have satisfied their desires for safe securities, they will be more willing to direct some of their buying to locally issued bonds, and perhaps in some future time frame they will buy locally issued common stocks.

Savers like Jane in rich countries are logical buyers for the new issues of bonds that will come from middle-income and poor countries. Savers like her can tolerate the risk of owning those bonds, and can easily vary how much of their portfolios they invest in them. They can diversify their holdings among bonds from many middle-income and poor countries, and that diversification will help stabilize the rate of return they earn. For those reasons, Jane is better suited than Pedro to own bonds issued in poor countries.

Neither Jane nor Pedro is suited to own common stocks issued in poor countries. In recent years rich savers and poor savers alike have shunned the local stock markets in poor countries. These markets are small; in 1998, for example, the aggregate value of all stocks listed on local stock markets in the middle-income countries was only $1.5 trillion, a puny 31 percent of their combined annual GDP. For comparison, the same source gives the aggregate value of all stocks listed on stock markets in the rich countries as $21.7 trillion, a more reasonable 97.8 percent of their combined annual GDP.[3] These figures show the potential for stock market development in poor countries and also show that those stock markets do not compete successfully for funds.

Ideally, savers in rich countries will diversify their holdings internationally, and so will savers in middle-income and poor countries. If they do this in the proper magnitudes and in the proper time frame, the happy outcome proposed in this chapter becomes feasible.

The Main Prosperity Diffusion Scenario

In a few middle-income countries, savers already hold appropriately diversified portfolios and are adding to those at the needed rate each month. In this scenario the pattern spreads to other middle-income and then to poor countries.

Every year the number of buyers from the middle-income and poor countries must increase. After savers in middle-income countries become buyers, savers in the poor countries must be in condition to buy stocks and bonds. That creates pressure for savers in the poor countries to have enough income to be able to save, and for the national financial systems in those countries to function well.

The diffusion scenario is already making progress. Savers like Jane in the rich countries are buying more bonds issued in the emerging countries. The people who issue those bonds are already making them more appealing. They are buying credit enhancements so that the returns to investors will be more stable. The new-look bonds with credit enhancements are proving to be more marketable, so the middle-income and poor countries are placing growing amounts of bonds in international markets. The potential demand is huge, because savers like Jane in rich countries can prudently hold much larger amounts of these bonds than they currently do.

As savers in the rich countries direct a portion of their portfolios to buying bonds issued in the middle-income and poor countries, their buying will ease the chronic foreign exchange shortage in those countries. Savers like Pedro in those countries would then be able to acquire dollars more easily to achieve the international diversification they desire.

When people like Jane buy emerging-market bonds, their buying will accomplish something else that is important enough to underscore: It will raise the market prices of businesses and real estate in the middle-income and poor countries. This will give capital gains to the current holders of those assets. The magnitude of these capital gains could be very large. For example, the total value of all the productive assets and businesses in the middle-income countries might rise by an amount equal to one or two times the aggregate annual GNP of those countries, which in a recent year was $5.3 trillion. That increase would only be the beginning. An immediate response to the capital gains would be that local companies would issue more bonds. Savers like Jane in the rich countries would then buy the new bonds, and their buying would fuel a self-reinforcing asset boom in the middle-income and poor countries.

In the aggregate, middle-income and poor countries already are taking the first steps to implement this proposal. Data from world financial markets show that they are improving their performance as issuers of bonds. Many of those countries have been able to come to market with new issues of bonds and place them successfully in the international market. The International Monetary Fund reported that in 2000 emerging-markets bond issuance reached \$216 billion, a 32 percent increase over 1999. This continues a healthy trend. Emerging countries are getting more financing by issuing bonds and are relying less on loans from international banks and multilateral agencies like the World Bank. Loans from international banks used to be a bigger source of financing for these countries than international bond issuance was. Another healthy sign is that emerging countries were able to sell enough bonds so that they could use the proceeds to pay off bank loans and old, higher-cost bonds. These refinancing transactions lowered their cost of borrowing and also spread out the maturity of their foreign debt. The emerging countries were able to build up their deposits at international banks in 1999 and 2000. These improvements and steps toward modernization came partially in response to the Asian crisis of 1997. International banks demanded repayment and demanded that private borrowers in Asia restructure. The improvements also came in response to other pressures, including internal pressures for reform in the emerging countries themselves.

The evidence that internal pressures exist and are producing results is the rapid growth of domestic bond markets in the emerging countries. Local markets for long-term bonds hardly existed in the past, but in recent years have grown very rapidly. This is very good news because the long-term bonds are denominated in local currency, and local buyers are buying the bonds willingly. In the past in those countries neither savers nor lenders would tie up money for a long period of time at a fixed interest rate. Risk of inflation was too great. Further hopeful evidence is that credit ratings of emerging country governments, which dropped sharply after the Asian crisis and the Russian default, have improved since then.

Yields on emerging-markets bonds were −11.5 percent in 1998 because of the Russian default, but then rebounded strongly to 24.2 percent in 1999, and then went to a more normal 14.4 percent in 2000. Emerging-markets bonds have, on average, yielded more than enough in a typical year to compensate for the risk of holding them. Savers in rich countries gain from dedicating a small portion of their portfolios to emerging markets bonds, provided that they hold these bonds for a long enough time period so that short-term fluctuations smooth out. This fact makes the prosperity diffusion scenarios in this chapter feasible. Issuers in emerging markets will be able to sell more bonds each year as long as this pattern holds. In contrast, emerging-markets common stocks have not yielded high enough returns to compensate for the risk of holding them. Savers in the rich countries have bought emerging-markets stocks, but since 1994 have not benefited from doing so. The return on emerging markets stocks was −25.3 percent in 1998, rebounded to 66.4 percent in 1999, and then sagged to −31.8 percent in 2000.[4] This roller-coaster volatility is typical for emerging-markets common stocks. This asset class does not have a track record good enough to attract inflows of money from savers. After national financial systems in the middle-income and poor countries modernize fully, the yield on emerging-markets common stocks will rise and become more stable. Until that happens, savers like Jane will not buy large amounts of emerging markets common stocks. They will buy only emerging-markets bonds, and only those that are appropriately structured.

There is reason to hope that the yields on emerging-markets bonds will remain high even if issuers succeed in issuing large amounts of new bonds. There are enough profitable projects, and the deals can be designed so that enough of the returns go to the bondholders. The proceeds of each bond issue will be earmarked for specific uses, and auditors will verify that the proceeds went to the intended uses. Each project's backers will do a road show and make their pitch to expert bond buyers. The backers will get the money if the deal is well-designed, and if there are adequate safeguards for the bond buyers.

An equally essential part of this prosperity diffusion scenario is that savers in the middle-income and poor countries obtain easier access to blue-chip stocks, such as Nestlé, IBM, and Vodaphone, trading on international markets, and to bonds, including U.S. and European government bonds. Savers in middle-income and poor countries currently resort to circuitous ways of buying top-rated securities. They need to be allowed to buy mutual funds sponsored by world-class financial services firms. Local savers will trust those financial services firms and will put money into mutual funds those firms sponsor. Those financial services firms are already lobbying to be allowed to offer these mutual funds in the middle-income and poor countries. Barriers to international competition in financial services are falling. For this diffusion scenario to work, savers in all countries—rich, middle-income, and poor—must diversify their portfolios internationally to a much greater extent than they have done previously.

As this diffusion scenario unfolds, the magnitudes of cross-border portfolio investment increase greatly. For example, if savers in rich countries direct 20 percent of their annual saving to buying newly issued emerging markets bonds, they would buy about $480 billion per year of those high-yielding, volatile bonds. These purchases would provide foreign exchange for the countries that issue the bonds. It is not clear how much foreign exchange savers like Pedro would demand, because they have not been free to allocate their savings in line with their true preferences. The assumption is that savers like Pedro start out buying $400 billion a year of world-class blue-chip stocks and very safe bonds, and increase their buying 7 percent every year.

Feasibility of the Main Prosperity Diffusion Scenario

This section presents a simple calculation to gauge whether the main scenario can deliver enough buying power to remedy the looming shortage of buyers in the rich countries. The calculation works with macroeconomic data and makes assumptions about the total amount people like Pedro will save and what they will do with the money they save.

Using a figure for annual savings in the middle-income and poor countries of 20 percent of output gives $1.71 trillion of annual savings. The main scenario assumes that savers in those countries buy world-class blue-chip stocks and very safe bonds with $400 billion of the $1.71 trillion and invest the rest locally. In the early years of the scenario savers in rich countries buy $480 billion of new bonds issued in these countries. With that amount of investment, the annual growth rate of the middle-income and poor countries could reach 7 percent a year.[5] This growth rate can be achieved if the available capital would be invested in projects that bond investors willingly support, and would not go to white elephants or politically motivated waste. A growth rate in that range rapidly raises the amount of top-rated bonds and common stocks that savers in middle-income and poor countries would be able to buy. If they start out buying $400 billion a year of those securities and increase their buying 7 percent each year, their annual buying would exceed $1 trillion a year by 2017. In the main scenario savers in middle-income and poor countries would be buying the securities as retirees like Jane are selling, and would also be investing enough in their home countries to sustain economic growth there. The middle-income and poor countries would receive net inflows of portfolio investment in the early years of the scenario, and after that their buying would exceed the amounts coming in from rich-country savers.

The results indicate that it is feasible for savers in the middle-income and poor countries to buy enough securities to forestall the retirement crisis facing the rich countries. To completely bridge the gap, savers like Pedro must buy more each year than the main scenario indicates.

This diffusion scenario is a win for both groups of savers even if it does not completely bridge the gap. Savers in rich countries earn higher returns on their savings. Savers in the middle-income and poor countries gradually obtain the internationally diversified portfolios they desire. They earn steadier returns, and their savings become less vulnerable to the vagaries of their national financial systems.

The main scenario, however, is imperfect. It does not fully solve the rich countries' retirement crisis and does not bring prosperity to all the people in the middle-income and poor countries very rapidly. It showers capital on the middle-income and poor countries that choose to participate, and relegates the other countries to irrelevancy. In the main scenario prosperity spreads but does not permeate to all corners of the earth. There is a more grandiose diffusion scenario that will accomplish more of the desired outcomes.

A More Grandiose Prosperity Diffusion Scenario

By the year 2028 the amount of securities retirees may want to sell might exceed the amount young people in the rich countries are able to buy by as much as $10 trillion a year. In the time frame 2020–2030 all the baby boomers will have retired, and a large proportion of them probably still will be alive. Their combined holdings of financial assets would have reached $200 trillion by that time, and could have reached $300 trillion. If their holdings are of that magnitude, it is plausible they might try to sell $20 trillion of their financial assets each year. The younger cohorts in the rich countries would be able to buy only $10 trillion a year. Savers like Pedro in countries that today are middle-income and poor would have to bridge the gap, and buy $10 trillion a year worth of securities. Is there any way those savers can possibly do that?

There is a way. The world would have to work single-mindedly to raise the incomes of the people in middle-income and poor countries. To see that those people can acquire enough buying power, first consider that the dollar value of world output at that time will be in the range of $90 to $95 trillion a year. That assumes annual growth of 3 percent per year in the rich countries, 7 percent per year in the middle-income and poor countries, and no inflation. Next consider that the dollar value of all the stocks and bonds in the world could be as high as $450 trillion and might easily be higher, for example $600 trillion. This is five to seven times the lower figure for annual output. Both the $450 trillion figure and the $600 trillion figure assume that all the world's assets are securitized, and that national financial systems are all modern and are all working smoothly. The $450 trillion and $600 trillion figures are not theoretical maximum amounts; they bracket a practical range.

The dollar value of stocks and bonds in the world, in this scenario, would have gone up by a factor of four, or perhaps by a factor of six, while world output only increased by a bit more than a factor of two. The biggest increase in the dollar value of bonds and stocks would have happened in the countries that today are poor. These countries would have dramatically improved their performance as issuers of securities. They would be highly successful as issuers of bonds and would also have become successful at issuing common stock. The common shares they issue would still fluctuate, but only in response to changes in business conditions, not in response to manipulations. The value of businesses, real estate, local brand names, and other property in these countries would be much higher than it is today.

The owners of farms, apartment buildings, gas stations, restaurants, and factories in the emerging countries would have benefited from a steady, sustained asset boom. The owners of these businesses and the people who work in them would be, in the aggregate, wealthy enough to buy $10 trillion worth of securities each year. They would get the money to buy the securities by selling some of their assets to younger people in the countries where they live. The younger people would then operate those assets and add value to them.

In this grandiose scenario there would be enough buying power to prevent stock and bond prices from falling and to sustain the gradual asset boom in the middle-income and poor countries. This scenario harnesses the potential buying power of hundreds of millions of young adults who will be living and working in the countries that today are poor.

This approach entirely prevents the retirement crisis in the rich countries. In this scenario there is more buying than selling in the world's stock and bond markets every year from 2005 onward. The steady upward march of bond and stock prices that began in 1982 continues, with the usual transitory fluctuations, to 2040 and beyond. In this scenario the people in the rich countries who are now saving for their retirement can safely assume they will make high yields on their portfolios for the rest of their lives. No long, disheartening slide in the prices of stocks and bonds happens. The people in rich countries who start saving late in their working lives, for example at age 55, can make high enough returns on those savings so that they avoid becoming a burden on the younger people in the rich countries.

To see how enough people in the middle-income and poor countries can become buyers quickly enough, and how they can possibly buy enough, it is necessary to look beyond those countries' current output levels. The combined annual output of the middle-income and poor countries was $7.8 trillion in a recent year, and that seems too low to support much buying. The picture looks more promising if the focus shifts to the value of all the assets and businesses in those countries. The picture looks extremely promising if the focus shifts to what those assets can be worth in the near future.

The value of all the assets and businesses, in the poor and middle-income countries in 2002 was probably no higher than $35 trillion. That figure includes the value of crude oil and minerals in the ground; it is so low because these countries do not give priority to maximizing the market prices of businesses or properties. If these economies shift their emphasis, they can initiate an upward trend in asset prices. They could raise the value of assets that already exist and attract funding to build new assets. With consistent, dedicated effort, they can increase the value of these assets to $150 trillion or $200 trillion by 2020. This implies that the aggregate market value of assets and businesses in these countries would increase by 10.2 percent a year from 2002 to 2020. This increase may sound high, but it is feasible because there are so many assets that can be worth more. For example, Hernando de Soto estimates that the houses in the third world would be worth more than $10 trillion as of 2001 but are of questionable value because the homeowners do not have clear title to their homes.[6] His reasoning applies to other categories of assets too. Many businesses in these countries can rise in value if their owners attune their thinking to the needs of portfolio investors. For the value of assets and businesses to reach $150 trillion to $200 trillion, annual output of these countries would probably have to reach $30 trillion. This implies a 6.6 percent annual growth rate from 1999 to 2020. This growth rate is high, but many countries have grown at that rate or faster. One way of reaching and sustaining the needed growth rate is to emphasize policies to raise the market value of assets and businesses. If those countries can initiate an asset boom, the rising wealth can fuel high real economic growth.

Conclusion

There are hopeful signs that the distribution of income in the emerging countries is becoming more egalitarian. A new force that will exert the most pressure to raise incomes in the poor countries has scarcely begun to make itself felt. That force will gain strength in the near future and will then grow even stronger.

The new force is external. Savers in rich countries need more buyers for the securities they will be selling after they retire, and they will press for reforms so that people in middle-income and poor countries can become buyers.

The value of businesses and properties in the middle-income and poor countries can rise rapidly. The value is currently low and easy to raise, and there is external pressure on those countries for reforms that will foster a rise. Once asset values begin rising, those countries will benefit from the rise and will assign higher priority to sustaining the rise. They will find that raising the value is a feasible route to prosperity and a good way of accelerating their economies' growth rates.

Wealth will spread to many more people than it has reached so far. A major force that will spread it is the self-interest of the people who now buy stocks and bonds every month.

Chapter 11 concludes this book. It recounts a brief, revealing conversation I had in 1976, when the struggle for economic development was raging, the outcome was teetering between disaster and hope, and the driving motivations for working in economic development were altruism and charity.

11 Conclusion and Implications

There have always been optimists predicting that everyone on earth will someday have the necessities of life. They trust man's ingenuity to overcome all obstacles. Now the evidence that validates their optimism is at hand. The triumph, however, is only an accidental by-product of man's ingenuity; it is an achievement of man's selfishness, greed, and desire for opulent leisure. For that reason the cynics who quote Hobbes can claim to have been right: Man's baser instincts have prevailed. The cynics can also dismiss as premature this claim of victory.

The darkest time in the struggle for world prosperity, however, was a quarter of a century ago. The world economy really did appear to be floundering, and indicators of the quality of life were wavering. During the 1970s it was particularly hard to hang onto the dream of progress. There were crop failures and two oil crises. World population growth was roaring at a terrifying rate: more than 2 percent a year, and not yet slackening. Malnutrition and outright starvation were everyday realities, not theoretical threats. Working in economic development at that time was nerve-wracking and exhilarating. There was a constant sense of urgency and sometimes an air of desperation. It felt like working to prevent a natural disaster, like struggling to shore up a levee with the river rising and the rain pouring down. The threat seemed imminent, as if the rising water were going to spill over the levee and wash everything away.

My own darkest moment came in 1976, after I had been working in Nicaragua for a few weeks. Nicaragua was a very tough challenge, because the country was an absolute dictatorship and the dictator had no tolerance for reform. The country was poor but had the resources to be much more prosperous. The institutions were all rigidly against bold initiatives; they allowed only little experiments and pilot projects. These bits of tinkering around the edges were strictly for show, to impress visiting diplomats and keep the foreign aid coming in. The oligarchy put on a facade of tranquility, signaling that business was carrying on as always, but behind the facade the oligarchs were worried. Most were already sliding into a bunker mentality. The country was a hard place to work, but I was ready to face the challenges head-on. I expected to find a latent undercurrent of support for new initiatives. The darkest moment was a brief conversation with a new friend, when my confidence in that undercurrent of support suffered a setback.

"You seem to think the economy here isn't very good," he said. He spoke in a matter-of-fact tone, as if he were remarking on the weather, but he held my attention. I waited for him to continue.

"Well, let me tell you something," he said in the same calm, matter-of-fact voice. "It will save you a lot of trouble and frustrations. We know what's wrong with it, and we like it the way it is."

A second later, after he saw that I had heard him, he smiled and said, "So, why not just relax and enjoy your time here."

The country was poor, and part of its poverty was due to neglect. The capital city was still in ruins following the earthquake that hit almost five years earlier. Its central plaza had been on the edge of the lake, and its downtown business district had begun at the central plaza and extended away from the lake in the direction of the Interamerican Highway. Then the earthquake had flattened the downtown and damaged the buildings around the central plaza. The dictator had never bothered to rebuild the downtown. Instead he had stolen most of the foreign-assistance funds for earthquake relief and for rebuilding the downtown, so the city no longer had a core. The surviving businesses had moved out of the downtown and now occupied makeshift facilities that sprawled along the Interamerican Highway. Before the earthquake, the Interamerican Highway skirted the city, bypassing the downtown business district. In the four years since the earthquake the Interamerican Highway had gradually become the main street of the city. Everybody accepted this and did not remark on how inefficient it was.

Before the earthquake, north-south traffic could go around the down-town and continue without slowing down. After the earthquake, because of the neglect, traffic on the Interamerican Highway no longer flowed smoothly. The businesses that relocated along the highway were constantly sending workers with heavily loaded carts onto the highway. The carts would go some distance to another business on the other side of the highway. Businesses that previously had been in close proximity to each other were now spread along the highway, sometimes several kilometers apart. All the cars and trucks now had to go slowly through the traffic. The carts and the workers on foot or on bicycles constantly caused delays. Street vendors and pedestrians milled around, causing additional delays.

Many people in that country really wanted to improve the situation. But there were others who feigned sincerity without having any real desire for change. They would willingly discuss alternative ways of doing things, and sometimes they seemed to believe that they were really seeking to make their businesses more efficient. But, at heart, they were fearful of change and especially resistant to macro-level change. The guerrilla movement was building strength and scoring small victories against the National Guard. As my two-year assignment went on, the business oligarchs became more and more insistent that everything was fine, and the economy was going to grow rapidly and provide good jobs for everyone. They had to show a good face to everyone, and I could not get them to take me into their confidence and confess to me how they really felt. My years there were exciting, and I often felt satisfaction with the progress I was making, but my friend's words kept coming back to me. My little triumphs were pleasant, and sometimes I allowed myself to savor them for a few days. But even as I was enjoying a momentary success, I felt hollow and unsatisfied, and I was often inclined to concede that my friend was right, at least about Nicaragua at that time. There were barriers to progress I would not succeed in pushing aside.

The conversation with my friend was a moment when the quest to bring an adequate standard of living to everyone in the world seemed particularly hopeless. Such a highly educated young man should have been progressive, and instead he was blandly defending the status quo and urging me to relax and enjoy my time in the country. In retrospect I later saw him as a savvy guy who was caught in a web of local conventions. For him the least disruptive alternative was to hope that the guerrillas would fade back into the jungle and the dictatorship would continue. Two and a half years later the Sandinistas defeated Somoza's National Guard and overthrew the dictatorship. The upheaval shattered the world that my friend knew, and the Somoza-era oligarchs dispersed to Miami and to adjoining countries.

Now the tide has turned. Savvy young men like my Nicaraguan friend do not say things like that. They do not blandly assume that the people in control can continue running an unfair economy. There is too much international scrutiny and too many inquisitive outsiders asking pointed questions. The questions keep coming until the right answers come back. Nobody silences the questioners, and nobody successfully keeps a veil of secrecy around a scandal. The secrets all come out, and the ugly details all come under public scrutiny. Too many people want to know what is really going on, and there are too many ways for them to find out. Hundreds of millions of people need to make investments that will yield high returns. For years investors dismissed countries like Nicaragua, but now they see such countries as potential places for portfolio investment, suitable in every respect except for some pesky local predators. The predators are local business people who take more than their share of the profits of investments that foreigners finance. The foreigners keep watching, knowing the predators are still there, and the foreigners invest only very small amounts. They keep asking if the predators are still there, and why they are still there. Sooner or later they hear the answer they are waiting for, and then they invest much larger amounts.

While my friend was informing me that I was not going to be able to accomplish much to improve the Nicaraguan economy, there was a transition taking place in the rich countries. That transition determined the outcome of the struggle to raise all people out of poverty. Middle-class people in the rich countries gained control over their own financial destinies. They fought and won many battles in their long struggle, and they gradually prevailed over entrenched groups of rich people in their own countries. Middle-class people in the rich countries fought for their own financial security. They fought to create favorable conditions for saving, and they succeeded, and then went on to earn high yields on their savings. People in poor countries benefited from that successful struggle, but they benefited by accident, not by design. In the 1980s the rich countries created savings mechanisms that at that stage did not need to involve the poor people or the poor countries. Now the middle-class savers in the rich countries need the poor countries, and they especially need the middle-class people in the poor countries. They need the poor countries to become credible issuers of high-quality securities, and they need middle-class people in the poor countries to start buying large amounts of stocks and bonds.

In 1976 the main geopolitical question was whether modern capitalism was really superior. The capitalist countries did not know at that time how close they were to a resolution of that question. The campaign for economic development went along in parallel with the Cold War and was sometimes caught up in it. In the years following my friend's smug remarks, the rich countries gradually abandoned some of their Cold War preoccupation and started prioritizing new objectives. Voters in the rich countries saw that they might live long enough to become elderly, and they began to worry how they would support themselves in retirement. They thought about saving, and many of them tried to save the way their parents had, by putting money into banks. That did not work very well, and in the 1970s buying bonds did not help either. The recession in the mid-1970s was deep, and oil-price rises destabilized the rich countries' economies. Inflation in the 1970s eroded the value of long-term bonds, and it pushed many middle-class households into high tax brackets. They found that to accumulate a nest egg it was better to borrow money and buy a house than to save.

The middle classes in the rich countries faced an uncertain economic future in the late 1970s. The dollar was weak and inflation was high. The poor countries were gaining leverage in international markets because commodity prices were high. Then came the 1980s. Inflation fell, and Americans began to take advantage of tax-deferred savings schemes like individual retirement accounts (IRAs). Commodity prices fell, and the poor countries went into a long recession. Ordinary people in the rich countries no longer paid much attention to the poor countries. The Americans who were opening IRAs in the early 1980s did not imagine that later they would need middle-class people in the poor countries to become buyers of stocks and bonds.

The U.S. stock market, meanwhile, was poised to offer a solution to the floundering, frustrated middle-class savers in the rich countries. The stock market had shared with the banks the role of whipping-boy during the Depression. Its abuses had been laid bare and its cozy tradition of self-regulation had been completely supplanted. With the new regulatory framework, the U.S. stock market had become an institution that could deliver high returns to unsophisticated savers. Certainly, it still had defects, but it had fewer than other countries' stock markets and fewer defects than banks. From the second half of 1982 onward, it prospered mightily and became the mainspring of the resurgent U.S. economy.

The U.S. stock-market-driven prosperity was different from all earlier waves of prosperity. Breakthroughs in manufacturing did not underpin it. Increases in real output and productivity happened in synchronization with the stock and bond market boom but were not the prime mover. The stock market rally rose on a foundation of complex, highly refined legal and social conventions. There had never been a solid, stress-tested national financial system before. Earlier national financial systems had seemed robust but suffered from flaws that caused them to collapse. The U.S. financial system showed that it was strong and resilient enough to support a huge pile of financial assets. The characteristic that made the new prosperity possible was that people who managed money operated in full view, under close scrutiny, and with restraints on their autonomy. They kept their jobs only as long as they performed well, and they faced jail terms and financial penalties if they misbehaved. The new prosperity needed a stable currency, a clear set of laws and a judiciary to enforce them, and a vigilant regulatory structure. It also needed a large number of investors who trusted its fairness and ability to produce results.

Other countries did not have so many preconditions for stock-market-driven prosperity. Japan had a stock-market-driven boom in the second half of the 1980s, but it came crashing down. Europe had too many currencies and too many national coalition governments, so it could not create the preconditions for stock-market-driven prosperity until 1994 or 1995, when its coming monetary convergence began to lift stock prices. Emerging countries did not have the preconditions either, but many of them appeared to be putting the preconditions in place.

Savers, especially younger, highly educated people in rich countries, responded enthusiastically to every favorable signal. Whenever they thought they saw a stock market rally beginning in any country, they bought enthusiastically, and drove up stock prices. They paid too much for Japanese stocks in the late 1980s, then overpaid for emerging markets stocks from 1992 to 1994, and then paid too much for U.S. and European tech stocks in 1999 and 2000.

From the vantage point of 2003 the savers who overpaid for common stocks look like lemmings, foolishly following each other off one cliff after another. But from a longer-term perspective they will probably look like pioneers. Despite their many setbacks, as a group they are earning higher rates of return on their savings than their parents did. The volatility they have experienced is an inconvenience, and for some savers the volatility has made their rate of return negative. But the overriding fact is that common stocks can yield more than bonds, provided there is political and economic stability, and that shareholders have enough clout.

The need for portfolio investment to yield high returns has become urgent. Today's savers need to earn high returns on their savings, and one way for them to accomplish that is to invest in countries that are now poor and help those countries grow more quickly. Savers cannot invest in poor countries, however, until the poor countries make themselves attractive to portfolio investors. The poor countries already are feeling pressure to reform their laws and put a stop to white-collar crime. The poor countries that successfully make themselves attractive to portfolio investors will experience asset-price booms. Those can happen quickly and spur economic growth.

The need for high returns requires that poor countries improve their internal living conditions. People in the poor countries need to earn enough so that they can save and become buyers of stocks and bonds. The need for high returns is a force that will lobby for improvements in incomes in the middle-income and poor countries.

Implications for Investors

Investors must develop their own personal responses to several arguments that this book presents. The first response is to forecast when the period of net selling will begin and how severe it will be. The Boomer generation in the United States has already begun to retire, and when that generation really moves en masse into retirement, Americans will become net sellers of stocks and bonds. Every investor needs to have a forecast of the date when Americans will become net sellers, and needs to monitor and update this forecast frequently. Large numbers of baby boomers might retire sooner than expected, or upon turning 65, or they may delay retirement. In some scenarios baby boomers become net sellers of stocks and bonds before 2010. Soon after that, Boomer selling would exceed Generation X's buying by a growing amount each year. The selling pressure could be severe and protracted, and the annual excess of selling over buying could be in the trillions by 2015.

Alternatively, enough foreign buyers may add their purchases to the buying power of Generation X savers, thereby forestalling the date when the shortfall of buying power occurs. In the most rosy scenario, there may never be a period of net selling. If enough new foreign buyers come into the market each year, their buying can absorb the avalanche of stocks and bonds the Boomers will be selling. In that case the long stock-market boom would be able to continue for many decades into the future. Several favorable events must coincide for this rosy scenario to happen. First, the buying power of people in the poor countries would have to rise quickly. Second, the total amount of new common stock and bonds that will be issued each year around the world would have to be less than the amount that savers choose to buy each year. These felicitous events can happen, but other less favorable outcomes are more likely.

The second response that investors must develop is almost as important. They must decide which countries will become good places for portfolio investment. Some countries already have become good places for portfolio investors to put money. The United States has acquired a reputation as a good place to put money and will try to maintain its good reputation. Some countries, however, have gained and then lost their reputations as hospitable places for foreign portfolio investors, whereas other countries have never had reputations as safe or profitable places for foreigners to put money. The question, therefore, is Which of those countries will make a serious effort to attract foreign portfolio investment?

For a country that has not successfully attracted foreign portfolio investment in the past, putting the necessary institutions in place is hard. In each country there are groups that benefit because the national financial system is opaque and inequitable. These groups often have enough political clout to protect their privileges. There are moments of optimism and there are investors who buy early, hoping to get in before the cautious ones come in later. That is why so many emerging countries' stock markets have had furious rallies followed by collapses. The adventuresome pioneers get in early, but the country does not give them enough protection. The local powerful groups use their clout to take some money that should have gone to foreign portfolio investors, who then become disillusioned and start selling. Once the foreign portfolio investors start selling, their departure turns into a disorderly rout.

Savers can refuse to participate in this drama. They can invest only in the rich countries, but if they do, they forego the potentially high returns. There is a better way for them to deal with the volatility of investing in emerging countries. They can use scientific diversification techniques. These techniques allow each saver to determine how much to invest abroad, and how much to invest in emerging countries. For example, a mix of investments for a typical person in a rich country who will not retire in the next twenty years and who is moderately tolerant of risk might be 70 percent investments in the home country, 20 percent in other rich countries, and 10 percent in emerging countries. In many emerging countries, the national financial system gives better protection to bondholders than to minority shareholders. In consequence, the 10 percent of the typical investor's portfolio that is invested in emerging countries should be allocated mostly to bonds. This 10 percent should be sprinkled over 15 or 20 emerging countries, with no more than 1 percent invested in any single emerging country. Finally, investors must take a long view and be prepared for violent fluctuations in that part of the portfolio.

Emerging countries try to signal that they are hospitable and safe for foreign portfolio investors. They build state-of-the-art stock transactions processing systems. They do road shows to persuade investors to buy securities. They often succeed in raising amounts of money that seem large but are nowhere near as large as their underlying economic potential would justify. Despite their hard work, they do not succeed easily or quickly in convincing the outside world that they are truly hospitable. The reason is that foreign portfolio investors are weak compared to local oligarchs, politicians, judges, and bankers. For this to change, there must be many occasions over a long period of time when local controlling shareholders or politically connected local financiers try to swindle or underpay foreign portfolio investors and fail. Local authorities must be the ones who stop them. After there is enough evidence that the country protects foreign portfolio investors, the country rises into a more privileged category in investors' minds. They begin to think of it as a serious place to put larger amounts of money.

The third response that investors must develop is an estimate of how much cross-border portfolio investment there will be. The answer to this question is important because if there is not enough cross-border investment, today's savers will probably not earn high returns.

There are reasons to believe that cross-border portfolio investment in the future will be sufficient. Until now middle-class savers in the rich countries have shown a strong and persistent preference for investing in their home markets. Savers in poor countries have not been able to reveal their true preferences for investing abroad because many of them are not allowed to send money abroad. In the future, people in rich countries will probably invest more abroad and more in emerging countries. Their international holdings will partially offset the volatility of their home-country holdings, and may outperform them. People in poor countries will probably prevail on their governments to allow them to invest abroad. When more of them are allowed to invest abroad, they will probably buy bonds and stocks in the rich countries.

Investors need to monitor the growth of cross-border portfolio investment and track the development of national financial systems in the poor countries. If national financial systems in poor countries do not improve, and if middle-class savers in poor countries do not find ways of investing abroad, the outcome will be bad. Savers in rich countries will refuse to make portfolio investments in poor countries, and savers in poor countries will put money into the stock and bond markets of the rich countries. This combination of events would concentrate too much buying power in the rich country stock and bond markets. That could drive prices of stocks and bonds in the rich countries to very high levels. At those high levels, the stocks and bonds would not yield very much and would be vulnerable to steep price declines. Meanwhile, the poor countries would suffer from a shortage of capital.

A Happy Ending

If savers in the rich and poor countries all direct their investments according to the most optimistic scenario in this book, the outcomes can be very favorable. There can be enough buying power during every time period in the future to keep prices of bonds and stocks high, and savers can all earn high yields. The world can accomplish the transition from unfunded national retirement systems to fully funded individual savings plans without suffering major disruptions. During the same time frame the world can achieve rapid increases in the market values of stocks and bonds and steady real economic growth. Many of the prerequisites for these favorable outcomes are already in place, and pressure is building to put the remaining prerequisites in place.

For this transition to happen smoothly, many events must take place at the right time and in the proper magnitude. For the favorable scenario to occur, the most difficult requirement is that people in poor countries will have to buy enough stocks and bonds. They will have to buy in greater and greater amounts and keep buying for many decades into the future. They already are buying small amounts, but they will have to increase their purchases rapidly.

How can middle-class people in the poor countries become buyers for stocks and bonds? Most do not earn enough, and most are wary of putting their savings into their own national financial systems. There are two parts to the answer. First, they will need to earn more money than they do now, which means that the economies of the poor countries must perform better and grow more rapidly. Second, the national financial systems of the poor countries will have to improve; too many have been treacherous for unsophisticated investors.

The pressure to improve living standards in the poor countries has been intensifying. Historically, the pressure came from multilateral agencies and from well-intentioned individuals. Now it comes from Mr. Market, and the new pressure is capricious and impersonal, but ultimately relentless and inescapable. The pressure to improve national financial systems also comes from the grass roots. People will not willingly put money into a national financial system if it is defective or inequitable. A growing percentage of the world's population now has ways of moving money across national boundaries. There is no country that can be confident of capturing its citizens' savings and investing those savings according to a national plan or dictatorial edict. All countries now have to accept the reality that local savings can migrate abroad in search of better opportunities. Every country's national financial system has to make a serious and sincere effort to attract and retain people's hard-earned savings. There are now several national financial systems that treat savers fairly, and as they grow, they take market share and capital away from national financial systems that do not.

Endnotes

Chapter 2

1. The article my coauthor, Susan E. Moeller, and I published is: "International Equity Returns, Country Growth, and World Economic Recovery," *Management International Review* 28, no. 1 (spring 1988): pp. 45–50.

Chapter 3

1. The figure of 475 Internet startup companies in Buenos Aires came up several times in interviews I conducted in the fall of 1999. The report, written with Thomas McDermott and Marcos Espinel is "Venture Capital/Private Equity Financing of Early Stage Entrepreneurship in Latin America," (December 1999). Available from the Institute for Latin American Business Studies at Babson, (http://www2.babson.edu/Babson/BabsonHPp.nsf/public/international publications).

Chapter 4

1. The figure for total private debt of all types in the United States in 1960 comes from *Barron's*, (1 April 2002): p. 10.

2.   Data on time deposits at depository institutions comes from the Federal Reserve Economic Data service (FRED) (http://research.stlouisfed.org/fred/).

3.   Data on liquid assets, gross domestic product, and gross private saving is from FRED (http://research.stlouisfed.org/fred/).

4.   Data on U.S. stock market capitalization in 1960 came from the Security and Exchange Commission, *SEC 2000 Annual Report* (Washington, D.C.: GPO, 2000), p. 169.

5.   Corporate debt in 1960 comes from data published in *Barron's*, (19 August 2002): p. 30.

6.   Assets of insurance companies figures from *Historical Statistics of the United States,* Insurance Stock Company Resources: Operating Results, Table Series X 947–956; and from *Insurance Facts 1986–87*, Insurance Information Institute Consolidated Assets Table 1978–1985.

7.   Assets of mutual funds and other mutual fund data from the Investment Company Institute's *ICI Mutual Fund Fact Books* (1997): p. 110; and (2002): p. 105.

8.   Inflation and savings rate data from FRED (http://research.stlouisfed.org/fred/).

9.   The information about the mix of household assets in Japan contrasted with the US appears in the article "From Fear to Favor" in *Forbes*, dated April 2, 2002, and is available at http://www.forbes.com/global/2002/0204/044_print.html. For a more detailed discussion, see Jesper Edman, "Japanese Households and the Big Bang: Have Household Portfolios Changed with Financial Deregulation?" The European Institute of Japanese Studies, Working Paper 111, December 2000 (http://web.hhs.se/eijs/wp/111.pdf).

Chapter 5

1.   For a discussion of Venezuela's Banco Latino crisis, a good starting point is Nick Rosen's *Case Study: The Venezuelan Banking Crisis*, Initiative for Policy Dialogue (http://www.gsb.columbia.edu/ipd/j_bankingVEN.html).

2.   For a discussion of the design defects of the classic commercial bank, a good starting point is Edward S. Prescott's "Can risk-based deposit insurance premiums control moral hazard?" *Economic Quarterly*, (Federal Reserve Bank of Richmond), Spring 2002: pp. 87–100.

Chapter 6

1. Data on average annual return on common stocks in the United States is computed from values for the Standard & Poor's 500 index reported on http://table.finance.yahoo.com/ d?a=0&b=2&c=1990&d=11&e=31&f=2001&g=d&s=%5Egspc. The computed rate of return does not include dividends.

2. Annual private investment data for the U.S. economy are from FRED (http://research.stlouisfed.org/fred/).

3. Data for corporate profits, depreciation, and corporate income taxes are from FRED (http://research.stlouisfed.org/fred/).

4. Personal bankruptcy filings by quarter are shown on American Bankruptcy Institute's Web site (http://www.abiworld.org/stats/personalbk.pdf).

5. Samuelson. P.A. and Nordhaus, W. *Economics* (McGraw-Hill, 14th edition 1992), p. 519 discusses the value of capital assets relative to a country's annual output.

6. Data for the value of tangible reproducible capital assets in the United States is from the U.S. Department of Commerce, *Survey of Current Business* (Washington, D.C.)August 1994, p. 55; September 1997, pp. 37–38; and September 2001, pp. 27–28.

7. *Barron's*, the financial weekly, reports the average P/E ratio for the Standard & Poor's 500 index. See *Barron's* (18 February 2002): MW42; and *Barron's* (10 February 2003): MW42.

8. To verify that corporate profits would rise from 5.9 percent of GDP to about 10 percent of GDP, assume that the corporate tax rate is 30 percent. In that case pretax corporate profits would be 8.4 percent of GDP. Note that 8.4*(1–0.3) = 5.9. That leaves 10 percent – 8.4 percent = 1.6 percent to be explained. That 1.6 percent of GDP increase in corporate profits would come from lowering and stabilizing the cost of skilled labor and from extending the lives of patents.

9. The 300 million figure for the number of savers consists of 80 million in the United States, 100 million in Europe, 50 million in Japan, and the rest elsewhere. There are also between 200 million and 500 million more people who might start accumulating financial assets soon but have not done so yet.

10. The statement about Social Security eligibility is a simplification. The exact rule and the birth years are in flux.

11. Figures on output and population for the middle-income and poor countries are from the World Bank's *World Development Report 2000/2001*, Oxford University Press, p. 275.

12. The Institute for International Finance proposal for rules of corporate governance is described in detail at (http://www.iif.com/press/pressrelease.quagga?id=37) and reported in "New code aimed at emerging markets," *Financial Times* (13 February 2002).

Chapter 7

1. The three projects are described as I remember them. There were many similar projects that I saw, and could substitute for those three.

2. To verify the 47.6% annual rate of return, solve the equation $3/(1+r) + 13/(1+r)^2 = 8$. The solution is $r = 47.6\%$.

3. To verify the 107% rate of return for the institutional investors and the 29% rate of return for the new buyer, solve the equation $8(1+r)^{0.5} = 11.5$ giving $r = 107\%$ for the institutional investors and the equation $11.5 = 3/(1+z)^{0.5} + 13/(1+z)^{1.5}$ giving $z = 29\%$ for the new buyer.

Chapter 8

1. World population data is supplied by the Population Reference Bureau (http://www.prb.org) and by the U.S. Census Bureau (http://www.census.gov/ipc/www/worldpop.html).

2. To verify the 10.9 billion figure, consider that world population in 2002 was 6.13 billion, then compute $6.13*(1.012)^{48}$, which gives 10.87 billion.

3. To verify the 0.83% growth rate, solve the equation $6.13*(1+x)^{48} = 9.1$. Solving for x gives 0.0083.

4. To verify the 0.1% growth rate, solve the equation $9.1*(1+k)^{30} = 9.4$. Solving for k gives 0.001.

5. An article computing the slowdown in population growth is provided by Lutz, Sanderson, and Scherbov in "The end of world population growth," *Nature* 412 (August 2001): pp. 543–545.

6. An article giving a more extreme scenario for the slowdown in world population growth by Blain, Robert. is "The End of World Population Growth," posted on Blain's Web site (http://www.siue.edu/rblain/worldpop.htm).

7. Paul Erlich's book *The Population Bomb* (Ballantine Books, Reissue edition, August 1988) originally appeared in 1968 and drew attention to the population explosion in progress at that time.

8. The U.S. Census Bureau gives a projection for world population growth through 2050 and shows that the annual rate of increase is about to fall below 1 percent.

9. In the year 2000 the total population of the Americas was 824 million, computed from the World Bank's *World Development Report 2000/ 2001*, Oxford University Press, New York, pp. 278–279.

10. To verify this crude projection of when world population growth would reach zero, start with 13.6 percent and make the growth rate 1.6 percent lower each decade. The growth rate for each successive decade would be 12 percent, 10.4 percent, 8.8 percent, and so on. If growth slows by 3 percent each decade, start with 13.6 percent and make the growth rate 3 percent lower each decade. The growth rate for each successive decade would be 10.6 percent, 7.6 percent, 4.6 percent, 1.6 percent, and then negative.

11. Population Reference Bureau (http://www.prb.org) summary data sheets for 2001 and 2002 show these countries and these low or negative population growth rates.

12. To verify these compound annual average growth rates, solve the equation $(1+ y)^{49} -1 = 0.44$. Solving for y gives y = 0.0075.

13. The history of population programs is provided in the Center for Disease Control's "Achievements in Public Health, 1900–1999: Family Planning," *MMWR Weekly* (3 December 1999): pp. 1–2.

14. For a source on infant mortality rates, see Johns Hopkins University Center for Communication Programs Population Reports Data Table at http://www.jhuccp.org/pr/j49/j49table.shtml.

15. The reported decline in foreign aid appears in "The Politics of Compassion: Part 1 Foreign Aid Shrinks, but Not for All: With Clout in Congress, Armenia's Share Grows," *Washington Post*, 24 January 2001, p. A01.

16. Reported cuts in aid for family planning appear in "Family Planning Funds Put on Hold: Abortion Foes Press Bush to Deny Money for UN Population Fund," *Washington Post,* 12 January 2002, p. A02.

17. The 11 percent annual growth rate for financial wealth includes the value of stocks, bonds, bank deposits, mortgages, and other financial assets in the world. To the extent possible, the annual estimates eliminate double counting.

18. The $153 trillion is an estimate developed from estimates of the value of world output, the percentage of world assets that is securitized, and the average market multiples for securitized and unsecuritized assets. For example, if world annual output is $40 trillion, and 60% of world assets are securitized, and the securitized assets are worth 4.5 times their output on average, then securitized assets would be worth $108 trillion. If unsecuritized assets are worth 2.5 times their annual output on average, they would be worth $40 trillion, and the total value of world assets would be $148 trillion. The additional $5 trillion is for assets that owners conceal from government statistical surveys. In March 2003, the International Monetary Fund published a report giving estimates of world annual GDP of $31 trillion for 2001. The numerical examples in this book use $40 trillion in an attempt to take into account unreported economic activity. In the same document the IMF estimated the dollar value of gross world financial assets as $150 trillion in that same year. This figure includes bank assets of $79.4 trillion. Since banks usually own bonds and, in many countries, also own common stocks, the figure of $150 trillion probably includes some double counting. The $110 trillion figure used in this book is conservative, and the world total of financial assets may go past that level by 2001 and may be yet be higher in 2003 as this book goes to press. The report is International Monetary Fund, *Global Financial Stability Report: Market Developments and Issues*, March 2003, Statistical Appendix, Table 3, Selected Indicators on the Size of the Capital Markets, 2001, p. 121. Available on the Web at http://www.imf.org/external/pubs/ft/gfsr/2003/01/pdf/appendix.pdf.

Chapter 9

1. Data on population trends in Mexico are from Mexico's Instituto Nacional de Estadistica Geografia e Informatica, (http://www.inegi.gob.mx/difusion/espanol/fietab.html). For the period 2000–2002 several sources show slower growth rates for Mexico's population. The UN estimate for 2002 is 2.1 percent. Other sources give figures as low as 1.5 percent.

2. The amount of financial assets Americans will own in future years is projected using the stated growth rate and the starting figure from 2001–2002.

3. That the average person spends 1 percent to 4 percent of their increase in wealth comes from a speech by Alan Greenspan. The speech is reported in Richard Stevenson, "Tracking the Wealth Effect," *New York Times,* 24 February 2000, Section C, p. 1. If financial assets earn 8.5% on average, and if the owners spend 10% of the annual increase, they would spend 0.85% of their wealth each year, less than the 1 to 4% range that Greenspan cited.

Chapter 10

1. The argument that world income inequality peaked in the 1970s appears in David Dollar's and Aart Kraay's article "Spreading the Wealth," *Foreign Affairs,* January–February 2002, pp. 120–133.

2. For estimates of population and income per capita in the middle-income and poor countries, see the World Bank's *World Development Report 2000/2001* (Oxford University Press, 2001), pp. 275, 280–281.

3. Data on the market capitalization of stock markets appears in International Finance Corporation's *Emerging Stock Markets Factbook,* reported in the World Bank's *World Development Indicators* 1999, pp. 277–279 available at http://www.worldbank.org/wdr/2000/fullreport.html .

4. Data on annual flows and rates of return on emerging markets bonds and common stocks are from the International Monetary Fund's *World Economic and Financial Surveys, International Capital Markets: Developments, Prospects, and Key Policy Issues* (Washington, D.C., August 2001), pp. 40–57. Available at http://www.imf.org/external/pubs/ft/icm/2001/01/eng/pdf/chap3.pdf.

5. To grow at a rate of 7 percent a year, with a capital/output ratio of 3, the countries would be investing 21 percent of their annual output.

6. Hernando de Soto, *The Mystery of Capital* (Basic Books, New York: 2000, pp. 9 and passim).

Index

8 reasons why you should read the Financial Times for 4 weeks RISK-FREE!

To help you stay current with significant
developments in the world economy ...
and to assist you to make informed business
decisions — the Financial Times brings you:

❶ Fast, meaningful overviews of international affairs ... plus daily briefings on major world news.

❷ Perceptive coverage of economic, business, financial and political developments with special focus on emerging markets.

❸ More international business news than any other publication.

❹ Sophisticated financial analysis and commentary on world market activity plus stock quotes from over 30 countries.

❺ Reports on international companies and a section on global investing.

❻ Specialized pages on management, marketing, advertising and technological innovations from all parts of the world.

❼ Highly valued single-topic special reports (over 200 annually) on countries, industries, investment opportunities, technology and more.

❽ The Saturday Weekend FT section — a globetrotter's guide to leisure-time activities around the world: the arts, fine dining, travel, sports and more.

The *Financial Times* delivers a world of business news.

Use the Risk-Free Trial Voucher below!

To stay ahead in today's business world you need to be well-informed on a daily basis. And not just on the national level. You need a news source that closely monitors the entire world of business, and then delivers it in a concise, quick-read format.

With the *Financial Times* you get the major stories from every region of the world. Reports found nowhere else. You get business, management, politics, economics, technology and more.

Now you can try the *Financial Times* for 4 weeks, absolutely risk free. And better yet, if you wish to continue receiving the *Financial Times* you'll get great savings off the regular subscription rate. Just use the voucher below.

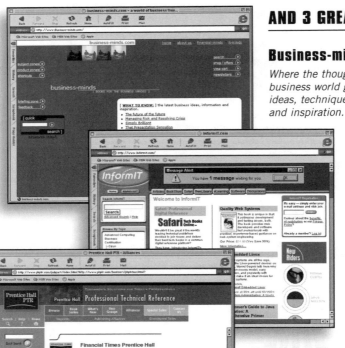